The Return of The King

A Prophetic Timeline of End Time Events.

Jeff Kluttz
www.returningking.com

Copyright © 2008, by ReturningKing.com

All Rights Reserved. No part of this book may be reproduced or transmitted in any form or by any means without the written permission of the author.

Cover artwork titled "King of Kings and Lord of Lords" by Pat Marvenko Smith © 1982, 1992 has been used by permission. For information on the artwork go to www.revelationillustrated.com.

Scripture taken from the HOLY BIBLE, NEW INTERNATIONAL VERSION® unless otherwise noted. Copyright © 1973, 1978, 1984 International Bible Society. Used by permission of Zondervan. All rights reserved.

To my King: in response to His clear calling to organize and write this work. All thanks and glory to Him for His gracious placement of my life in the loving hands of the greatest family, friends and church one could ever hope.

Table of Contents

Preface v
Introduction 1
Chapter 1: Pre-tribulational Events 7
    General Birth Pains 7
    The Re-establishment of Israel 15
    Rebuilding of the Jewish Temple 19
    The Gog-Magog War 23
    The One-World Government 36
    The Revealing of the Antichrist 50
    About The Antichrist 52
    A Period of Peace 69
Chapter 2: The Rapture 71
    The Rapture Event 72
    The Process 75
    The Transformation 78
    The Nature of The Resurrected Body 81
    The Timing of the Rapture 84
    The Judgment Seat of Christ 90
Chapter 3: The First Half of the Tribulation 97
    Notes on the Book of Revelation 97
    The Purposes of the Tribulation 99

Preface

- Events of the First Half 105
  - The Beginning of The Tribulation 105
  - The Seal Judgments 106
  - The Ministry on earth: The 144,000 Evangelists 115
  - Ministry on earth: The Two Witnesses 117
  - The Counterfeit Ministry on earth: Babylon The Great Harlot .. 121
  - The Rise of Babylon (The City) 125
  - The Seventh Seal: The Trumpet Judgments 129
  - The Woe Judgments 134
- Other Events of the First Half of the Tribulation: 139
- Chapter 4: The Middle of the Tribulation 145
  - Death of the Two Witnesses 145
  - Worship of Antichrist 148
  - The Abomination of Desolation 150
  - The False Prophet 157
  - The Mark of the Beast 161
  - The Breaking of the Seven Year Covenant 164
  - The Persecution of the Jews 166
- Chapter 5: The Second Half of the Tribulation 177
  - The First Six Bowl Judgments 178
    - The first Bowl Judgment: 178
    - The second Bowl Judgment 179
    - The third Bowl Judgment 180
    - The fourth Bowl Judgment 182
    - The fifth Bowl Judgment 183
    - The Sixth Bowl Judgment 183

- The Fall of Babylon 184
- Chapter 6: The Battle of Armageddon 187
  - Setting of the Stage: the Assembling of the Armies 187
  - Antichrist's purposes in the Battle of Armageddon 189
  - The First Wave 192
  - The Second Wave 196
  - The Salvation of Israel 197
    - God's purging of Israel 197
    - Israel Calls on Christ 199
- Chapter 7: The Return of the King 211
  - The Route 211
  - Christ Finishes The Battle 215
  - The Process 218
  - The end of the battle 221
  - The Seventh Bowl Judgment 222
  - The Judgment of the Gentiles 224
- Chapter 8: Prophecies Concerning The Messianic kingdom ... 233
- Chapter 9: The messianic kingdom 243
  - The Gap 243
  - Jesus Judges His Enemies 245
    - Satan is bound for 1,000 years 245
    - The Confinement of Demons 247
    - The First Resurrection 251
    - Marriage Feast of The Lamb 258
  - Life In The Messianic Kingdom 260
- Chapter 10: The Final Battle 275

Preface

Final Prophecies Fulfilled on earth	280
Chapter 11: The Great White Throne Judgment	283
Chapter 12: Eternity	293
A Description of Heaven	300
Chapter 13: Our Response	307
God's Offer: Now, and To Come	313
How to Receive God's Offer	316
Scripture Index	327

Preface

Never does one approach a piece of great literature, be it a masterful novel or a historical account, without regard for the narrative. While the events themselves may be central, even life changing for the reader, it is the *story* which guides one's perspective for each recorded action in the written account. A story is essentially a demonstration of conflict resolution. A problem arises and is dealt with by the end of the work. It is the finality of the resolution of such conflict in which a reader finds satisfaction and fulfillment in having taken the literary journey.

Strangely, when it comes to the biblical narrative, many have found themselves completely comfortable to remain in ignorance concerning the end of the story. Some understand that the great conflict of the Bible has been completely resolved by Jesus' atoning work of redemption on the cross. While it is certainly true that Jesus provided the means of the destruction of sin for the individual, the true conflict of sin remains, however. Sin and its destructive qualities still remains among mankind. It wreaks havoc on cultures, families and individuals; even among those who have found redemption in Christ. The scripture makes it utterly clear that the narrative of scripture did not end upon Christ's death, burial and resurrection. He rose to authority. He was given the name that is above every other name, "that at the name of Jesus every knee should bow, in heaven and on earth and under the earth, and every tongue confess that Jesus Christ is Lord, to the glory of God the Father."[1] This designation, however, is not the end of the story, for every knee has not yet bowed to him as King. While the promise of such a truth has been granted, the fruition of the promise remains a future event. The story continues.

Thus is the nature of eschatology, the theological term for the "study of end things." This work is designed to examine the remainder of the biblical narrative concerning the story of Christ's redemptive work and

---

[1] Philippians 2:10-11

Preface

establishment of himself as King of the universe with man's full acquiescence.

As this work is concerned with the end of the account, a short introduction is necessary to provide the reader some rough details concerning the beginning and the middle of the story. The first and most important detail to be observed is that the bible is not the account of man, but of God. It is *his* story, not mankind's, which the Bible is concerned. In a nutshell, God's story is that he created the heavens and the earth to reveal his own worthy glory. That creation was tainted by man's sin, inspired by God's earlier creation, Satan. At that moment, man became self-aware and antagonistic toward his God. And, from that very moment God put into place a plan of redemption; of man, the earth and the entire universe, to eradicate the sin which had entered it.

Scripture is chock full of prophecy which details the process by which God would renew the entire creation and destroy the sin within it. In Genesis God promised that an offspring of woman would destroy the work of Satan.[2] He later promised Abraham that he would be the father of a great nation who would produce this One and be a blessing to the entire earth.[3] He promised that a great King would arise from David's lineage which would rule the earth forever.[4] Promise after promise, the Lord ensured the conflict would be resolved through a future coming King.

There are two general categories of such promises which God revealed. The first was a categorical promise of an atoning for sin. This coming King would offer himself as a substitutionary payment for the penalty of sin, which God himself demanded was to be death.[5] God then promised that this King would rise from the dead and be exalted to God's right

---

[2] Genesis 3:15
[3] Genesis 12:2-3
[4] Isaiah 9:6-7
[5] Isaiah 53:4-5

hand.[6] Jesus has fulfilled these promises. They are historical realities.

It is the second general category of promise concerning this coming Messiah which is essential to the end of the story. He is to come a second time to be the King of the earth.[7] He is to rule the earth in person for a one thousand year term, after which he will usher in the final judgments of God upon the sin which remains in existence. He is to permanently re-create the earth and establish Heaven upon it.

The examination of the numerous remaining promises of God are the purpose of this work. While Jesus has indeed come and offered a glorious personal restoration to those who will receive him as their King today, he will come again and complete that restoration on a profoundly complete level. As such, the end of the story is as of yet unwritten in history. It is the supreme privilege of a future age, perhaps this very generation, to witness astonishing events which will unfold in light of God's judgment of sin, installation of his King, and restoration of his creation.

No story can be properly understood without knowledge of its end. Nor is a narrative complete without the expression of its true resolution. *The Return of The King* is the biblical account of that which remains untold historically. It is a scriptural expose' concerning the end of the story.

---

[6] Isaiah 53:11
[7] Mark 13:26, Revelation 3:3, Isaiah 9:6

Preface . . . .

Introduction

About This Work
Its Purpose

Many have undertaken the study of times and things to come. The goal of this particular writing is not to necessarily unearth any radically new insights nor to attempt to decisively debunk those which are contrary to the conclusions of the author. It seems, however, that most biblical studies in this field are written too far to one side or the other of two extremes. Either they are written with too much prerequisite knowledge for the average lay reader to comprehend or they are written in common language, yet with a sincere lack of biblical foundation, rendering the conclusions of the author more postulate than demonstrable theology. Neither is fitting for a serious work on the subject geared toward a broad range of readership.

It is the purpose of *The Return of The King* to find a medium between these two extremes. *The Return of The King* will attempt to present a clear and decisively biblically based set of conclusions on the subject of eschatology (or end time events) while also attempting to inform and educate the reader as to common theological terms and ideas which may be presumed knowledge in other works of this nature.

Furthermore, the purpose of this work is to attempt to build a timeline of eschatology, rather than to focus extensively on each event or series which makes up the whole. While most coming historical events will receive substantial attention, the goal is to paint an overall *portrait* of the events of eschatology, while giving careful attention to the underlying biblical texts which present the timeline.

This work is not intended to be divisive

The study of eschatology can easily span one's entire lifetime while leaving many questions unanswered. Additionally, *many exceptionally bright and doctrinally sound theologians disagree on the conclusions of their eschatological studies.* It would be simultaneously egotistical and naïve for anyone to believe themselves the final authority in this very difficult field. Some of the author's favorite theologians adhere to views vastly different from his own.

Eschatology should not be divisive. It is non-essential doctrine, for a large part, and is exceptionally colored with symbolic language. It is clear from scripture itself that elements of end time prophecy are intentionally shrouded until the times pre-determined for their unveiling are at hand.[8] It appears, therefore, by design that eschatology has questions which remain unanswered and can be interpreted differently by different individuals. While these elements will remain concealed until their proper time, it is still the responsibility and joy of the biblical student to ponder and understand that which *can* be known, which will inevitably lend itself to differing opinions.

This work is not unbiased.

This work will not contrast the many differing views on eschatology, but will be a study of the author's understanding, which is a wide-spread view known as *dispensational pre-tribulational premillennialism.*

> ***Dispensationalism*** is one of several frameworks which describes one's understanding of the flow of the Bible. Basically, dispensationalism is the understanding that God's work on earth follows time periods of differing purposes or revelations of his character. For instance, in the Garden of Eden a dispensation of innocence is commonly described by dispensationalists. After the giving of the Law of Moses, many see that a dispensation of law existed. After Christ's substitutionary death there existed a dispensation of grace. God's work during the church age, under grace, is far different than God's work was during the age of innocence or the age of law. Dispensationalism should not be

---

[8] Daniel 12:9-10

understood as a concept whereby God changes his attributes or character, but rather a process whereby God reveals himself to mankind through a series of sequential steps throughout history. Furthermore, characteristics of dispensationalism include the consistent literal interpretation of scripture and the understanding that Israel and the church are two separate entities in scripture.

Pretribulationalism is the belief that a removal of the church (or a "rapture") from the earth in bodily form will take place prior to a period known as "the great tribulation" (which will be discussed later in this work). This belief maintains that the church will not be present on earth during the great tribulation, but will be with Christ until he returns. This view is based to some extent on scriptural references indicating that believers in Christ are not subject to God's wrath. This does not mean that believers are not subject to other tribulations, but specifically the wrath which the great tribulation will hold for those who refuse to submit to God's lordship.

Premillennialism is a view focusing on a more stringently literal interpretation of the Bible in eschatological passages as opposed to a purely figurative or metaphorical view of these biblical texts. A more literal view of these texts leads one to understand that Christ will physically return to the earth and establish a one thousand year reign as King on earth. Contrasting views include *Amillennialism*, which teaches that the one thousand year reign of Christ spoken of in Revelation 20 is metaphorical, and began upon Christ's resurrection. While Amillennialists should not be considered as *not* interpreting the Bible literally, they do hold to metaphorical interpretations of scripture in areas where dispensationalists do not.

The author of this work maintains the Bible as a primarily literal work, even in apocalyptic literature (literature which prophetically reveals end time events). While some of the language is particularly metaphorical in apocalyptic literature, the underlying truths are literal, historical and tangible.

Introduction

Occasionally in this study alternative views will be mentioned to solidify the author's establishment of his premillennial position. Yet, this study is not intended to give a well-rounded overview of each alternative system.

This Study is not comprehensive.

A truly comprehensive study of this nature is a life-long venture which many have undertaken at great expense. The purpose of this study is to do a relatively thorough overview of the timeline from the period of the current generation through the eternal kingdom of Heaven as outlined in the Bible. Most major events will be covered in thorough detail, however, and this study will likely be more comprehensive than some.

While not comprehensive in its covering of biblical material, this study *will* be comprehensive in its coverage of future history. Some studies cover only the tribulational period and the return of Christ, for example. This study will cover events leading up to the tribulational period, through the very end of history in the eternal kingdom of Heaven.

About The Author's Conclusions

The author has served over twenty years in local church ministry and is a Biblicist; believing that the Bible is a literal work and that *all* essential doctrines of the Christian faith are discovered and defined by the writings it contains. He does not believe that doctrinal beliefs should be formulated based upon the writings of any man, creed or teacher beyond the biblical writers, whom he believes were inspired by God for their work in the assembly of the scriptures, which are God's very own account of himself, history and truth. While the teachings of theologians and ministers are essential for Christian growth, it is the author's understanding that all biblical teaching is to come fully from one's understanding of scripture, rather than one's political, ideological or cultural views.

To that end, every conclusion observed in this study will be formed by a careful examination of the biblical passages that teach it. The contents of this work is, in effect, a large-scale Bible Study which will topically address the timeline of eschatology. At times the author *will* give a personal opinion on the subject matter, but will always note such, and will support a purely biblical approach to conclusions made in this work.

Key Terms

There are a number of terms that will be used throughout this study. This section is to prepare the lay reader for the use of these terms, which may be referenced prior to their full explanations.

Tribulation: Biblically, a "tribulation" is simply a trial or extremely difficult season in the life of an individual. For the purposes of this study, "tribulation" will likely be referring to a specific tribulation, known as "the great tribulation," when the term is used in a specific historical reference.

The great tribulation will be defined as a seven year period prior to the return of Christ in which terrible judgments are poured out upon the earth and a final call to repentance will be given to the whole of mankind. A sizeable portion of this study will detail the events of The great tribulation, or "the tribulation."

Antichrist: The term "antichrist" refers to a systematized approach which is the polar opposite of the person, teachings and character of Jesus Christ, while attempting to present itself as authentically Christian. For the purposes of this study, the term will be most commonly used as a proper name, as it is used biblically in certain texts. Antichrist is the name of a world leader who will essentially rule the earth during the tribulation and who will establish himself as a false Christ.

Eschatology: Eschatology, simply put, is the study of end time teachings. Specifically, in this work, eschatology will refer to end time teachings from a uniquely biblical perspective.

Millennium: The term literally means "one thousand years." For the purposes of this work, it will refer to a specific one thousand years: the one thousand years in which Christ will rule the earth as King after his return.

Chapter 1: Pre-tribulational Events

Concerning the progression of the timeline of the end of this age, the seven year period known as the great tribulation is a focal season. It is the advent of the great tribulation which begins God's prophetic countdown to Christ's return. However, that season is not yet upon the earth. It is still to come, as prophecies remain to be fulfilled prior to its dawn. Categorically, these remaining forecasted marker events are known as "pre-tribulational events."

The study of pre-tribulational events, or those events which must precede the great tribulation, is a particularly fascinating venture because many of these predictions are now historical realities. In fact, *most* pre-tribulational prophesies have unfolded as of the writing of this work, causing many to believe that mankind is indeed relatively close to the period of the great tribulation, while causing others to incorrectly conclude that the great tribulation is now underway. Several of these predictions, now understood as mere history, were once thought unlikely at best and highly improbably at worst. The realized fulfillment of these biblical prophecies is the very confirmation of the Bible as God's own testimony to mankind. In this section several interesting biblical prophesies will be observed that could *only* have been predicted by men to whom God himself had truly spoken; the biblical writers. To be certain, the timeline of eschatology does not begin at some point in the future, but has begun already; much of which is now historical record.

General Birth Pains

Beginning with the most general in nature of the pre-tribulational prophesies are what Jesus categorically called "birth pains." While numerous pre-tribulational prophecies are highly articulate and specific, these events, described in Matthew 24:3-8, are of a very general nature. Being however broad in scope, one should note that these are the words of Christ, himself, warning his disciples that the advent of these particular events is a sign that the end is approaching. They are in effect the previews before the main event begins.

Chapter 1: Pre-tribulational Events

. . . .

Jesus' symbolic reference to these events as "birth pains" indicates a similarity between these events and literal birth pains. Just as birth pains are not indicative that a child is to be born at that very moment, so these events are a sign of the season only. They do not indicate that the end times have arrived, but that the end is drawing near. And, as birth pains increase in their intensity and regularity as birth approaches, many of these events will intensify historically to notify the earth of the pending advent of the end times.

> ***Matthew 24:3-8***
> *³As Jesus was sitting on the Mount of Olives, the disciples came to him privately. "Tell us," they said, "when will this happen, and what will be the sign of your coming and of the end of the age?"*
>
> *⁴ Jesus answered: "Watch out that no one deceives you. ⁵ For many will come in my name, claiming, 'I am the Christ,' and will deceive many. ⁶ You will hear of wars and rumors of wars, but see to it that you are not alarmed. Such things must happen, but the end is still to come. ⁷ Nation will rise against nation, and kingdom against kingdom. There will be famines and earthquakes in various places. ⁸ All these are the beginning of birth pains."*

Matthew 24 begins what is commonly referred to as "The Olivet Discourse." In this text, Jesus and the disciples are leaving Jerusalem when a conversation about the future destruction of the temple ensues. This discussion leads the disciples to ask three questions: *"when will this happen, and what will be the sign of your coming"* and [what will be the sign of] *"the end of the age?"* The Olivet Discourse will be observed in pieces throughout this work, but what is relevant at this point can be noted in verse 6, *"but the end is still to come."* From this statement, it is clear that Jesus actually begins by answering the third question, relating to the signs of the end of the age.

Scriptural interpretation requires one to utilize a historical-cultural interpretational method. Jesus and the disciples he spoke with were Jewish and communicated within the context of their cultural norms. In Jewish thought, the timeline of history was commonly relegated to two ages: the current age, and the age to come, which was the coming age of Messiah's reign. From the book of Genesis, throughout the Old Testament, prophesies existed which pointed to a coming Messiah. Jewish thinking toward the "age to come" yearned for the advent of Messiah's reign. The difficulty was that Jewish scholars, while they knew the prophetic writings very well, had not definitively discerned messianic prophesies (prophesies concerning the coming of the Messiah) into their two types. Some messianic prophecies spoke of the first coming of Messiah, when he would be offered as a substitutionary atonement (see Isaiah 52-53) and other messianic prophecies predicted his return, when Messiah would subdue the earth as its King. It appears from the New Testament that Israel was looking for her Messiah to arrive as the conquering King and had somehow managed to overlook or misinterpret messianic prophesies which spoke of the suffering servant, who would fulfill the Law of Moses and secure salvation for mankind. It is this misapprehension which some believe led Israel to completely reject Christ as their Messiah. He did not come and conquer Rome, for example, which had dominated Israel. Instead he lived a humble life which resulted in an untimely death on a cross. Perhaps because he did not fit the common profile of the King they desired to embrace, Christ was rejected as the Messiah of the "age to come" by Jewish leaders, and consequently by Israel as a whole.

Clearly from Matthew 23, although the whole of Israel had rejected Christ as their Messiah, the disciples *had* in fact received him as Messiah. While understanding that Messiah had come in the person of Christ, they still asked the question concerning the end of this age, which would signify the coming of the "age to come." They clearly were asking about his second coming, as he stood before them in the fruition of his first coming. Specifically, they were asking him "*what are the signs*" of the end of this age, which would then be the precursor to the next age, Christ's return as the Messiah of kingship for which Israel had long yearned. The disciples recognized that Jesus was the one who was

Chapter 1: Pre-tribulational Events

to establish the coming kingdom. Their question was simple; "*what will be the signs*" of that eventuality.

In the first part of Jesus' answer to this question, he notes several signs that will precede the end of this age, or will be "*the beginnings of birth pains,*" as he notes in verse 8.

The first sign is that false Christs will appear. Jesus notes, "*Watch out that no one deceives you. For many will come in my name, claiming, 'I am the Christ,' and will deceive many.*" Indeed, false Christs appeared even from the time of the early church. Yet, Jesus' prophecy in this text is that "*many*" will come claiming "*I am the Christ,*" and will deceive *many* people. Jesus' birth pain analogy will be observable as the increase of the frequency and intensity of this particular event advances. *Many* will come to deceive, and will have much success in their work.

Modern history has demonstrated a situation fitting to Jesus' words. At the time Jesus came, he was the first noted historical figure to have proclaimed himself the Christ. False Christs did follow thereafter, even in the first centuries following Jesus, but nowhere near the extent as they have appeared in recent history. Jim Jones, David Koresh & Sun Myung Moon are all examples of men who have claimed to be Christ in modern history. More recently, José Luis De Jesús Miranda is a current contender in the false Christ category. The Houston Press News reports, "Along with congregations scattered across the Americas, his ministry, Creciendo en Gracia (Growing in Grace), has a 24-hour cable channel, complete with sermons, news programs and music videos, that reportedly reaches over two million homes."[9]

Perhaps a man leading 75 Branch Davidians in a field near Waco doesn't fit the description of a "false Christ" to some, but when a man reaches 2 million homes in a 24 hour cable TV ministry, he clearly can be said to "*deceive many,*" as Christ warned. Miranda is only one of many who

---

[9] http://www.houstonpress.com/2006-11-30/news/this-man-thinks-he-s-jesus-h-christ/

have claimed to be Christ, and undoubtedly more will follow, as the words of the real Jesus indicate.

In the next birth pain, Jesus informs the disciples in verse 6 that they will hear *"of wars and rumors of wars, but see to it that you are not alarmed. Such things must happen, but the end is still to come."* He then adds in verse 7 that *"Nation will rise against nation, and kingdom against kingdom."* The idea presented by Jesus' warning here is one of truly global warfare. In modern history the advent of global warfare was introduced in World Wars I and II. Even the smaller modern Gulf Wars are not mere wars of two nations, but of coalitions of nations, with twenty or thirty nations involved in a singular conflict. Widespread warfare, as a sign of the beginning of birth pains, has been noted historically in these conflicts, and is a development on the scene of history which also is increasing in frequency and intensity.

Lastly, Jesus notes in verse 7, *"there will be famines and earthquakes in various places."* While this statement is very general in nature, being that it is referenced as a sign of the end of this age it must be concluded that the famines and earthquakes are of a non-typical nature. Either the severity of these disasters must be significant or their numbers must increase for this to be unique historically and thus understood as a sign. Birth pains increase both in frequency *and* intensity, so perhaps both should be considered as evidence of the season of the end nearing.

There are many eschatological works citing earthquake frequencies on the rise in modern times, yet rarely are sources given to verify the claims. However, the U.S. Geological Survey public website cites earthquake frequency findings from the past two decades which lends credible testimony to an increase in the numbers of earthquakes in recent history. USGS statistics for earthquakes world-wide indicate 16590 earthquakes in 1990[10], 22256 quakes in 2000 and 29673 in 2007[11]. While the year by year numbers vacillate, there is a notable increase in earthquake

---

[10] http://wwwneic.cr.usgs.gov/neis/eqlists/info_1990s.html
[11] http://wwwneic.cr.usgs.gov/neis/eqlists/eqstats.html

Chapter 1: Pre-tribulational Events

frequency, resulting in significant changes in just an eighteen year period.

In the end, any changes in the frequency or intensity of earthquakes and famines should be noted by the observant student. Jesus noted this birth pain as a sign that the end was approaching.

It should be again noted that Jesus' warning wasn't that an increase in global wars, false Christs, earthquakes and famines are a sign that the end has come, but that the time of the end is nearing. These signs are the beginning of birth pains. Just as a woman will begin birth pains well before the time of birth arrives, so these signs are illustrative of the times of the end nearing.

Jesus next illuminates another category of signs which will follow the general birth pains. These are the signs which would immediately precede the time of the end and are found in Matthew 24:9-14.

> [9] *"Then you will be handed over to be persecuted and put to death, and you will be hated by all nations because of me.* [10] *At that time many will turn away from the faith and will betray and hate each other,* [11] *and many false prophets will appear and deceive many people.* [12] *Because of the increase of wickedness, the love of most will grow cold,* [13] *but he who stands firm to the end will be saved.* [14] *And this gospel of the kingdom will be preached in the whole world as a testimony to all nations, and then the end will come.*

In verse 9, "*you will be handed over to be persecuted*" speaks directly to the disciples as Jewish men. "*You will be hated by all nations because of me*" speaks of their national affiliation being hated by the national affiliation of others. Some have understood this statement to be indicative of the persecution of the early church. This may be true in light of an interpretive rule called "the law of double reference," which will be discussed later in this work. It possibly speaks to Jesus' generation as well as a generation to come. However, in light of Jesus making this statement in the context of birth pains and the signs of the end, it is best understood to apply toward future times as a more general phenomenon of anti-Semitism. Jesus' direct warning is to the disciples, being Jewish men, and "*all nations*" of others who are to persecute them.

Perhaps at no time in history has anti-Semitism been as prevalent as the post-1948 period, since Israel has been re-established as a sovereign nation. While Israel has had ongoing conflicts with Arab nations throughout its entire history, Jesus noted her pending hatred "*by all nations*," which points to a more extensive anti-Semitism. It seems today that public sentiment is readily turned against Israel, even in favor or terroristic activities which target Israel. News media and citizens worldwide have a tendency to find Israel at fault when logic demands that she is not. This type of sentiment validates Jesus' warning that she will *"be hated"* by all nations. Some are also quick to note the holocaust, likewise, as a sign of Jewish hatred. The holocaust, however, was relegated to the hatred of a singular nation. Post-1948 history has wrought an increase of disdain for Jews on a more global level.

Verse 11 turns again to impostors of the faith, citing *"many false prophets will appear and deceive many people."* Differing from a false Christ, as Jesus noted earlier, the false prophet is one who claims to be a prophet of God but fails to meet biblical criteria for that position.

False prophets, in the Old Testament, were defined as men who claimed to be prophets of God, yet their prophecies did not come to pass with 100% accuracy. Deuteronomy 18:21-22 says,

> *"[21] You may say to yourselves, "How can we know when a message has not been spoken by the LORD?" [22] If what a prophet proclaims in the name of the LORD does not take place or come true, that is a message the LORD has not spoken. That prophet has spoken presumptuously. Do not be afraid of him."*

With the completion of the New Testament, prophets have an even

Chapter 1: Pre-tribulational Events

stronger biblical criteria in that their words must align with the scriptures[12]. Vast numbers of teachers exist today which have failed on both accounts. And, as Jesus prophesied, *"they will deceive many people,"* indeed. Today's false prophets have surpassed even the ministry of the false Christ, Miranda, and are instead infiltrating the church itself with bogus teachings through an impressive array of television programs aimed at propagating their unbiblical doctrines, and more times than not, filling their pockets with cash.

Benny Hinn is one well known example from among thousands who fit this criteria. Hinn "prophesied" in the 90's that before the year 2000 God would destroy America's homosexual community, Fidel Castro would die, America would elect its first female president and that the east coast would be devastated by earthquakes.[13] False teachings notwithstanding, Hinn establishes himself as one who hears God speak and presumes to forward that message to thousands of eager listeners. When God speaks, however, what God has said will actually happen. When one who presumes to speak on God's account is wrong, he is, by definition, a false prophet.

Clearly failing the Old Testament test in that his words did not come true, he also fails the New Testament test by preaching a supposed "truth" which he derives from his self-proclaimed "revelation knowledge," which is supposed supernatural information which does not appear in the Bible, but only to Hinn himself. 2 Peter 2:3 (NIV) notes *"In their greed these teachers will exploit you with stories they have made up."* Thus, the authority of scripture must be the sole basis for any and all genuine Christian prophecy. Clearly, Peter does not allow men to "make up" their doctrine as so many today are in the habit of doing. The church is not a self-help class. It is a congregation of people who submit themselves to the lordship of the God of the Bible. Thus, all teachings concerning God are to come from that very source.

In all fairness to Hinn, he is only one of multitudes who preach made up

---

[12] Heb 1:1-2, 2 Pe 1:20, 2:1-3; 21
[13] http://en.wikipedia.org/wiki/Benny_hinn

doctrines and lead astray millions for the sake of personal wealth, power or other reasons. It is the author's estimation that at no time in history has there been a greater deception in the church than the present, nor a greater breadth of existing false ministries. The airwaves of supposed "Christian" television reach untold millions of homes daily with the deceptions of false teachers. Truly it can be said that at this very time that "*many false prophets*" have appeared who "*deceive many people.*"

Jesus further states that "*this gospel of the kingdom will be preached in the whole world as a testimony to all nations."* This statement being a final warning before stating "*and then the end will come"* doesn't necessarily indicate that the preaching of the gospel to the whole world is the last thing that will happen before then end, but that the preaching of the gospel to the whole world will occur before the end can come. This phrase will be observed later in this work as an event which is fulfilled in the beginning of the great tribulation, which is that time most immediately preceding the end of this age. The preaching of the gospel to all nations, for that reason, perhaps should be understood as an event of the tribulation rather than a pre-tribulational event. The tribulation itself is not the end, but the final seven years before the end of this age.

The Re-establishment of Israel

One of the most fascinating pre-tribulational prophesies concerns a seemingly unlikely historical event. Israel is shown in Ezekiel 20 being restored as a nation, for the purpose of being judged and purged in preparation to repent and receive their Messiah, Christ. Israel will receive Christ toward the end of the tribulation but must be re-established as a nation prior to the beginning of the tribulation. This may not seem particularly fascinating on the surface, but considering that Israel was not a nation *at all* from the first century until 1948, this is actually a *quite* impressive prophecy which has come to pass in the lifetime of the current generation.

> ***Ezekiel 20:32-38***
> [32] *"'You say, "We want to be like the nations, like the*

Chapter 1: Pre-tribulational Events

> *peoples of the world, who serve wood and stone." But what you have in mind will never happen. ³³ As surely as I live, declares the Sovereign LORD, I will rule over you with a mighty hand and an outstretched arm and with outpoured wrath. ³⁴ I will bring you from the nations and gather you from the countries where you have been scattered--with a mighty hand and an outstretched arm and with outpoured wrath. ³⁵ I will bring you into the desert of the nations and there, face to face, I will execute judgment upon you. ³⁶ As I judged your fathers in the desert of the land of Egypt, so I will judge you, declares the Sovereign LORD. ³⁷ I will take note of you as you pass under my rod, and I will bring you into the bond of the covenant. ³⁸ I will purge you of those who revolt and rebel against me. Although I will bring them out of the land where they are living, yet they will not enter the land of Israel. Then you will know that I am the LORD.*

In verse 34 God informs Israel that he will "*bring you from the nations and gather you from the countries where you have been scattered.*"

This prophecy is two-fold regarding the sovereignty of the nation of Israel. First, it determines the scattering of the Israelites among the nations of the world at a future date from Ezekiel's writing. Secondly, it determines the gathering back of this people group into a nation once again. In historical retrospect it is understood that this timeline included almost 1900 years of the non-existent nation of Israel which would be brought back together and re-instituted by God's pre-determined plan.

In verse 36 God draws a simile between this event and the exodus, when he brought Israel out of Egypt and judged them in the Sinai dessert for their rebellion. At that time he purged the nation of those who dissented against him and allowed a new generation to enter the Promised Land. Verse 38 states, "*I will purge you of those who revolt and rebel against me,*" indicating that Israel will at this future date again be purged of those who have rebelled against God. The unveiling of God's program for

Israel will be outlined later in this work, but begins with God's bringing Israel back from the nations which she has been scattered for the purpose of this purging, which will be observed in chapters 3-5 concerning the great tribulation. In order for Israel to be subject to God's purging of her unbelievers, he will reconstitute her into a nation once again.

Verse 37 speaks of Israel being brought into the bond of the covenant. This refers to the national salvation of Israel, bringing them into the new covenant with Christ, after their purging as noted in Jeremiah 31.

> ***Jeremiah 31:31-33***
> *[31] "The time is coming," declares the LORD,*
> *"when I will make a new covenant*
> *with the house of Israel*
> *and with the house of Judah.*
> *[32] It will not be like the covenant*
> *I made with their forefathers*
> *when I took them by the hand*
> *to lead them out of Egypt,*
> *because they broke my covenant,*
> *though I was a husband to them, "*
> *declares the LORD.*
> *[33] "This is the covenant I will make with the house of Israel*
> *after that time," declares the LORD.*
> *"I will put my law in their minds*
> *and write it on their hearts.*
> *I will be their God,*
> *and they will be my people.*

This text indicates the final restoration of Israel as they receive their Messiah. Yet this prophecy can only occur after Israel is once again a nation and has undergone the purging of Ezekiel 20.

This reconciliation of Israel from the nations of the earth is an important pre-tribulational event. It will furthermore be demonstrated in this work that the great tribulation will begin with the signing of a seven-year

Chapter 1: Pre-tribulational Events

covenant between Israel and the Antichrist. For such to happen, Israel will be required to be a sovereign nation which is capable of accepting such a treaty.

Israel became a nation once again, gathered from the corners of the earth, in 1948, thus fulfilling the beginning, at least, of this prophecy.

Beyond this text, numerous other prophecies will be examined over the course of this study which will demand that Israel be a sovereign nation for their fulfillment to occur. If there is no Israel, these prophesies have no subject. It is essential to a literal interpretation of biblical prophecy that Israel would be re-established as a nation at some point prior to the great tribulation.

Surely there was a great period in history when such prophecies would have seemed an impossibility to be literally fulfilled. Israel had truly been scattered to the corners of the earth, as the nation was decimated by AD 70, seemingly never to be heard of again. Yet, through God's providence a miraculous series of events transpired to bring Israel back into national status nearly two millennia after her demise.

Many questions must have existed to a pre-1948 prophetically inquisitive mind. How would Israelites retain a national identity 1900 years after the destruction of their nation? In America, known as a "melting pot" for its ethnic diversity, after only a few hundred years of history as a nation, many do not fully, or even partially know their ethnic heritage. Yet, the Jews always knew who they were, even after having been scattered among the nations and having countless generations integrated into other cultures. Prophecy teaches overwhelmingly that God is not finished with Israel as a nation. He therefore had forged their national identity into their collective memories, while so many other conquered people groups in history have forgotten their roots in very few generations. For 1900 years, Jews remained Jews although thoroughly distributed and ingested into other societies world-wide.

One also may have wondered how a group of people would be motivated to return to their homeland after fifty generations had passed from the demise of their national status. What is the call that would cause one to leave the only home one has known in order to resettle in an ancient homeland? Yet, Jews in great numbers desired to return to Israel when given the opportunity. For several hundred years prior to the re-establishment of a Jewish nation the descendants of Israel were migrating back to their geographical homeland. Truly nothing in history has come close to the perplexing migration of Jews back to their historical homeland.

While beyond the scope of this work, another phenomenal historic event was the very process of Israel's re-establishment as a nation. That a group of people could re-emerge on their geographical homeland and defend themselves against sovereign nations intent on their removal has defied all logic numerous times over. Israel has outfought, outlasted and outdone herself in ways that can only be understood in light of a divine intervention on her behalf.

Today, Israel is a highly developed nation with exceptional world potential and one of the most educated populations on earth. As improbable as this must have seemed only one hundred years ago, it is an impeccable demonstration of the power of God's hand in history and the firm grasp his Word has in reality. He has brought it to pass exactly as prophesied. Israel is a nation again after almost two millennia, in her place and prepared to receive her lot as God unfolds the destiny he has written for her.

Rebuilding of the Jewish Temple

Another group of prophecies which tell an astounding story are those writings which speak of the use of the Jewish temple in the tribulation as well as the millennial kingdom of Christ. There is, of course, no temple in Jerusalem currently to give fulfillment to such forecasts. The first temple, Solomon's Temple, was destroyed in 586 BC by the Babylonians. The second temple was destroyed by the Romans along with the dismantling of the nation in 70 AD. Since Israel has become a

Chapter 1: Pre-tribulational Events

nation again, the temple has not been rebuilt. To some, the idea of the Jewish temple being rebuilt is as unlikely as was the re-establishment of a Jewish nation.

While prophetic passages depict the temple playing a noticable role in tribulational events, it is unclear if the temple will be actually built prior to the beginning of the tribulation or shortly thereafter. Thus, the inclusion of this subject in a chapter entitled "Pre-tribulational Events" is based on some amount of speculation. While the timing of the beginning of construction on a new Temple is not certain, what is known with certainty from scripture is that the Temple will be built and will be in use by the middle of the tribulation, as is described below by Daniel. To that end, it seems very *likely* that the construction on the temple will have at least begun by the advent of the tribulation, as the last temple took many decades to complete.

> ***Daniel 9:27***
> *^{27} He will confirm a covenant with many for one 'seven.' In the middle of the 'seven' he will put an end to sacrifice and offering. And on a wing [of the temple] he will set up an abomination that causes desolation, until the end that is decreed is poured out on him".*

The "he" in this text refers to Antichrist, a world ruler and the key character of Satan's own agenda work during the great tribulation. This assertion will be demonstrated later when Daniel 9 will be studied in more detail, but at this time it must only be gleaned that "he" will "*put an end to sacrifice and offering*" in the middle of the tribulation (the middle of the seven) and establish an abomination on a wing of the temple. Thus, a temple must be built and fully operational by the middle of the tribulation. It must obviously be built by its very reference in the text. Yet, it must also be operational, as Antichrist will "*put an end to sacrifice and offering*," which will require the temple to actually be functioning as a center for sacrificial worship.

Jesus referenced this text from Daniel as an end time prophecy in Matthew 24:15. "*So when you see standing in the holy place 'the*

abomination that causes desolation,' spoken of through the prophet Daniel--let the reader understand-- ^{16} *then let those who are in Judea flee to the mountains."* This *"abomination of desolation"* references Daniel 9:27 in the same context as the earlier observation of the Olivet Discourse, answering the questions *"what will be the sign of your coming and of the end of the age?"* Thus, the abomination of desolation, which will occur in the temple, also requires that the temple must be rebuilt.

Yet another text referencing the temple in the tribulation is found in 2 Thessalonians. While speaking of the day of the return of Christ, Paul writes,

> ***2 Thessalonians 2:3-4***
> *³ Don't let anyone deceive you in any way, for that day will not come until the rebellion occurs and the man of lawlessness is revealed, the man doomed to destruction. ⁴ He will oppose and will exalt himself over everything that is called God or is worshiped, so that he sets himself up in God's temple, proclaiming himself to be God.*

Paul speaks also of the man who will be known as "Antichrist," citing the same *"abomination of desolation"* noted by Daniel and Jesus. Once again, an end time prophetical text speaks of an active temple during the period of the great tribulation. Thus, the non-existent temple must be built and operational by the middle of the tribulation. (This timing will be demonstrated in Chapter Three.)

While much of modern Israel seems relatively unconcerned with their religious heritage, having a temple in Israel has been a long-standing desire of some modern Jews. In existence today is an organization known as *The Temple Institute*, which states on its website the goal of being "dedicated to every aspect of the Biblical Commandment to build the Holy Temple of G-d on Mount Moriah in Jerusalem."[14] While the building of a third temple faces seemingly insurmountable obstacles, so

---

[14] http://www.templeinstitute.org/about.htm

did the re-emergence of a nation lost for 1900 years.

The historical site of the former temples in Jerusalem is commonly referred to as the "Temple Mount". At that location, in roughly the exact place where the former temple stood, the Dome of The Rock now exists. The Dome of The Rock is considered one of the most holy of Islamic sights. It is the oldest extant Muslim building and is considered by Muslims as the place where Mohammad ascended into Heaven.

The Temple Mount was acquired by Israel in the 1967 Six Day War, yet Israel has allowed Muslim control of it for the sake of the poor relations between the two groups. Muslims have since forbidden Jewish prayer in that location. The use of the temple compound is a volatile issue between Jews and Muslims on an ongoing basis. It will be interesting to see how both Jews and Muslims will come to terms with God's plan for a temple to be rebuilt on that site. Both groups consider the site their most revered and holy ground. Surely a great issue must be resolved. It is unimaginable that Israel would desire to build their future temple on any other piece of real estate. Nor is it fathomable that Muslims will allow the Dome of The Rock to be destroyed without a fight.

Some have suggested that the treaty between Antichrist and Israel, which will be discussed later in this work, may include the solution to this issue by Antichrist somehow negotiating the building of the temple on that site in exchange for Israel's commitment to a peace treaty with him. That suggestion is extra-biblical and purely speculative, however. Moreover, it will be determined from scripture that Israel's safety will be the primary reason for her covenant with Antichrist, rather than a peaceful resolution to the Temple Mount issue. God will reveal his plan in due time concerning how the rebuilding of the temple will come to fruition. But, in whatever way it is to happen, a temple must be constructed prior to the middle of the tribulation. And, scriptural descriptions concerning the location of the Millennial Temple, which will be examined later, strongly indicate that it will be built at that very location.

The Gog-Magog War

Another event understood to be pre-tribulational involves a future battle concerning Israel. Ezekiel prophesies an attack against that which must be understood to refer to modern Israel, as the conditions of this event are such that it cannot refer to a former time in Israel's history. This attack is another event which has not yet happened as of the writing of this work. This prophecy is outlined in Ezekiel 38 with substantial detail. Commonly referred to as a war, it could perhaps be more accurately thought of as a battle, as it will be brief and not widespread, though it will certainly be noteworthy.

Amusingly, prophecies concerning the Gog-Magog War have led many students of eschatology to continually postulate any and all attacks against Israel as somehow connected to this particular forecast. When a rogue terrorist group launches an isolated attack across Israeli borders, people immediately begin speculating the advent of the Gog-Magog war. However, the events prophesied by Ezekiel concerning this conflict make it abundantly clear that this particular event will be easily discernable to students of eschatology. It will not be something that will slip through the news cycle at media outlets without a great deal of attention. It will be large-scale, calculated and will end in such a miraculous way that the world will be forced to ponder in great awe what exactly had happened when it is over.

Ezekiel describes this attack in a nearly perfect who, what, when, where, how and why fashion.

Who are the attackers?

> ***Ezekiel 38:1-6***
> *[1] The word of the LORD came to me: [2] "Son of man, set your face against Gog, of the land of Magog, the chief prince of Meshech and Tubal; prophesy against him [3] and say: 'This is what the Sovereign LORD says: I am against you, O Gog, chief prince of Meshech and Tubal. [4] I will turn you around, put hooks in your jaws and*

Chapter 1: Pre-tribulational Events

> *bring you out with your whole army--your horses, your horsemen fully armed, and a great horde with large and small shields, all of them brandishing their swords. ⁵ Persia, Cush and Put will be with them, all with shields and helmets, ⁶ also Gomer with all its troops, and Beth Togarmah from the far north with all its troops--the many nations with you.*

Magog, Rosh, Meshech, and Tubal are ancient tribes that occupied the geographical area of modern day Russia, and parts of Iran and Turkey. Magog, Meshech and Tubal were sons of Japheth. Magog's descendants, according to Josephus[15], were the Scythians. The Scythians occupied an area above the Black Sea in modern day Ukraine and western Russia.

Gog and Magog are mentioned also in the book of Revelation, which will be covered toward the end of this study. However, it is the author's understanding that in Ezekiel, Magog is a geographical reference, along with Rosh, Meshech and Tubal, while in Revelation Gog and Magog are symbolic references to all nations without Christ which are susceptible to Satanic deception.

Meshech is understood by many biblical and historical scholars as the ancestors of the Russian people. It is believed that several Russian geographical names, such as Moscow, the Meschera tribe and the Meshchera Lowlands, could be related to Meshech.

Tubal, also being a son of Japheth, is almost always coupled with Meshech in scripture. Tubal's descendants are understood to be the Tiberini of the Greek historian Herodotus, a people of the Asiatic highland west of the Upper Euphrates, the southern range of the Caucasus, on the east of the Black Sea.[16] In modern terms, this area would include modern day Georgia, and could include Turkish and

---

[15] Flavius, Josephus: "Jewish Antiquities", book 1 chapter 6 page 123. Boston: Harvard University Press, 1930.
[16] Easton's Illustrated Dictionary

Iranian areas to the south and Russian areas to the north.

Rosh was the seventh son of Benjamin in Genesis 46:21. The geographical location of Rosh's descendants are difficult to trace, but in this text are relegated to the same general area *"far from the north"* as the other ancient nations referenced. Coincidentally, tracing *"from the far north"* from Israel, in a straight line, one arrives at Moscow, Russia.

The prophecy is spoken against *"Gog,"* who is referenced as the ruler of Meshech and Tubal. Specifically he is named as "*the chief prince of Meshech and Tubal.*" To that end, Gog should be understood as a title, such as "Caesar." Because the prophecy is spoken against Gog, it is apparent that the area consistent with modern day Russia is the leading nation in this attack, as Gog is the chief prince of nations which formerly occupied that geographical area. This is a coalition attack of numerous people groups, in retrospect, fitting well with Jesus' words examined earlier in Matthew 24 of wide-spread warfare as a birth pain pointing toward the times of the end.

Verses 5 and 6 note other nations involved in the attack: Persia (present day Iran), Cush (modern day Ethiopia), Put (modern day Somalia), Gomer, referred to as *Germania* in the *Midrash* and the *Talmud* (modern day Germany) and Togarman (Armenia).

Many have attempted to determine the nations involved in this attack by historical evidences rather than the Bible itself. This has led many to turn away from the "Russian" leadership of this attack due to the fall of the former Soviet Union. However, the Bible speaks of the geographic areas of its own day rather than referencing specific modern nations. The fall of the former Soviet Union is irrelevant to the interpretation of this prophecy. Perhaps Russia itself will fall and be named another name. The biblical geography is what is relevant to understanding who is involved, not the names of the modern nations, themselves.

It is tempting to try to interpret the Bible in light of current events. However, the student of eschatology should understand that current

Chapter 1: Pre-tribulational Events

events are, in fact, determined by the Bible. The presupposition of this work is that the Bible is unfailing in its teaching and that history will unfold as it has been prophesied. Thus, regardless of the future outcomes of any nations currently occupying these areas, the people who occupy this geography at the time of the attack are being specified in this text.

This coalition is said to be *"from the far North"*, though not all of these nations are North of Israel. The indication is that they are attacking from the North and that their leadership is from the far North (modern day Russia).

In summary, the attackers, unless their names or borders are changed between now and this attack, appear to be Russia, Georgia, possibly Turkey, Iran, Ethiopia, Somalia, Germany and Armenia.

Who Is Attacked?

It's clear that Israel is being attacked, but specifically, it should be noted that it is *modern* Israel which is being attacked, as opposed to the former Israel destroyed in the first century. Only modern Israel fits the description of the text.

> ### *Ezekiel 38:7-9*
> *[7] "'Get ready; be prepared, you and all the hordes gathered about you, and take command of them. [8] After many days you will be called to arms. In future years you will invade a land that has recovered from war, whose people were gathered from many nations to the mountains of Israel, which had long been desolate. They had been brought out from the nations, and now all of them live in safety. [9] You and all your troops and the many nations with you will go up, advancing like a storm; you will be like a cloud covering the land.*

Verses 8 and 9 specify the mountains of Israel as the location of this attack, and note that it will be a massive attack *"covering the land."*

26

Likewise, verse 8 describes what can only be understood as modern Israel, rather than ancient Israel, because it is a land *"that has recovered from war, whose people were gathered from many nations to the mountains of Israel, which had long been desolate."* These statements are not true of Israel in any time prior to current history. Israel has reunited as a nation, from many peoples, and have been rebuilding the communities in the mountains that had long been desolate from their former national existence. While parts of Israel have been desolate for long periods of time, only today are those places of desolation fully rebuilt and flourishing with life again. And, only today can it be accurately said that the rebuilding of those desolate places coincides with the people having been *"gathered from many nations,"* concurrent with the convergence of Jews to the land of Israel prior to and since Israel's rebirth as a nation in 1948. Israel has re-gathered from exile to its homeland at former times in history, but not from *"many nations"* as its existence today can be very literally described.

Why will they attack?

Why this coalition will attack Israel is answered in two parts by the text. The first answer is seen in verses 10-13:

> ***Ezekiel 38:10-13***
> *[10] "'This is what the Sovereign LORD says: On that day thoughts will come into your mind and you will devise an evil scheme. [11] You will say, "I will invade a land of unwalled villages; I will attack a peaceful and unsuspecting people--all of them living without walls and without gates and bars. [12] I will plunder and loot and turn my hand against the resettled ruins and the people gathered from the nations, rich in livestock and goods, living at the center of the land." [13] Sheba and Dedan and the merchants of Tarshish and all her villages will say to you, "Have you come to plunder? Have you gathered your hordes to loot, to carry off silver and gold, to take away livestock and goods and to seize much plunder?"'*

Chapter 1: Pre-tribulational Events

Verses 10-12 define the incentive for the attack to be for the spoils of war, or, "plunder & loot."

> *I will plunder and loot and turn my hand against the resettled ruins*
>
> *"Have you gathered your hordes to loot, to carry off silver and gold, to take away livestock and goods and to seize much plunder?"*

Noted specifically are silver, gold, livestock, goods and general plunder. Understanding Ezekiel's ancient world view, each of these products most likely represent a generalization of the "spoils of war" consistent with Ezekiel's day. In short, the motive will be greed. Israel will have something which the attackers desire to have for their own.

One possible source of desired plunder has been suggested to be the Dead Sea. The Dead Sea is the second largest salt lake on earth, and contains sodium, chlorine, sulfur, potassium, calcium, magnesium & numerous other minerals and chemicals which could be harvested. Its salt content is over 8 times that of the ocean[17] and among many other anomalies it produces asphalt deposits.[18] Any number of potential future chemical or mineral needs could cause the Dead Sea to become a commodity of great interest.

Other potential plunder could be energy, as Israel is a global leader in areas of geothermal energy,[19] diamonds, or Israel's general wealth, being exceptional throughout the Middle East. Whatever the coalition may say of their purpose when this day comes, the Bible states the real purpose for the attack will be greed for some element of plunder.

---

[17] Goetz, P.W. (ed.) *The New Encyclopaedia Britannica* (15th ed.). Vol. 3, p. 937. Chicago, 1986

[18] http://en.wikipedia.org/wiki/Dead_sea

[19] Ginsburg, Mitch. "A Hotter Holy Land", The Jerusalem Report, 2007-05-28.

Ezekiel 38:13 indicates that there are nations which will speak against the coalition for this attack, but in word only. There is no mention of intervention on Israel's behalf by any nation of earth, only God himself.

> *Sheba and Dedan and the merchants of Tarshish and all her villages will say to you, "Have you come to plunder? Have you gathered your hordes to loot, to carry off silver and gold, to take away livestock and goods and to seize much plunder?"*

Sheba and Dan are the areas of modern day northern Arabia, while Tarshish and all her villages is a bit more difficult to discern. *"All her villages"* probably indicates offspring nations spawned from Tarshish, but determining exactly which geographical area is indicated by the name "Tarshish" is a bit puzzling.

There are several historical regions which have been named Tarshish. Of those which have spawned other nations, one is the city of Tartessos in Southern Spain, or a Tarshish existing in England.

If the Tarshish of Spain is that which is referenced by Ezekiel, then "*her villages*" would refer to South and most of Central America. If England is the Tarshish referenced by Ezekiel, "*her villages*" would include the USA, Canada, Australia, New Zealand & some other western lands.

Who precisely opposes this attack is not relevant to the outcome, however, since their opposition is that of word only, and nothing is done to defend Israel in the attack. What is perhaps the most important deduction from this part of the text is that Sheba, Dan and Tarshish at least understand the true motives of the attack to be that of greed and are not fooled by any other potential excuse.

The second answer to the question of "why will they attack" is answered from God's perspective. Clearly the coalition who is attacking has their own motives, but Ezekiel 38 informs us that God himself has a motive for this attack, for it is he who allows it to take place, and even more so,

Chapter 1: Pre-tribulational Events

it is he who instigates this coalition to embark on this attack.

> ***Ezekiel 38:14-16***
> *¹⁴ "Therefore, son of man, prophesy and say to Gog: 'This is what the Sovereign LORD says: In that day, when my people Israel are living in safety, will you not take notice of it? ¹⁵ You will come from your place in the far north, you and many nations with you, all of them riding on horses, a great horde, a mighty army. ¹⁶ You will advance against my people Israel like a cloud that covers the land. In days to come, O Gog, I will bring you against my land, so that the nations may know me when I show myself holy through you before their eyes.*

Verse 16 says, *"I will bring you against my land, so that the nations may know me when I show myself holy through you before their eyes."* From God's perfect perspective, the purpose of this attack is to reveal his glory. Specifically, his glory is to be revealed to "*the nations*." When this battle is complete, God will have revealed himself in a very powerful way to the world at large. In fact, the conflict will be resolved with God's direct intervention so profoundly that the world will wholly realize that it is God himself who has redeemed Israel from her attackers.

It may seem problematic to some that God himself would inspire nations to do that which could otherwise be considered wrong and ungodly. However, this will certainly not be the first time God has done such a thing. Romans 9:17 states *"For the Scripture says to Pharaoh: "I raised you up for this very purpose, that I might display my power in you and that my name might be proclaimed in all the earth."* God chose for Pharaoh, an ungodly king, to rise to power and hold Israel under the bondage of slavery so that God could demonstrate his power through Pharaoh to the world by destroying his stronghold over Israel. A similar condition will exist in the Gog-Magog war. God will personally instigate this coalition to come against his chosen people so that he can demonstrate his power to the nations of earth.

The context of Ezekiel 38 indicates that this attack will happen in close historical proximity to the beginning of the great tribulation. In chapter 37 God speaks of a coming time when he will do a work which will bring Israel back together as one nation under one king, the Messiah, David's heir. Then, following this text in chapter 40, a description of the Millennial Temple is given which sandwiches this story between the time God begins his work of redeeming Israel and the time when that redemption is complete, under Christ's rule. Thus, this invasion is understood to be close in proximity to the period of the great tribulation, but it cannot be during the great tribulation for reasons which will be seen later in the text.

It seems, then, that this invasion is a catalyst for the world to begin paying attention to Israel and her estranged God, who will bring her back into his fellowship just a few short years in the future from this event. Being a pre-tribulational event itself, perhaps this invasion is another occurrence likened to the signs of Matthew 24, which will quicken mankind to begin watching the stage of world events for the coming of God's judgments on the whole of the earth.

It will also soon be observed that God's program for the great tribulation has as its secondary purpose to draw men to repentance. The comprehension of God's glory will certainly play a role in that draw. His resolution of this battle will focus the attention of the world to his work.

What will happen as a result?

Essentially, the "what" is answered next.

> ### *Ezekiel 38:17-18*
> *[17] "'This is what the Sovereign LORD says: Are you not the one I spoke of in former days by my servants the prophets of Israel? At that time they prophesied for years that I would bring you against them. [18] This is what will happen in that day: When Gog attacks the land of Israel, my hot anger will be aroused, declares the Sovereign LORD.*

Chapter 1: Pre-tribulational Events

The end result of the attack is that God's "*hot anger*" will be aroused against the attackers. While the text informs us that God ultimately is behind the attack for his own glory, the attackers desire to loot and plunder Israel of their own sinful accord. God's anger will bring him to rise against the attackers in a most impressive way.

> **Ezekiel 38:19-23**
> *[19] In my zeal and fiery wrath I declare that at that time there shall be a great earthquake in the land of Israel. [20] The fish of the sea, the birds of the air, the beasts of the field, every creature that moves along the ground, and all the people on the face of the earth will tremble at my presence. The mountains will be overturned, the cliffs will crumble and every wall will fall to the ground. [21] I will summon a sword against Gog on all my mountains, declares the Sovereign LORD. Every man's sword will be against his brother. [22] I will execute judgment upon him with plague and bloodshed; I will pour down torrents of rain, hailstones and burning sulfur on him and on his troops and on the many nations with him. [23] And so I will show my greatness and my holiness, and I will make myself known in the sight of many nations. Then they will know that I am the LORD.'*

God's retaliation against the attackers begins with a massive earthquake. In this quake, even the fish of the sea and the birds of the air are impacted. The statement "*mountains will be overturned*" certainly invokes a realization of the stark magnitude of this event. It will be very impressive and "*all the people on the face of the earth will tremble*" at God's presence. While earthquakes occur daily throughout the earth, rarely is one so significant that it draws world-wide attention. In this case, the whole earth will take note and will fear God, at least in that moment.

With the earthquake drawing the world's attention, what God does next will captivate the world audience, so that his glory can truly be seen by all. Following the quake, the armies begin a conflict within their own ranks. *"Every man's sword will be against his brother,"* perhaps from the panic of the quake itself or from the fear of God's presence which accompanies it.

Following the civil conflict is a series of plagues of Old Testament reminiscence. *"Torrents of rain, hailstones and burning sulfur"* will be rained down from the heavens upon the enemy of Israel. This is done *"in the sight of many nations."* Surely in a modern setting the earthquake itself will draw international attention. News crews and dignitaries will flock to the sight. While the world gazes upon the invasion and the earthquake, supernatural intervention will literally rain down upon Israel's enemy in the form of rain, hailstones and literal fire from Heaven. How impressive it will be to see burning sulfur raining down from heaven on the seven o'clock news! Indeed, God will make himself known and *"they will know that I am the LORD."*

Formerly it was considered an impossibility that the entire earth could witness this event as described. Even biblical commentators who lived prior to today's global media had difficulty understanding the possibilities of an event being seen by the whole earth. Yet, today, truly global news coverage is a common occurrence. It is actually somewhat amusing to look at scripture retrospectively through the lens of history. The pragmatically impossible has become reality time and again. Israel *did* become a sovereign nation from the far corners of the earth. And, world-wide spectacles have become a common event. Even prior to man's ability to comprehend the possibilities of scriptural foresight, God had spoken that which was to be.

When will this happen?

The first observation as to when this attack will happen must be the conclusion that it has not already occurred in the past. For this battle to be prophetically accurate, several historical facts must come together perfectly, the first of which is the general description of the condition of Israel. The land is described in Ezekiel 38:8 as a *"land that has*

Chapter 1: Pre-tribulational Events

recovered from war," and *"whose people were gathered from many nations to the mountains of Israel, which had long been desolate."* As has been noted, this demands an Israel of modern description rather than historic Israel. Additionally, Israel is said to *"live in safety,"* in verse 8, and is said to be made up of *"unwalled villages"* and *"without gates and bars."* Categorically, these statements describe modern Israel, and no other historical version.

Furthermore, there have been no historic battles against Israel which fit the description of this text: a coalition of numerous nations, led by Gog of modern day Russian geography, which was thwarted by God's hand via plagues of hail, fire and torrential rain, and conducted while the world watched. Clearly this fits no account afforded by recorded history.

Furthermore, the placement of this battle in the context of Ezekiel puts it in between God's drawing Israel together in preparation for the reign of Messiah and the fulfillment of his reign. Thus, this is an event which must take place between the current date and the messianic kingdom. Chapter 39, however, further limits the possibilities of the timeline of this battle.

> ### *Ezekiel 39:9-12*
> *⁹ "'Then those who live in the towns of Israel will go out and use the weapons for fuel and burn them up--the small and large shields, the bows and arrows, the war clubs and spears. For seven years they will use them for fuel. ¹⁰ They will not need to gather wood from the fields or cut it from the forests, because they will use the weapons for fuel. And they will plunder those who plundered them and loot those who looted them, declares the Sovereign LORD.*
> *¹¹ "'On that day I will give Gog a burial place in Israel, in the valley of those who travel east toward the Sea. It will block the way of travelers, because Gog and all his hordes will be buried there. So it will be called the Valley of Hamon Gog.*
> *¹² "'For seven months the house of Israel will be*

> *burying them in order to cleanse the land. ¹³ All the people of the land will bury them, and the day I am glorified will be a memorable day for them, declares the Sovereign LORD.*

Continuing his discourse on this battle, Ezekiel states that Israel will use the weapons left behind in this battle for fuel for seven years. Specifically mentioned are shields, bows and arrows, war clubs and spears. This has led some to conclude that this army would attack with ancient weapons, and has led to all sorts of speculations as to why such would take place in a modern setting. It seems more reasonable to understand the text as demonstrating a general reference to weapons of war using the known war implements of Ezekiel's day. Obviously God is speaking here, and Ezekiel is simply the mouthpiece. However, it seems unlikely that God would speak the names of gunpowder, rocket fuel or diesel to Ezekiel's generation, which would have no idea what was being discussed. To that end, it seems likely that the reference to weapons of war could be limited by Ezekiel's world view, and instead be understood to indicate an assortment of war hardware.

In either interpretation, the arms left behind by the invaders will be gathered and used for fuel for seven years. That insight itself lends more understanding to the timeline of this battle. It will be demonstrated later in this work that beginning at the mid-point of the tribulation, Israel will be under continual persecution and attack by the armies of Antichrist. And from that moment, 3 1/2 years into the tribulation, Israel will be either in flight or in a defensive posture for the duration of the tribulation. In such a position, they would not be wandering the mountains in search of fuel, as the armies of Antichrist will have Jerusalem surrounded, and will occupy a vast area in Israel, making it impossible for the Israelites to wander the open country in search of abandoned weaponry.

Because Antichrist's assault on Israel will begin 3 1/2 years into the tribulation and the collecting of the fuel from the weapons of the Gog-Magog war will last seven years, it can be reasonably assumed that the Gog-Magog war will complete at least 3 1/2 years before the beginning

Chapter 1: Pre-tribulational Events

of the tribulation. This timeline alone will allow a full seven years to collect fuel before Israel is shut into a defensive stance.

Lastly, it can be concluded from the text that this battle cannot be referring to the battle of Armageddon, as some have erroneously asserted. In Ezekiel 38:8, while describing Israel prior to this attack, it is stated that "*they had been brought out from the nations, and now all of them live in safety.*" The Hebrew word for "*safety*" in the NIV is transliterated *betah*, and indicates that the nation lives securely, or safely from oppression by enemies. As will be demonstrated later in this study, the battle of Armageddon (which may actually be best understood as several battles) will begin near the end of the great tribulation. It will also be demonstrated that Antichrist will begin to bring hostilities upon Israel in the middle of the tribulation. To that end, they cannot be described as a people "*living in safety*" at the point of the Battle of Armageddon, as they will have been under siege for some time prior to that event. At no time past the mid-point of the tribulation can Israel be described as living in safety, but rather quite the contrary.

In conclusion, the Gog-Magog war can be concluded to occur at least 3 1/2 years prior to the beginning of the tribulation, and is one of several pre-tribulational events which should be watched for. For the news-watchers who desperately search for an eschatological sign from every middle-eastern fireworks display, this is one that will not be missed. When this conflict has ended, no one will have to ask if this were in fact the Gog/Magog conflict. Unless fire from Heaven becomes a regular occurrence between now and that time, it is relatively safe to assume this event will easily define itself.

The One-World Government

A disturbing pre-tribulational event which will also be readily perceptible will be the advent of a one-world government upon the whole earth. The understanding of a coming one-world governmental power is observed in two visions from the book of Daniel, found in Daniel 2 and

Daniel 7. Both texts will be presented below, followed by a comparison of their similarities.

Daniel 2:26-45

26 The king asked Daniel (also called Belteshazzar), "Are you able to tell me what I saw in my dream and interpret it?"
27 Daniel replied, "No wise man, enchanter, magician or diviner can explain to the king the mystery he has asked about, 28 but there is a God in heaven who reveals mysteries. He has shown King Nebuchadnezzar what will happen in days to come. Your dream and the visions that passed through your mind as you lay on your bed are these:
29 "As you were lying there, O king, your mind turned to things to come, and the revealer of mysteries showed you what is going to happen. 30 As for me, this mystery has been revealed to me, not because I have greater wisdom than other living men, but so that you, O king, may know the interpretation and that you may understand what went through your mind.
31 "You looked, O king, and there before you stood a large statue--an enormous, dazzling statue, awesome in appearance. 32 The head of the statue was made of pure gold, its chest and arms of silver, its belly and thighs of bronze, 33 its legs of iron, its feet partly of iron and partly of baked clay. 34 While you were watching, a rock was cut out, but not by human hands. It struck the statue on its feet of iron and clay and smashed them. 35 Then the iron, the clay, the bronze, the silver and the gold were broken to pieces at the same time and became like chaff on a threshing floor in the summer. The wind swept them away without leaving a trace. But the rock that struck the statue became a huge mountain and filled the whole earth.
36 "This was the dream, and now we will interpret it to the king. 37 You, O king, are the king of kings. The

Chapter 1: Pre-tribulational Events

God of heaven has given you dominion and power and might and glory; [38] in your hands he has placed mankind and the beasts of the field and the birds of the air. Wherever they live, he has made you ruler over them all. You are that head of gold.

[39] "After you, another kingdom will rise, inferior to yours. Next, a third kingdom, one of bronze, will rule over the whole earth. [40] Finally, there will be a fourth kingdom, strong as iron--for iron breaks and smashes everything--and as iron breaks things to pieces, so it will crush and break all the others. [41] Just as you saw that the feet and toes were partly of baked clay and partly of iron, so this will be a divided kingdom; yet it will have some of the strength of iron in it, even as you saw iron mixed with clay. [42] As the toes were partly iron and partly clay, so this kingdom will be partly strong and partly brittle. [43] And just as you saw the iron mixed with baked clay, so the people will be a mixture and will not remain united, any more than iron mixes with clay.

[44] "In the time of those kings, the God of heaven will set up a kingdom that will never be destroyed, nor will it be left to another people. It will crush all those kingdoms and bring them to an end, but it will itself endure forever. [45] This is the meaning of the vision of the rock cut out of a mountain, but not by human hands--a rock that broke the iron, the bronze, the clay, the silver and the gold to pieces.

"The great God has shown the king what will take place in the future. The dream is true and the interpretation is trustworthy."

Daniel 7:1-28

1 In the first year of Belshazzar king of Babylon, Daniel had a dream, and visions passed through his mind as he was lying on his bed. He wrote down the substance of his

dream.

2 Daniel said: "In my vision at night I looked, and there before me were the four winds of heaven churning up the great sea. [3] Four great beasts, each different from the others, came up out of the sea.

[4] "The first was like a lion, and it had the wings of an eagle. I watched until its wings were torn off and it was lifted from the ground so that it stood on two feet like a man, and the heart of a man was given to it.

[5] "And there before me was a second beast, which looked like a bear. It was raised up on one of its sides, and it had three ribs in its mouth between its teeth. It was told, 'Get up and eat your fill of flesh!'

[6] "After that, I looked, and there before me was another beast, one that looked like a leopard. And on its back it had four wings like those of a bird. This beast had four heads, and it was given authority to rule.

[7] "After that, in my vision at night I looked, and there before me was a fourth beast--terrifying and frightening and very powerful. It had large iron teeth; it crushed and devoured its victims and trampled underfoot whatever was left. It was different from all the former beasts, and it had ten horns.

[8] "While I was thinking about the horns, there before me was another horn, a little one, which came up among them; and three of the first horns were uprooted before it. This horn had eyes like the eyes of a man and a mouth that spoke boastfully.

[9] "As I looked,
"thrones were set in place,
  and the Ancient of Days took his seat.
His clothing was as white as snow;
  the hair of his head was white like wool.
His throne was flaming with fire,
  and its wheels were all ablaze.
[10] A river of fire was flowing,
  coming out from before him.
Thousands upon thousands attended him;

Chapter 1: Pre-tribulational Events

*ten thousand times ten thousand stood before him.
The court was seated,
    and the books were opened.
[11] "Then I continued to watch because of the boastful words the horn was speaking. I kept looking until the beast was slain and its body destroyed and thrown into the blazing fire. [12] (The other beasts had been stripped of their authority, but were allowed to live for a period of time.)
[13] "In my vision at night I looked, and there before me was one like a son of man, coming with the clouds of heaven. He approached the Ancient of Days and was led into his presence. [14] He was given authority, glory and sovereign power; all peoples, nations and men of every language worshiped him. His dominion is an everlasting dominion that will not pass away, and his kingdom is one that will never be destroyed.
[15] "I, Daniel, was troubled in spirit, and the visions that passed through my mind disturbed me. [16] I approached one of those standing there and asked him the true meaning of all this.
"So he told me and gave me the interpretation of these things: [17] 'The four great beasts are four kingdoms that will rise from the earth. [18] But the saints of the Most High will receive the kingdom and will possess it forever--yes, for ever and ever.'
[19] "Then I wanted to know the true meaning of the fourth beast, which was different from all the others and most terrifying, with its iron teeth and bronze claws--the beast that crushed and devoured its victims and trampled underfoot whatever was left. [20] I also wanted to know about the ten horns on its head and about the other horn that came up, before which three of them fell--the horn that looked more imposing than the others and that had eyes and a mouth that spoke boastfully. [21] As I watched, this horn was waging war against the saints and defeating them, [22] until the Ancient of Days came and pronounced judgment in favor of the saints of the Most High, and the time came when they possessed the*

40

> *kingdom.*
> *[23] "He gave me this explanation: 'The fourth beast is a fourth kingdom that will appear on earth. It will be different from all the other kingdoms and will devour the whole earth, trampling it down and crushing it. [24] The ten horns are ten kings who will come from this kingdom. After them another king will arise, different from the earlier ones; he will subdue three kings. [25] He will speak against the Most High and oppress his saints and try to change the set times and the laws. The saints will be handed over to him for a time, times and half a time.*
> *[26] "'But the court will sit, and his power will be taken away and completely destroyed forever. [27] Then the sovereignty, power and greatness of the kingdoms under the whole heaven will be handed over to the saints, the people of the Most High. His kingdom will be an everlasting kingdom, and all rulers will worship and obey him.'*
> *[28] "This is the end of the matter. I, Daniel, was deeply troubled by my thoughts, and my face turned pale, but I kept the matter to myself."*

While this is a lot of text to consider at once, it is necessary to consider both visions as a unit, because both are of future world-dominating kingdoms; the same kingdoms, seen by Nebuchadnezzar and Daniel in different visions at different times. It is clear from each context that an unfolding of world history is being presented through the observation of these global dynasties which are to exist in Daniel's future.

History has clearly depicted these kingdoms to modern readers, yet the fourth kingdom has qualities which have not yet been fully realized historically.

Chapter 1: Pre-tribulational Events

The First Kingdom

Daniel 2	Daniel 7
[32] The head of the statue was made of pure gold... *Daniel 2:37-38 (NIV)[37] You, O king, are the king of kings. The God of heaven has given you dominion and power and might and glory; [38] in your hands he has placed mankind and the beasts of the field and the birds of the air. Wherever they live, he has made you ruler over them all. You are that head of gold.*	*[4] "The first was like a lion, and it had the wings of an eagle. I watched until its wings were torn off and it was lifted from the ground so that it stood on two feet like a man, and the heart of a man was given to it.*

The first kingdom is represented with the head of gold and the winged lion beast. This was the Babylonian Empire of Nebuchadnezzar himself, which was an empire of the known world in Daniel's day.

The Second Kingdom

Daniel 2	Daniel 7
[32] ...its chest and arms of silver, its belly and thighs of bronze,	*[5] "And there before me was a second beast, which looked like a bear. It was raised up on one of its sides, and it had three ribs in its mouth between its teeth. It was told, 'Get up and eat your fill of flesh!'*

The second kingdom, represented by the arms and breast of silver and

42

the bear-like beast, refers to the Medo-Persian Empire which was the global kingdom emerging after the Babylonian Empire.

The Persian Empire overthrew the Medes and the remaining territories of the Babylonians, giving rise to the next consecutive world kingdom noted historically in Daniel's vision.

The Third Kingdom

Daniel 2	Daniel 7
32 ... its belly and thighs of bronze *39 ... Next, a third kingdom, one of bronze, will rule over the whole earth. 33 its legs of iron, its feet partly of iron and partly of baked clay.*	*6 "After that, I looked, and there before me was another beast, one that looked like a leopard. And on its back it had four wings like those of a bird. This beast had four heads, and it was given authority to rule.*

The third kingdom, with belly and thighs of bronze and depicted as a leopard with wings, is the Hellenistic Empire of Alexander the Great.

The Greeks conquered the remaining Persian territories, forming the next historical global empire of Daniel's dream.

The Fourth Kingdom

Daniel 2	Daniel 7
40 Finally, there will be a fourth kingdom, strong as iron--for iron breaks and smashes everything-- and as iron breaks things to pieces, so it will crush and break	*7 "After that, in my vision at night I looked, and there before me was a fourth beast--terrifying and frightening and very powerful. It had large iron teeth; it crushed and*

Chapter 1: Pre-tribulational Events

all the others. ⁴¹ Just as you saw that the feet and toes were partly of baked clay and partly of iron, so this will be a divided kingdom; yet it will have some of the strength of iron in it, even as you saw iron mixed with clay. ⁴² As the toes were partly iron and partly clay, so this kingdom will be partly strong and partly brittle. ⁴³ And just as you saw the iron mixed with baked clay, so the people will be a mixture and will not remain united, any more than iron mixes with clay.	*devoured its victims and trampled underfoot whatever was left. It was different from all the former beasts, and it had ten horns.* ²³ *"He gave me this explanation: 'The fourth beast is a fourth kingdom that will appear on earth. It will be different from all the other kingdoms and will devour the whole earth, trampling it down and crushing it.*

The fourth kingdom, different from the others, was the world dominating kingdom of the Roman Empire. What becomes difficult is the determination of how the rest of the vision will come to fruition.

Clearly the Roman Empire was the next world empire historically. And noticeably, as Daniel 7:23 indicates, it was "*different from all the other kingdoms*" and devoured the earth. Its differences will be discussed shortly, but the most essential question which must be answered is the question of how the Roman Empire, long since lost to the annals of time, can be the empire after which Daniel 2:44 states, "*the God of heaven will set up a kingdom that will never be destroyed, nor will it be left to another people. It will crush all those kingdoms and bring them to an end, but it will itself endure forever.*"

One solution exists in Amillennialism, which teaches that Christ's resurrection began this final kingdom which would crush the others. Surely Christ's kingdom came, surely he reigns supremely, surely he is the final authority. However, in Daniel's vision, each kingdom was literal prior to the fifth kingdom that will never be destroyed, which demands that the fifth kingdom itself must also be interpreted as a literal kingdom. Amillennialism describes a symbolic kingdom of Christ in

Heaven rather than a literal kingdom of Christ on earth. Additionally, the destruction of the ten kings which ruled the fourth kingdom must be interpreted literally in light of the literality of the other kingdom's descriptions.

The simple reality of life on earth today is that Christ's kingdom has not *literally* obliterated the ten kings of a one-world government, which demands that this prophecy is not completely fulfilled, if indeed a consistently literal interpretive method is to be applied to scripture. To be honest, a metaphorical interpretation is much easier to understand for this text, yet it does not keep the interpretations concerning each kingdom consistent. It makes no sense for Daniel and Nebuchadnezzar to have visions of four empires which will come to literal power, only to be *figuratively* destroyed by a fifth and final kingdom. In actuality, each of the first three *were* literally destroyed as the next succeeding empire came into power. In the Amillennial view, the fourth empire fails to realize a literal destruction as did the others. As difficult as it is to wrestle with the Roman empire being the empire which Christ will *literally* destroy, the consistent interpretation of the text demands that it be understood in this manner. Christ will destroy, literally, the fourth empire, which is the Roman empire.

One key to understanding the nature of the fourth kingdom is found in Daniel 7:23, in that it was "*different from all the other kingdoms.*" It was unique. The Roman Empire, unlike prior empires, gave rise to a new way of governing. The Roman Empire gave rise to what is commonly known today as imperialism. While some would argue that elements of imperialism existed in former governments, it was not until the Roman empire that imperialism was fully developed or that it was demonstrable in a truly global economy. The Romans, for example, allowed a conquered nation to keep its social structure, religions and even government offices intact insomuch as the nation submitted to Rome as its ultimate authority. This idea is represented in Daniel 2:40 "*and as iron breaks things to pieces, so it will crush and break all the other*" and 2:43 "*just as you saw the iron mixed with baked clay, so the people will be a mixture and will not remain united, any more than iron mixes with clay.*" This characteristic of the Roman empire is clearly visible in New

Chapter 1: Pre-tribulational Events

Testament Israel, observable in the narrative of the arrest and trial of Jesus.

In Matthew 26, Jesus was arrested in accordance with the laws of Israel, a nation under Roman imperialistic rule. In Matthew 26:57 Jesus is taken to the high priest after his arrest. Once found guilty by that court, a sentence was given, as "*all the chief priests and the elders of the people came to the decision to put Jesus to death.*" Then, in Matthew 27:11 Jesus was taken to the Roman court and placed before Pilate, the roman governor, who held the final authority over such a sentence. Without Rome's consent Israel would have been unable to legally put Jesus to death. Roman imperialism was indeed a new global system which allowed Israel to maintain their religion, laws and even certain governmental offices while being subject to Rome on the larger scale.

This type of government dominates the world today, with the United States being a shining example, though with its own unique qualities. Each U.S. state has its own government, which submits to the Federal government. Many other nations follow a similar pattern of imperialism, which had the Roman Empire as its root model of origin.

Among nations, furthermore, there exists today the United Nations, which is not currently a governing head per se, but is growing increasingly stronger in its influence each passing year, even to the point of managing the sovereignty of any nation foreseen to be a threat to the whole. Many believe the UN will provide the platform for Antichrist's authority, however this idea is only speculation. The UN is, however, another form of modern imperialism. It is in effect, even today, a form of global government having its own world court, the International Court of Justice. The ICJ has heard cases related to war crimes, illegal state interference and ethnic cleansing, among others. While each nation retains its sovereignty, the UN serves as a governing board negotiating relations between member nations such as the intervention into Iraq during the 1991 Gulf War, which was authorized by the UN. These examples each follow the same general model demonstrated on a global level by the former Roman Empire. Imperialism permeates the modern world.

Historically, the Roman empire itself was split into an east/west balance of power in 364 by Valentinian. The world continues in an east/west balance of power today. Daniel 7:7 says *"it crushed and devoured its victims and trampled underfoot whatever was left."* No historical kingdom has fit this description on a global level since the Roman Empire.

Daniel 2 reveals the messianic kingdom of Messiah – or the rock that becomes a mountain, to be the destruction of this fourth kingdom. Daniel 2:44 states *"the God of heaven will set up a kingdom that will never be destroyed, nor will it be left to another people."* All variants of eschatological study agree that this kingdom is the kingdom of Christ. Where they disagree on is whether this kingdom is literal, observed by the future return of Christ to rule on the physical earth, or figurative, that Christ rules vicariously from Heaven until the time of his return to restore the earth. Once again, history has defined each kingdom in the text to be literal up until the time of the final kingdom. It should not be suddenly rendered figuratively due to the difficulty of the subject matter.

If, then, this kingdom is literal, it represents the Roman Empire, and the contention must be that an element of this empire exists today, and will give rise to the ten kings noted in both Daniel 2 and 7. Some conclude that the East/West balance of power is the remnant of the Roman Empire. Some contend that imperialism is that which has lived on. In either case, this empire will give rise to ten kings who will rule the earth.

> ***Daniel 7:23-25***
> [23] *"He gave me this explanation: 'The fourth beast is a fourth kingdom that will appear on earth. It will be different from all the other kingdoms and will devour the whole earth, trampling it down and crushing it.* [24] *The ten horns are ten kings who will come from this kingdom. After them another king will arise, different from the earlier ones; he will subdue three kings.* [25] *He will speak against the Most High and oppress his saints and try to change the set times and the laws. The saints will be handed over to him for a time, times and half a*

Chapter 1: Pre-tribulational Events

time.

Verse 24 reveals the next vital step which will unfold, namely the advent of a one-world ruler which will speak against God and oppress his saints. More will be developed about this portion of Daniel 7 later in this work.

Essentially, it appears that this one-world government will in fact have a Roman imperialistic approach, as it will establish its kings in various places in the world to rule it, fitting the imperialistic model.

Historical speculations have pointed to the European Common Market (or more recently, the European Union) as the ten horns of this coming government. Yet in the text, the ten divisions are created after the formation of the kingdom, not before. Also, practically, it does not seem pragmatic that ten kings, all based in Europe, would rule the entire world, but rather kings who were dispersed throughout the world.

Still other speculation points to the United Nations as the substance of the ten kings. Assuming the UN were given more power that it currently has, this postulate may have merit. The UN is the epitome of imperialism, having each nation ruling itself under the global supervision of the whole. While this is a more pragmatic speculation, it should be noted that it is still a speculation, and should not be placed into one's eschatological lens in an unhealthy way. One can observe the UN to see if perhaps it will have a role in a future one world government, or if it could perhaps *become* a rigid governing institution of the world. But, one should not allow history to predict the Bible. Calling the UN the one world government is not a valid assertion, at least at this point in history.

However, those who follow this speculation do propose a realistic postulate: if the rapture (which will be covered later) occurs early enough, the UN would have a global catastrophic event which *could* in fact elevate their authority rapidly, especially if world leaders are taken quickly out of the picture from larger nations.

What can be know with certainty from the text is that there will be ten kings who will rule on behalf of a future one-world government. The

Bible does not reveal who each of these kings are, but only that the king which will lead them all will be overthrown by Christ.

More About the One-World Government

> ### Daniel 7:23
> *"He gave me this explanation: 'The fourth beast is a fourth kingdom that will appear on earth. It will be different from all the other kingdoms and will devour the whole earth, trampling it down and crushing it.*

The fourth kingdom will devour the whole earth like the three former kingdoms had done. The Roman Empire has devoured the whole earth formerly in history, but will also do so while under the auspices of the ten kings, and the one king who will rise above them all. The rising of the kings remains a future set of events. This is clear due to the fact that Christ will overthrow them. In literal history, Christ has not yet overthrown a government of any stature. Since a literal interpretation is called for because each additional kingdom referenced is literal, a time is coming when Christ will overthrow this literal government and the literal king who will be identified as "Antichrist" in the course of this work.

Daniel 7:20-22 continues to reference three of the ten horns bowing to the "*little horn*" that comes up among them. This little horn spoke boastfully and waged war against the saints until the Ancient of Days pronounced judgment on him.

> ### Daniel 7:24-25
> [24] *The ten horns are ten kings who will come from this kingdom. After them another king will arise, different from the earlier ones; he will subdue three kings.* [25] *He will speak against the Most High and oppress his saints and try to change the set times and the laws. The saints will be handed over to him for a time, times and half a*

Chapter 1: Pre-tribulational Events

time.

The antichrist will conquer three kings and kill them[20]. In Revelation 17 it is learned that the remaining kings will submit to him as well (in the middle of the tribulation) and will do his bidding, so that he will be the ruler of the earth for a season. More will be presented on that subject in the chapters concerning the great tribulation.

The Revealing of the Antichrist

> *2 Thessalonians 2:1-4*
> *¹ Concerning the coming of our Lord Jesus Christ and our being gathered to him, we ask you, brothers, ² not to become easily unsettled or alarmed by some prophecy, report or letter supposed to have come from us, saying that the day of the Lord has already come. ³ Don't let anyone deceive you in any way, for that day will not come until the rebellion occurs and the man of lawlessness is revealed, the man doomed to destruction. ⁴ He will oppose and will exalt himself over everything that is called God or is worshiped, so that he sets himself up in God's temple, proclaiming himself to be God.*

The phrases *"the coming of our Lord"* and *"our being gathered to him"* have created many questions for students of eschatology. At the heart of the issue is the determination of whether this phrase refers to one event or two. If "*the coming of our Lord and our being gathered to him*" refers to one event, whereby the Lord comes and we are simultaneously gathered, then the question is spawned, "does this refer to the Lord's return to reign, or is it referring to a rapture theology?" If, however, the phrase represents two ideas, the Lord's return and separately, our being gathered to him, then the question may be simpler to answer.

---

[20] Chapter 3 will discuss this in further detail

In either case, the apostle refers to "*our being gathered to him*" almost parenthetically in this announcement that "*that day will not come until the rebellion occurs and the man of lawlessness is revealed.*" Clearly, "*that day*" refers to the "*day of the Lord,*" or the return of Christ to rule, which is separate from "*our being gathered to him*" if one sees that phrase as a rapture event. Contextually, Paul was already speaking specifically about the day of the Lord. It is this event alone which he speaks to. Yet, he does add "*our being gathered to him*" to the thought, creating the question as to whether he is referring to a separate event which fits well into a rapture theology.

In the end, it is not possible to know for certain if Paul parenthetically refers to a rapture from this text alone. Nor is it essential to determine for Paul's warning to be understood. Neither interpretation changes the timing of the revealing of "*the man of lawlessness,*" or the Antichrist, as an event which will precede the coming of the day of the Lord.

At this point, some devotion to the phrase "*day of the Lord*" must be given. The "day of the Lord" is a common theme in prophetic writings and is an exceptionally important phrase in eschatology. How nice it would be if there were an answer key in the back of the Bible to inform readers of key phrases and their meanings. But, as there is no such key, repetitive phrases such as "*the day of the Lord*" must be determined systematically, by examining their usage throughout the Bible.

When the phrase "*day of the Lord*" occurs in scripture, it has two nuances, both of which refer to the last days, specifically, the great tribulation. The most common usage is a general depiction of the great tribulation. A more rare and specific usage articulates the very end of the tribulation, notably the specific moment of the return of Christ. While this work is not a systematic study on this phrase, it will be examined numerous times which will assist in demonstrating this truth. To that end, further examination of this phrase will not be conducted in this chapter. Suffice it to say, however, that the phrase "*day of the Lord*" will always refer to the great tribulation in scripture. At times it will refer specifically to the very end of the tribulation, the return of Christ, but most commonly it is a general depiction of the great tribulation, which

Chapter 1: Pre-tribulational Events

concludes with Christ's return.

The usage of *"the day of the Lord"* in this text is of the more general nature. It refers to the general season of the great tribulation rather than the specific event of the return of Christ. Contextually, in 2 Thessalonians 1, Paul had set up this usage with a discussion of the events of this coming day of the Lord. He notes in 1 Thessalonians 1:7 of the coming judgments of Christ, *"This will happen when the Lord Jesus is revealed from heaven in blazing fire with his powerful angels."* As this study continues, it will be observed that the judgments of the great tribulation will involve fire from Heaven and are usually administered by angels. More on this will be discussed in the chapters on the great tribulation, but for important note at this time is the understanding that the *"day of the Lord"* refers to the pouring out of these judgments, which precede the specific return of Christ, and render the more general usage of "day of the Lord" in this context.

To conclude the timing of the revealing of Antichrist from this text, then, it is understood that he will be revealed prior to the day of the Lord, or prior to the great tribulation; the day Paul speaks of which will be the period of punishment for those who have rebelled against the Lord. Thus, the revealing of Antichrist is a pre-tribulational event.

Furthermore, it will be observed later in this study that the beginning of the tribulation period is *defined* by a specific act of Antichrist: the signing of a covenant between himself and Israel. One does not sign a treaty with a sovereign nation without a well-established identity and a position of power from which to barter such an agreement. Antichrist will be revealed, then, by merit of his position and other indicators which will be discussed shortly, before the beginning of the great tribulation.

About The Antichrist

This *"man of lawlessness"* bears the name "Antichrist" in First and Second John. Antichrist is one of the most key players on earth during the great tribulation, filling an important role as an agent of Satan. And, although Antichrist is a being of satanic origins and purpose, he is used of God to bring judgment to the earth and to unfold God's own foretold plans among the nations.

As his name indicates, Antichrist will appear as a divine entity, doing miraculous things, even being resurrected. He is of Satan, not God, and is not divine, but he is a great deceiver and will proclaim himself to be divine and will exalt himself as God. While some people have difficulty with the idea of a being having supernatural powers, biblical theology teaches that Satan and the angelic realm are created on a higher order than that of man. As such, they have powers beyond those of man, yet are not divine. They are created beings, lower than the creator himself, but higher and more powerful than man.

To that end, Antichrist is a false Christ in every way, even down to his supernatural incarnation, which will be discussed momentarily, and will make his life's work the deception of as many as possible. He will cause men to follow him, and vicariously, his master, Satan.

An early biblical description of Antichrist's campaign is seen in the book of Daniel. In chapter 9 a picture is given of Antichrist's role in the tribulation.

> ### *Daniel 9:24-27*
> *[24] "Seventy 'sevens' are decreed for your people and your holy city to finish transgression, to put an end to sin, to atone for wickedness, to bring in everlasting righteousness, to seal up vision and prophecy and to anoint the most holy.*
> *[25] "Know and understand this: From the issuing of the decree to restore and rebuild Jerusalem until the Anointed One, the ruler, comes, there will be seven 'sevens,' and sixty-two 'sevens.' It will be rebuilt with streets and a trench, but in times of trouble. [26] After the sixty-two 'sevens,' the Anointed One will be cut off and will have nothing. The people of the ruler who will come will destroy the city and the sanctuary. The end will*

> *come like a flood: War will continue until the end, and desolations have been decreed. ²⁷ He will confirm a covenant with many for one 'seven.' In the middle of the 'seven' he will put an end to sacrifice and offering. And on a wing [of the temple] he will set up an abomination that causes desolation, until the end that is decreed is poured out on him".*

The term "*sevens*" is likened to the English term "dozen." It refers to a seven of something, as dozen indicates a twelve of something. And like using the term "dozen," the only way to determine what the "*seven*" is of, is the context from which one speaks. In the context of Daniel's writing, he had been speaking in terms of periods of time. And, in each case, his time periods have consistently been rendered in years. Thus a "*seven*" in this context is a seven of years.

Daniel begins in verse 25 with "*seven sevens*," or 49 years. 49 years, or the first seven sevens, was described as the time required to rebuild Jerusalem after the decree was issued to do so.

Daniel follows with "*sixty two sevens*," or 434 years in verse 25 as the time from the completion of the rebuilding of Jerusalem until the Messiah would come.

Following the sixty two sevens a break is observed in the text:

> ²⁶ *After the sixty-two 'sevens,' the Anointed One will be cut off and will have nothing. The people of the ruler who will come will destroy the city and the sanctuary. The end will come like a flood: War will continue until the end, and desolations have been decreed.*

At this point, the "*Anointed One*," or Jesus, is "*cut off*," which in historical retrospect, demands to be understood as referring to his crucifixion. It is at this time that the first reference to Antichrist is observed.

> *The people of the ruler who will come will destroy the city and the sanctuary.*

This phrase bears two important notices concerning Antichrist. First, it speaks of a ruler "*who will come*" at a future point in history. This ruler does not come immediately, but after a break, which is described next. This ruler is understood from a systematic study of scripture to be the Antichrist. As this work continues, it will be seen that this ruler fits the description of Antichrist from numerous New Testament references.

Secondly, this phrase notes that Antichrist is of the same people as those who will destroy the city, or Jerusalem. Jerusalem was destroyed in AD 70 by Rome. Therefore, Rome is the people of "*the ruler who will come,*" which demands that the Antichrist will also be of Roman descent. While it is increasingly difficult to determine Roman descent in modern times, still this clue to Antichrist's heritage is given and should be considered when the time comes for attempting to discern Antichrist's identity.

Verse 26 then states, *"War will continue until the end, and desolations have been decreed."*

This sentence stands alone in the series of sevens. It is not part of the former seven, but refers to a period which connects the sixty two sevens from the last seven. It is a break in the timeline between the last two groupings of sevens. "*The end*" refers to the last seven. War continuing "*until the end,*" then, notes a gap of time whereby Israel will continue in war until the time of the end arrives. Consequently, Israel has not had peace from the time of the destruction of the city to this very day. Fighting in the Gaza strip is a normal condition of life. Attacks by Hezbollah and other terrorist groups are continual; so much so that life in Israel will hardly give pause after a suicide bombing or direct military attack.

War continuing until "*the end*" refers not only to the last seven, but to the end of the story, or the end of times, when "*desolations have been*

Chapter 1: Pre-tribulational Events

decreed" and God is ready to put the wheels into motion and begin the last seven of the series. In eschatological study, "*the end*" is concurrent with the last seven, or the tribulation period. When the tribulation period ends, so does the current age, and the new age of the millennial reign begins.

With the ending of the break and the beginning of the final seven, the last seven years of life in this age begin with Antichrist playing his very important role.

Verse 27 describes the final seven:

> *"He will confirm a covenant with many for one 'seven.' In the middle of the 'seven' he will put an end to sacrifice and offering. And on a wing [of the temple] he will set up an abomination that causes desolation, until the end that is decreed is poured out on him".*

"*He*," or Antichrist, is one and the same as the "beast" of the book of Revelation, and the final seven is the final seven years of life on earth prior to the Millennial Reign of Christ. Daniel only shows a glimpse of Antichrist's program in this text, yet it is clear that he is a key player, having the authority to halt temple worship and the audacity to exalt himself as God in the temple. These actions will be demonstrated in detail later in this work, but for now, as an introduction to Antichrist it should be observed that his is a person of great political and religious relevance in the great tribulation. He will exalt himself to the highest possible positions in both realms. Politically, he will essentially be the king of the world, while religiously he will exalt and proclaim himself to be the very God of Heaven. His title of "Antichrist" is very fitting; for he is everything in substance which is opposed to the legitimate Christ, all the while imitating Christ's program through counterfeit measures in an attempt to gain the trust and worship of the inhabitants of earth.

Antichrist's nature

Another key truth to grasp about Antichrist, in order to understand his role in the tribulation, is to note that he is in some way satanic in nature. In the context of any serious study of eschatology from a literal perspective, one understands clearly that Antichrist is given a great amount of power. He will be a master deceiver, yet will have an impressive array of supernatural abilities which will give credibility to his false claim to godhood. It is at this point that the biblical student must come to terms with Antichrist's nature so as to determine exactly how he is empowered to do the things he will be able to do. He is either fully demonic, demon possessed, or in some other way receiving a great amount of dark spiritual power. The question is, "exactly how?" Being fully demonic is easily ruled out, because Antichrist is noted to be a man in 2 Thessalonians 2:3, being called "*the man of lawlessness*." And, being *only* a man is also ruled out by a truth which will be observed later in this work, whereby Antichrist will be cast into the Abyss, a place where throughout the Bible only demons are sentenced to.

These truths lend one to lean toward Antichrist being a sort of hybrid man/demon, since he clearly exhibits characteristics of the demonic while also being called a man. But how does one come to be a hybrid between demon and man? How would such an entity come to be?

There are several scriptural clues as to how exactly Antichrist draws his Satanic power, and more specifically, how he came to his unique nature. One clue is found in 2 Thessalonians.

> ***2 Thessalonians 2:9***
> *"The coming of the lawless one will be in accordance with the work of Satan displayed in all kinds of counterfeit miracles, signs and wonders."*

The phrase rendered "*in accordance with the work of Satan*" in the NIV is translated from the Greek term *energeo*, which means *"to be energized of"* Satan. This term reveals that it will be Satan himself who will empower "*the coming*" of Antichrist. To understand that Antichrist is

Chapter 1: Pre-tribulational Events

. . . .

energized of Satan is not a terribly fascinating revelation. Yet, the text specifically notes that *"the coming of"* Antichrist is energized of Satan, or stated differently, "his advent" is energized of Satan. Thus, Antichrist's very existence is inspired in some way from Satan's power and work. It will be Satan's work and energy which will render Antichrist onto the playing field, albeit with God's full permit, as nothing happens without God's knowledge and permission.

A second clue to his nature is found in Genesis.

> **Genesis 3:15**
> *¹⁵ And I will put enmity between you and the woman, and between your offspring and hers;*
> *he will crush your head, and you will strike his heel."*

Spoken in judgment against the serpent for the deception leading to man's fall, Genesis 3:15 is noted from almost every theological background and perspective to be a Messianic prophesy. The "*offspring*" of the woman is understood by biblical students of vastly differing viewpoints alike to represent the coming Christ, who would crush the head of the serpent. And, most who accept this position also allow that the prophecy is spoken to Satan himself, rather than to the serpent. The prophecy "*you will strike his heal*" clearly doesn't speak to all serpent-kind, but uniquely to an individual; "*you.*" It is Satan's head which Christ will crush, not the head of some future random snake. While this position is accepted throughout Christendom, what is not as frequently discussed is the answer to the question, "who is Satan's offspring?" If Christ is the woman's offspring, who is the offspring of Satan that will have enmity toward Christ?

If the offspring of the woman is a unique individual, then the offspring of Satan must also be understood to be unique personage. That person will be demonstrated to be the coming Antichrist; the offspring to be energized of Satan himself.

The mere mention of the idea that Satan, a fallen angelic being, could have an offspring sends many scurrying for the cover of another possible translation for Genesis 3:15. The text itself, however, simply states its prophecy and moves on. It is up to the biblical student to uncover the ramifications of the text and build a theology concerning the future offspring of Satan which is noted.

The questions remaining lead to a place which many dare not tread. Those questions are beyond the latitude of acceptance of many, yet find their answers clearly from scriptural study. The first question is "how will Satan produce an offspring?" The second question is, "how can Satan's offspring be called a man and yet have a demonic nature?" The answers are found in a single statement of answer: Satan will procreate Antichrist through a human host. This answer is not one of convenience, but rather, one which comes from biblical consideration on the subject. Indeed, there is a wealth of scriptural content concerning this issue which will shortly be examined.

This answers to these questions are simple and biblical, yet are difficult to accept by many. Likewise the concepts of Virgin birth, the resurrection of the dead and the eternal nature of the spirit are simple and biblical, yet hard to accept by many. Never in Bible theology are the strange or supernatural characteristics of a principle grounds for dismissal. If they were, one may dismiss the Lord himself on the grounds that he cannot possibly be "eternal." In fact, nearly every attribute of God's own character is supernatural in origin. Never should the difficulty of human grasp be a cause to reject a biblical principle. The following section will give a biblical roadmap of evidence which supports not only the *possibility* of Antichrist being spawned of Satan himself, but also evidence that all processes required to achieve such demonic procreation have been formerly observed in scripture.

The thread which introduces biblical revelation of how demonic procreation can happen begins only a few short chapters further into Genesis, in the portrayal of the Nephilim of Genesis 6.

Chapter 1: Pre-tribulational Events

The Feasibility of Angelic/Human Procreation

The objection of many to the proposition that Antichrist is the product of the copulation of Satan and a human host is that it is impossible for angels to procreate. After all, Satan is a cherub; an angelic being for which there is no biblical description of family life, marriage or procreation.

That objection, however, is not accurate, for an objective examination of scripture tells another story.

> ***Genesis 6:1-4***
> *[1] When men began to increase in number on the earth and daughters were born to them, [2] the sons of God saw that the daughters of men were beautiful, and they married any of them they chose. [3] Then the LORD said, "My Spirit will not contend with man forever, for he is mortal ; his days will be a hundred and twenty years."*
> *[4] The Nephilim were on the earth in those days--and also afterward--when the sons of God went to the daughters of men and had children by them. They were the heroes of old, men of renown.*

The narrative of Genesis 6 reverences a specific group of Nephilim, a race of giants which lived on the earth at one time. The term "*Nephilim*" has a simple meaning, being literally defined as "giants." Nothing more should be noted about the term Nephilim unless otherwise gleaned from the text in which that term appears. Certainly there are giants referenced later in scripture, such as the offspring of Anak in Numbers 13. Nothing curious is noted of the sons of Anak except that they were in fact Nephilim, or giants. They were perhaps large because of normal genetic processes, much like is observed in the animal kingdom. Any given species of creature can vary from very small members, such as the miniature pony, to larger members, such as the Clydesdale, without any requisite supernatural intervention. Truly it is possible for normal genetic processes to vary the size of any species, including man. Thus, the term "*Nephilim*" doesn't necessitate an outside supernatural influence to account for the size of a race of people.

The Nephilim of Genesis 6, however, were in fact noted to be unique to other Nephilim which are mentioned in scripture. These Nephilim originated through a special set of circumstances.

> *The Nephilim were on the earth in those days--and also afterward--when the sons of God went to the daughters of men and had children by them.*

Specifically, it is noted that the Nephilim of those days were the product of "*the sons of God*" and "*the daughters of men.*" There was something distinctive about the combination of the sons of God and the daughters of men which created a unique species of giants. The Nephilim of Genesis 6 were a product of the breeding of these two groups.

Biblical students have challenged this text throughout history to answer the question "who are the sons of God which procreated this race of giants?" The "daughters of men" is simple enough to understand, but who are the sons of God, and why are they given that particular name? Some contend that the sons of God refer to godly people who were true to their fellowship with the Lord and the daughters of men were ungodly people who rebelled against God. Yet this interpretation does not account for how the marriage of the godly and the ungodly would produce a race of giants. Godly people have married ungodly people throughout history. While it is not a good idea nor a biblical practice, never has it been observed that a godly person having children with an ungodly person will produce an offspring which will grow into a giant. It seems the earth would team with giants if that were the case. One could not rightly restate this text to inform that "giants were on the earth from when godly people went to ungodly people and had children by them." While it is a simpler, and perhaps easier to accept position, it clearly falls short of the intent of the text, which is to demonstrate *how* the Nephilim came to be upon the earth. Godly people and ungodly people simply do not produce giants in demonstrable genetics.

Furthermore, this interpretation does not account for God's sudden destruction of the earth via the flood, which is the very next event in the

Chapter 1: Pre-tribulational Events

narrative. If there are a number of godly people called "the sons of God" who married ungodly people, the "daughters of men," then why does God proclaim his judgment later in the chapter against the entire world on the basis of there *being no godly people* on the earth other than Noah's family? It is clear from the text that Noah's family alone found favor in God's eyes. It is not likely, then, that the sons of God would refer to godly people of only one generation prior.

There is a more accurate and meaningful interpretation of this phrase.

The phrase "*sons of God*" is translated from the Hebrew term *bane 'elohiym,* which is quite literally rendered "*sons of God*" in English, yet is phrased differently throughout the Old Testament in several English translations. This is one of thousands of scriptural references in which a metaphorical term is used as a reference for something literal. "Sons of God" is a Hebrew idiom for angelic beings in the Old Testament. Just as Jesus is referred to as a "lamb" throughout the New Testament, angels are referred to as the "sons of God" in Old Testament passages. Several examples are found in Job, using the same exact Hebrew phrase, *bane 'elohiym,* yet being translated "angels" rather than "sons of God."

> ***Job 1:6-7***
> *⁶ One day the angels (bane 'elohiym) came to present themselves before the LORD, and Satan also came with them. ⁷ The LORD said to Satan, "Where have you come from?"*

The NIV translates *bane 'elohiym* as "angels" in Job 1:6, as do various other translations. While many prominent translations use the more literal rendering, "sons of God," the context clearly exhibits that "angels" is the intended interpretation of the expression. It is not possible for a human "son of God" to have approached the throne of God and presented himself to the Lord. When this text is taught and preached throughout the globe *bane 'elohiym* is almost universally understood to be referring to angels in this text. Whether the English translation states "sons of God" or "angels," the interpreter knows from the context that the *meaning* of the phrase concerns angels.

Likewise, Job 38:6-7 states:

> *6 On what were its footings set,*
> *or who laid its cornerstone--*
> *7 while the morning stars sang together*
> *and all the angels (bane 'elohiym) shouted for joy?*

Once again the NIV uses the term "angels" to translate *bane 'elohiym* while others, such as the KJV, use the more stringent "sons of God" for the same text. Yet clearly, again, the context indicates that "angels" is a proper translation, for the context dictates that *bane 'elohiym* refers to angels rather than a human "son" of God. Furthermore, the parallelism in the text compares the "sons of God" to the "morning stars." Parallelism, in Hebrew poetry, is a means of presenting a verse by stating a phrase two times in two different ways. In this case, the first phrase uses the term "morning stars," a metaphorical name for literal angels, and the second phrase uses the term "sons of God," also a metaphorical name for literal angels.

While *bane 'elohiym* only occurs a few times in the Old Testament, every usage is consistent in its meaning, and in each usage the phrase refers to "angels" rather than common man. If *bane 'elohiym* refers to angels elsewhere, why should it not have the same meaning in Genesis 6? The common sentiment seems to be that using the translation of "angels" creates problems with interpretation. In reality, however, using the term "angels" clears up many problems with interpretation, since that understanding alone gives a proper light to the context. If ungodly people have children with godly people, they produce common people of normal genetic stature; not giants. However, if angels have children with humans, however disconcerting it sounds, it certainly fits the context of Genesis 6 in that the product of that conception could create an unpredictable outcome; in this case, a race of giants.

Some claim Matthew 22:30 as a hindrance to the doctrine of angelic-human procreation.

Chapter 1: Pre-tribulational Events

> *Matthew 22:30*
> *[30] At the resurrection people will neither marry nor be given in marriage; they will be like the angels in heaven.*

This text clearly notes that the angels in heaven neither marry nor are they given in marriage. However, the phrase *"like the angels in Heaven"* does not indicate that angels are incapable of procreation, but it indicates that the angels *of Heaven* are not given in marriage, which leads some to the understanding that they do not procreate. It is biblically plausible, however, that the angels of Heaven are in fact *capable* of sexuality. The fact that they are not given in marriage does not negate the possibility of having reproductive capabilities. It is entirely logical that they do have the capability to procreate, but are obedient to not utilize their sexuality. One may rightly state also that the angels of Heaven do not serve Satan. Yet, angels were clearly *capable* of serving Satan, for one-third of the angels at a previous point in history chose to rebel against God, and currently *do* serve Satan, while the angels of Heaven do not. Jesus' note concerning marriage is not that it is impossible for angels to procreate, but rather, that the angels of Heaven- righteous angels who serve God- do not do so. Jesus' response concerned itself with what is proper rather than what is possible.

Men are created with the capability for procreation, yet obedience to Christ mandates that a man restrain himself until marriage to utilize that capability. Thus, the godly man who is unmarried will restrain himself from his God-given capability for sexual intimacy out of obedience to God while the ungodly man may not.

Likewise, the *"angels of Heaven"* are elect angels; righteous angels who did not sin when Satan rebelled against God. This text does not mention, however, the demonic angels that did rebel. Demonic angels are disobedient by their very nature. In fact, all scriptural evidence suggests that a demonic angel would certainly fulfill the fruition of any sinful action possible. If it is *possible* for the angels of Heaven to procreate, yet they do not do so out of obedience, then it is possible- and even likely- that the disobedient angels would choose to go against their nature and procreate out of disobedience to God, and perhaps even in obedience to a direct call of Satan. Numerous theologians who accept this interpretation of Genesis 6 believe this demonic intervention into the lives of mankind, or the daughters of men, was an attempt to corrupt the seed of woman. In this attempt, it is thought that Satan desired to thwart the prophecy of Genesis 3:15 and prevent the offspring of woman, Jesus, from bashing the head of Satan, as prophesied.

Interestingly, the very next verses following the account of the Nephilim demonstrate that God's favor was turned against mankind.

> ***Genesis 6:5-8***
> *[5] The LORD saw how great man's wickedness on the earth had become, and that every inclination of the thoughts of his heart was only evil all the time. [6] The LORD was grieved that he had made man on the earth, and his heart was filled with pain. [7] So the LORD said, "I will wipe mankind, whom I have created, from the face of the earth--men and animals, and creatures that move along the ground, and birds of the air--for I am grieved that I have made them." [8] But Noah found favor in the eyes of the LORD.*

Genesis 6:11-12 continues,

> *[11] Now the earth was corrupt in God's sight and was full of violence. [12] God saw how corrupt the earth had become, for all the people on earth had corrupted their ways.*

Clearly the action of the "*sons of God*" having children with the "*daughters of men*" was a serious offense to God; so much so that it is referenced as an example of the wickedness on earth and as a precursor to God's destruction of it.

Further evidence of a demonic perversion of the seed of man is found in the book of Jude.

Chapter 1: Pre-tribulational Events

> ***Jude 1:6-7***
> *⁶ And the angels who did not keep their positions of authority but abandoned their own home--these he has kept in darkness, bound with everlasting chains for judgment on the great Day. ⁷ In a similar way, Sodom and Gomorrah and the surrounding towns gave themselves up to sexual immorality and perversion.*

Jude's account requires some knowledge of the book of Enoch, from which he references his illustration. The book of Enoch is a non-canonical and extra-biblical book. It is not the basis of biblical theology. Yet, Jude quotes Enoch directly in verses 14-15, giving credibility to the idea that Jude writes verse 6 with Enoch's writings in mind as well. Jude is using Enoch's testimony to make his own argument. And, the book of Enoch, though extra-biblical, tells the story of demons procreating with humans to create a race of Giants. It further tells of God locking those angels away in the deepest regions of fire and torment because of their actions.

For Jude to make the statement, *"And the angels who did not keep their positions of authority but abandoned their own home--these he has kept in darkness, bound with everlasting chains for judgment on the great Day"* in context with other quotes from Enoch indicates that it is in fact Enoch's account of demonic and human conception which these angels are guilty of committing. While Enoch is not part of the Bible, Jude is. And, Jude is giving credibility to that specific part of Enoch's writing by quoting it.

Continuing, Jude 7 gives an even more direct indication of the actions which caused these particular angels to be bound when he states, *"In a similar way, Sodom and Gomorrah and the surrounding towns gave themselves up to sexual immorality and perversion."* Setting the book of Enoch aside, Jude clearly determines that the offense of the angels who were bound is equated in some way to the sexual perversion which existed in Sodom and Gomorrah.

These angels have clearly done something specifically evil in God's sight that they are bound in "*everlasting chains*." Being bound in eternally is a unique state for demons during this earth age. The only other time angels are referred to as being put into everlasting chains are those cast into "tartarus" in 2 Peter 2:4. Other angels are cast into the "Abyss" periodically (the Abyss will be dealt with later in this work) which is a temporary holding place for disobedient demons. These are later released, as their sentence is not eternal. Tartarus, however, is eternal, as is the punishment of the Jude 6 angels who committed a certain specific act of sin that God sentenced them firmly to this place until the time of their judgment, at the end of earth history.

In conclusion, there is a clear biblical thread of evidence that demonic angels, hurled to earth in rebellion, gave themselves up to sexual perversion, and they, the *bane 'elohiym*, interbred with the daughters of men creating the Nephilim of Genesis 6:4, "*when the sons of God went to the daughters of men and had children by them.*"

This is a difficult teaching for many to accept, but it plays an important role in the understanding of Antichrist. Suddenly, the designation of Antichrist's advent being "*in accordance with the work of Satan*," or literally being *energized* of Satan has fuller meaning. It is well within the realm of scriptural latitude for Satan to impregnate a woman and create a demonic human who will serve as his counterfeit son, Antichrist.

Antichrist's Role in Satan's Counterfeit Program

Though it is too rarely focused on in eschatological study, there is a clear teaching in scripture of Satan's counterfeiting work in his final program. Through the course of this study this counterfeiting will be identified on several levels.

The name "Antichrist" is not accidental in scripture. As the name implies, this being will be the antithesis of the person of Jesus Christ, yet will do all he can to emulate what Christ did in his ministry on earth. Just as Pharaoh's magicians performed their demonic versions of the miracles of Moses, so Satan will attempt to re-create the person of Jesus

Chapter 1: Pre-tribulational Events

Christ in Antichrist. Antichrist will, in effect, be Satan's attempt to "do Jesus" better than Jesus did. More importantly, Antichrist will be Satan's attempt to deceive the nations into believing that Christ has come to earth in the flesh prior to his actual return. In the Olivet Discourse discussed earlier, Jesus notes this reality specifically.

> ***Matthew 24:23-25***
> *[23] At that time if anyone says to you, 'Look, here is the Christ!' or, 'There he is!' do not believe it. [24] For false Christs and false prophets will appear and perform great signs and miracles to deceive even the elect--if that were possible. [25] See, I have told you ahead of time.*

"*At that time*" refers back to verse 15, "*so when you see standing in the holy place 'the abomination that causes desolation.'*" It will be demonstrated later in this work that the timing of the abomination of desolation is in the middle of the tribulation. Thus, "at that time" in Matthew 24:23 refers to the timing of the center of the great tribulation. Jesus warns, then, that "*at that time*" people will say, "*Look, here is the Christ!*" or "*There he is!*" Satan will repeatedly attempt to convince the world that Antichrist is the returning King. These facets of tribulational deception will be discussed in detail in chapters 4 and 5. But at this point it should be understood that Antichrist will be presented in every possible way to appear as the true Christ.

The first step in Satan's deception is realized from Antichrist's illegitimate conception. Through this process, Antichrist will become Satan's counterfeit "son." Just as the true Son, Jesus Christ, had a legitimate virgin birth, so Satan's program will demand that the false christ have a virgin birth via Satan's own copulation with a human woman, of Roman descent.

As Satan's program for the earth unfolds, it will be demonstrated that the counterfeit son will establish a covenant with Israel, who rejected the true Christ's covenant. Antichrist will establish himself as God in the Temple, creating the abomination of desolation. He will have a counterfeit death and resurrection. Satan will also produce a counterfeit

Holy Spirit, who will be known as "the False Prophet," leaving Satan himself as the counterfeit "father" of the unholy trinity of a great false religion on earth. Thus, the illegitimate demonic copulation of Antichrist involves more than a strange incarnation. It involves an attempt at counterfeiting the person of Christ, being born of supernatural conception, but by Satanic means.

A Period of Peace

One of the final pre-tribulational events is not really an event at all, but rather a season of a particular attitude. Understood from 1 Thessalonians, the advent of the tribulation will follow a peaceful period on the earth. Ironically, in today's culture, those interested in eschatological events find every aggressive act imaginable from the world news stage to predict that the end is upon us. In fact, the *season* of the end may be. However, scripture indicates that a more volatile world may not be the best indicator concerning the advent of the great tribulation. While these types of events - wars & rumors of war- are indicators of the *season*, they are not the best gauge as to the very advent of the tribulation. Quite the opposite is true.

> ***1 Thessalonians 5:1-3***
> *[1] Now, brothers, about times and dates we do not need to write to you, [2] for you know very well that the day of the Lord will come like a thief in the night. [3] While people are saying, "Peace and safety," destruction will come on them suddenly, as labor pains on a pregnant woman, and they will not escape.*

Paul's marker concerning the coming of the great tribulation is that it will follow a period of peace and misappropriated hope. *"While people are saying peace and safety"* the *"day of the Lord"* will come.

The "*day of the Lord*," once again, always refers to the period of the great tribulation in scripture. At times generally, and at times specifically the very return of Christ. In this instance the phrase refers

Chapter 1: Pre-tribulational Events

generally to the period of the tribulation. In this text, the common sentiment prior to the sudden advent of the day of the Lord is one of *"peace and safety."* Peace and safety can only be a general reference to the day of the Lord, for peace and safety will not be the climate prior to the moment of the return of Christ. Therefore, as one watches the world stage for signs of the coming day of the Lord, one must surely watch for the signs of birth pains, but one must also understand that the final moments prior to the advent of the day of the Lord will be filled with thoughts of security and peace.

Often times a world event receives great attention in the minds of those keeping watch, only to be rejected as coincidence the moment the news story diminishes to the third page of the paper. However, one must not be fooled into thinking that a cataclysmic prophetic birth pain or sign of the end will be the moment before the dawn of the tribulation. Clearly the moment before the tribulation will be one of security, when the latest fearful prophetic warnings are most likely waning from memory.

History will unfold with the revealing of the Antichrist, who is the *"little horn"* of Daniel 7, which demands that the ten kings of the one world government are already in place, since Daniel 7 demonstrates the little horn appearing after the ten original horns. It seems unlikely that the mere advent of a new world-wide government or the revealing of Antichrist would give way to a period of peace and false hope. People are typically skeptical of change, especially change of governmental influence. For people to truly be saying *"peace and safety,"* presumably the new government will have been at work time enough for the normal human suspicions of change to have been quelled.

Thus, it appears that the new government will have great success in winning the trust of the world and ensuring its stability as people will feel a genuine sense of peace and security in the season immediately before the tribulation begins. It should be noted, however, that it is a misappropriated sense of peace and hope, for the day of the Lord which will follow this season will be anything but peaceful or hopeful to those who endure it.

Chapter 2: The Rapture

While the previous chapter concerned itself with pre-tribulational events, one exceptionally significant pre-tribulational event remains; the rapture event.

The term "rapture" never appears in scripture. Some students of eschatology are inhibited from believing in the rapture merely because of that fact. However, while the precise term does not appear, the teaching does, and, one must be careful using such a litmus test for excluding doctrines which are otherwise taught in scripture. Another term which does not appear in scripture is the term "Trinity," and, like a theological understanding of the Trinity, one must come to understand the rapture systematically through a full study of scripture rather than from any singular scriptural term or sentence, although several singular texts do speak of a rapture event.

For a term or idea to be biblical does not require that the exact terminology be stated in an English translation of scripture. There are many terms which may be substituted for an identical definition. To subscribe to that position would be tantamount to stating that Jesus did not raise Lazarus from the dead. For technically Jesus stated, "Lazarus, come forth." Clearly the definition and the semantics are not at odds with one another in such circumstances.

The term "rapture" is defined as "the carrying of a person to another place or sphere of existence."[21] While one may claim that the actual theological term "rapture" is not used in scripture, the definition of the rapture certainly is clearly spoken in John 14, which will be discussed in

---

[21] "rapture." *Dictionary.com Unabridged (v 1.1)*. Random House, Inc. 25 Jun. 2008. <Dictionary.com http://dictionary.reference.com/browse/rapture>.

Chapter 2: The Rapture

detail in the next section. Jesus clearly states in that text, "*I will come back and take you to be with me that you also may be where I am,*" which is precisely the definition of rapture: to carry a person to another place of sphere of existence. Consequently, the term "rapture," and its definition are in fact scriptural in light of that definition. The absence of a specific English term is irrelevant to the teaching of that term, as the scriptures were not written in English, but translated.

The Rapture Event

The existence of the rapture is an issue of such great debate that eschatology is divided into major divisions over the issue. As noted in the foreword, this work is not an attempt to identify and explain all eschatological theories, but rather is a conclusion drawn from the examination of scripture which will define itself as believing in a pre-tribulational rapture. Concerning the rapture, a key text which will enlighten the issue in this work comes from Jesus' promise in John 14.

> ### *John 14:1-4*
> *¹"Do not let your hearts be troubled. Trust in God ; trust also in me. ² In my Father's house are many rooms; if it were not so, I would have told you. I am going there to prepare a place for you. ³ And if I go and prepare a place for you, I will come back and take you to be with me that you also may be where I am. ⁴ You know the way to the place where I am going."*

Jesus states in verse 2 that he is preparing a place for his disciples in his "*Father's house*," or in Heaven, the location of God's throne. No divisions of eschatology fail to recognize Heaven as the location of Jesus' preparations. Jesus then promises to "*come back*" and take his followers to be where he is. Where he will be prior to his coming back has already been established; he will be in Heaven, where he is preparing the place for his followers. Where he will take believers to upon his coming back is quite well stated in the text. He is taking them to the "place" He has been preparing for them; in Heaven.

This text is problematic for post-tribulational theories, because Jesus' promise to take his disciples to Heaven does not leave room for the typical post-tribulational assertions. Post-tribulational theories generally teach (though with variation) that during the rapture the church will meet Christ in the air and then return to earth to reign with him during his millennial kingdom. If that is the case, where is he preparing a place for the church right now? He was on earth when he made this statement, so where did he have to go in order to prepare this place? He clearly stipulated where he was to go; he was to go to his father's house. And he further stipulated that it was that very location from which he would come to take his people "back" to be with him. Thus, Jesus cannot establish his kingdom on earth as he meets his church. He must take them back to Heaven at this time, then establish his kingdom on earth at a future time.

Likewise, this text contains difficulties for Amillennial views of eschatology. The Amillennial position teaches that Christ will return to earth and establish his permanent kingdom of Heaven here, without a millennial reign or a rapture. While scripture does teach that Heaven proper will exist on the new earth in eternity, it does not exist on earth at this time. If the Amillennial position is to be understood from John 14, then how will Jesus both "*come back*" and "*take you to be with me*" if he will not be returning to Heaven after coming back? It would make more sense to believe Amillennialism if Jesus had said "I will come back and remain with you," but that is not what Jesus said. Clearly Jesus is teaching that he will leave Heaven, return to earth and collect his saints, then return *to Heaven* with them.

"*I will come back*" is indicative of both his return for the rapturing of the saints, and of the fact that the place he is preparing for them is not here, but somewhere else; in his Father's house. Thus, the rapture is best understood as an event taking the church from the earth, where his believers dwell, to Heaven, where he prepares them a new dwelling.

Some take issue with the pre-tribulational rapture position claiming this process demands both a second and "third" return of Christ to the earth. The contention is that Jesus must have a second coming to receive the

Chapter 2: The Rapture

church, as noted here in John 14, and that he must then return a third time to establish his millennial kingdom. It is arguable that Christ can be said "to come" and take his church, yet the rapture should not be understood as the second coming, while Christ's return to reign be understood as a third coming. The second coming is different from his return to rapture in that it will mirror his first coming in ways which the rapture event does not.

I Thessalonians 4, which will be the substance of the next section, states, that the church will "*meet the Lord in the air*" during this rapture process. The second coming of Christ, however, is described in detail in Zechariah with the Lord's feet firmly planted on the Mount of Olives.

> ***Zechariah 14:4-5***
> *⁴ On that day his feet will stand on the Mount of Olives, east of Jerusalem, and the Mount of Olives will be split in two from east to west, forming a great valley, with half of the mountain moving north and half moving south. ⁵ You will flee by my mountain valley, for it will extend to Azel. You will flee as you fled from the earthquake in the days of Uzziah king of Judah. Then the Lord my God will come, and all the holy ones with him.*

In the rapture process the Lord's action of meeting the church in the air does not fulfill the description of Zechariah for the event commonly known as "the second coming." Therefore, the rapture is not to be understood as a second of three "comings" of Christ. His feet do not touch ground, but rather he will "pass by" the earth while collecting his bride in the air. Thus, the rapture is not a second coming while the return of Christ to rule is a "third" coming. The rapture is an event contrary to the description of the second coming. It is a collection of the church from the air. There are several texts, however, which speak of a return of Christ, which can be understood contextually to speak of the rapture rather than his second coming to rule. Other texts speaking of a return, do speak of his return to rule. One must observe context carefully to determine the differences. This work will explain numerous such texts, that the reader can see the contextual qualities which differentiate between the two.

The Process

The process of the rapture is actually well articulated in scripture as well. As with all things, in the rapture process, the Lord is demonstrated to be a God of great order.

> ***1 Thessalonians 4:13-18***
> *[13] Brothers, we do not want you to be ignorant about those who fall asleep, or to grieve like the rest of men, who have no hope. [14] We believe that Jesus died and rose again and so we believe that God will bring with Jesus those who have fallen asleep in him. [15] According to the Lord's own word, we tell you that we who are still alive, who are left till the coming of the Lord, will certainly not precede those who have fallen asleep. [16] For the Lord himself will come down from heaven, with a loud command, with the voice of the archangel and with the trumpet call of God, and the dead in Christ will rise first. [17] After that, we who are still alive and are left will be caught up together with them in the clouds to meet the Lord in the air. And so we will be with the Lord forever. [18] Therefore encourage each other with these words.*

To begin this orderly process a shout, followed by the command of an angel is given:

> *For the Lord himself will come down from heaven with a loud command, with the voice of the archangel....*

Some have expressed difficulty understanding why the Lord would respond to the command of an archangel. However it is not stipulated in this text that the angel is he who grants the command, only that a

Chapter 2: The Rapture

command is *given* "with the voice" of an archangel. Angels are creatures of order as well, each with a rank and responsibilities. They are not called the hosts of Heaven without reason. They follow orders. Even to grant a command would be done in response to an order; the order of the Father that the time has come for the rapture event to take place. Accordingly, this order is given "*with the trumpet call of God,*" while an angel vocalized God's order with a shout.

Trumpets are used typically in scripture either for a call to battle or for a worship summons. The rapture begins with a similar summons from God, followed by the command shouted from the archangel, followed by the invocation of the rapture event.

The process of the rapture is also of a definitive order. All saints are not raptured simultaneously, but each in their turn, beginning with the dead in Christ, as "*the dead in Christ will rise first.*"

Prior to the living, the bodies of dead believers will rise to meet Christ. It should be noted for clarity that the sentiment of *rising* speaks of a physical resurrection of the dead. The spirits of the righteous dead will return with Christ from Heaven to meet up with their bodies, as referenced in verse 14, "[14] *We believe that Jesus died and rose again and so we believe that God will bring with Jesus those who have fallen asleep in him.*" As a result, the spirit is rejoined with the body of those dead in Christ. The spirit returns with Christ while the body rises from the dust of the earth to meet its body.

A literal resurrection of the dead is a difficult event to picture. Many in this resurrection will have been dead for thousands of years. In such cases, their bodies will have been completely consumed by the elements and redistributed in numerous compounded manners. Yet, the God who promises this resurrection is the same God who created man from that very dust of the earth. He is capable of doing precisely what he says. What a fascinating illumination it will be to witness how precisely the Lord will reconstitute the bodies of those who have been dead for such long periods of time!

The term "*in Christ*" in this text limits the resurrection to those who have the Holy Spirit, the church. "*In Christ*" is a uniquely New Testament post-conversion term indicating the indwelling Christ through the Holy Spirit. Those which have not received the Holy Spirit are not referred to as being "*in Christ*" in scripture. Thus it should be noted that the Old Testament saints are not a part of the rapture process, but will be raised at a later time, which will be observed in chapter nine.

Verse 17 then observes, *"After that, we who are still alive and are left will be caught up together with them in the clouds to meet the Lord in the air."*

Some argue the phrase *"we who are still alive and are left"* as evidence of a post-tribulational rapture. They understand *"still alive"* to refer to those which Antichrist has not killed during the tribulation. While that position does appear plausible in this text, nothing is indicative of the tribulation in the context. Rather, in the context, "*we who are still alive, who are left till the coming of the Lord*" refers to those who have not formerly died, but continue to live until the Lord's coming to rapture them. "*We who are still alive*" is simply the antithesis of "*the dead in Christ will rise first."* The purpose of this text is to speak to the order of the resurrection noted in the rapture event. The dead will rise first, followed by the living. The great tribulation needs not to be underway for some to have died and others to be left living. The text is making a very general assertion; some will have died, and they will be taken first. Others will still be living and will be taken thereafter. Thus, "*we who are still alive, who are left till the coming of the Lord, will certainly not precede those who have fallen asleep.*"

"*And so we will be with the Lord forever,"* indicates that the church will never again be separated from the Lord. The church will be where Christ is for the duration of eternity, including his return in glory and the Millennial Reign. The church's position with Christ for all eternity will be demonstrated throughout this work, as will the positions the church will fill during various elements of future history.

Chapter 2: The Rapture

The Transformation

A fascinating element of observation concerning the rapture event involves a physical transformation which will occur to all who are taken to be with Christ. Just as humanity is given a body which is appropriate for life on earth, so the inhabitants of Heaven are to be granted a spiritual body which is equipped for life in Heaven.

> *1 Corinthians 15:50-58*
> *[50] I declare to you, brothers, that flesh and blood cannot inherit the kingdom of God, nor does the perishable inherit the imperishable. [51] Listen, I tell you a mystery: We will not all sleep, but we will all be changed-- [52] in a flash, in the twinkling of an eye, at the last trumpet. For the trumpet will sound, the dead will be raised imperishable, and we will be changed. [53] For the perishable must clothe itself with the imperishable, and the mortal with immortality. [54] When the perishable has been clothed with the imperishable, and the mortal with immortality, then the saying that is written will come true: "Death has been swallowed up in victory."*
> *[55] "Where, O death, is your victory?*
>   *Where, O death, is your sting?"*
> *[56] The sting of death is sin, and the power of sin is the law. [57] But thanks be to God! He gives us the victory through our Lord Jesus Christ.*
>   *[58] Therefore, my dear brothers, stand firm. Let nothing move you. Always give yourselves fully to the work of the Lord, because you know that your labor in the Lord is not in vain.*

1 Corinthians 15 describes the rapture event and the essence of the translated body which will be allowed to enter Heaven. The primary idea of this text is that an inconsistency exists between earthly matter and heavenly matter. *"[50]I declare to you, brothers, that flesh and blood cannot inherit the kingdom of God, nor does the perishable inherit the imperishable."* Clearly, one cannot enter Heaven as one currently is. A change must take place from the earthly corruptible state to a heavenly

incorruptible state.

The state of man, of course, is sinful and perishable. Such a state is not suitable for Heaven. While man possesses the promise of salvation, he remains sinful. He lives under grace, but still has a sinful nature. Thus a foundational change in essence is required.

> *[W]e will all be changed--* [52] *in a flash, in the twinkling of an eye, at the last trumpet. For the trumpet will sound, the dead will be raised imperishable, and we will be changed.*

That this change occurs "*in a flash*" indicates an instantaneous process whereby the imperishable replaces the perishable.

The phrase, "*at the last trumpet,*" has been taken by some to indicate the seventh trumpet judgment of Revelation, which would fit well with mid-tribulational theories. However this does not seem likely, as it appears that Paul assumes the church would know what he's talking about. He knowingly mentions *the last trumpet* without any further explanation. The book of Revelation, which details the seventh trumpet judgment, however, had not yet been written at the time Paul wrote his letter to the Corinthians. 1 Corinthians was written in roughly AD 56, while Revelation was written around AD 95. The Corinthians could not have known of the seven trumpets of the Revelation and would not have recognized which trumpet Paul referred to if in fact he were referring to a trumpet judgment. It seems that Paul would offer an explanation of exactly what this trumpet were if he were writing of something new. He is, after all, detailing the events to come. To refer to a trumpet no one knew of would have fit the purpose of his writing very well if he had only explained it. But, he did not, so it appears he is referring to a trumpet of which the church would be previously familiar.

The trumpets the church would have known of are the trumpets of Old Testament worship. One trumpet Paul may have been referencing bears the very name, "the last trumpet," and was the final trumpet blast at the

Chapter 2: The Rapture

Feast of Trumpets (*Rosh Hoshanah*).

The Feast of Trumpets called for numerous trumpet blasts in the synagogue service, each with differing characteristics and each having differing symbolic meanings. The last one was called the "tekiah gedolah" or, in English, the "*last trumpet*." The tekiah gedolah blast was a very long and sustained blast. It was very well known in Jewish tradition as "*the last trumpet*" and symbolized the very hope for the future redemption of Israel.

This redemption is secured for the church, both dead and living, at this moment, for *"[54]When the perishable has been clothed with the imperishable, and the mortal with immortality, then the saying that is written will come true: 'Death has been swallowed up in victory.'"*

In this manner the dead in Christ are raised with their new glorified bodies and those living are immediately translated into theirs. The hope of a future redemption will be realized as the bodies of death are converted into glorious new perfection.

Other trumpets the church would have known of are the general trumpets used in the Old Testament, such as in Numbers 10, which either mobilized the people to move or led out in a great celebration.

> ***Numbers 10:8-10***
> *[8] "The sons of Aaron, the priests, are to blow the trumpets. This is to be a lasting ordinance for you and the generations to come. [9] When you go into battle in your own land against an enemy who is oppressing you, sound a blast on the trumpets. Then you will be remembered by the LORD your God and rescued from your enemies. [10] Also at your times of rejoicing--your appointed feasts and New Moon festivals--you are to sound the trumpets over your burnt offerings and fellowship offerings, and they will be a memorial for you before your God. I am the LORD your God."*

Verse 10 notes a very possible understanding of the "last trumpet" as the signal of a time of rejoicing.

Precisely what trumpet Paul notes as the "last trumpet" in 1 Corinthians 15 remains in great debate among students of eschatology. What is certain is that a trumpet call of God will be sounded. Beyond that a debate will undoubtedly continue.

The Nature of The Resurrected Body

1 Corinthians 15:35-49
[35] But someone may ask, "How are the dead raised? With what kind of body will they come?" [36] How foolish! What you sow does not come to life unless it dies. [37] When you sow, you do not plant the body that will be, but just a seed, perhaps of wheat or of something else. [38] But God gives it a body as he has determined, and to each kind of seed he gives its own body. [39] All flesh is not the same: Men have one kind of flesh, animals have another, birds another and fish another. [40] There are also heavenly bodies and there are earthly bodies; but the splendor of the heavenly bodies is one kind, and the splendor of the earthly bodies is another. [41] The sun has one kind of splendor, the moon another and the stars another; and star differs from star in splendor.
  [42] So will it be with the resurrection of the dead. The body that is sown is perishable, it is raised imperishable; [43] it is sown in dishonor, it is raised in glory; it is sown in weakness, it is raised in power; [44] it is sown a natural body, it is raised a spiritual body.
  If there is a natural body, there is also a spiritual body. [45] So it is written: "The first man Adam became a living being" ; the last Adam, a life-giving spirit. [46] The spiritual did not come first, but the natural, and after that the spiritual. [47] The first man was of the dust of the earth, the second man from heaven. [48] As was the earthly

Chapter 2: The Rapture

> *man, so are those who are of the earth; and as is the man from heaven, so also are those who are of heaven. ⁴⁹ And just as we have borne the likeness of the earthly man, so shall we bear the likeness of the man from heaven.*

While this text does not speak in terms of the rapture event, it does give a broad description of the resurrected body which believers will have in eternity. Consequently, it also speaks of the glorified bodies the church will receive at the time of the rapture. 1 Corinthians 15:5, examined sentences ago, declares the fact of a spiritual body which finds its description in this text.

A chief observation of the spiritual is described in verse 42, "*The body that is sown is perishable, it is raised imperishable.*" The imperishable nature of the resurrected body, simply stated, demands that the spiritual body will not deteriorate. It will not die. Because it will not die, a second deduction can be drawn, which is that it cannot sin. Scripture teaches clearly that sin yields death to the body.[22] Hence, a body which is guaranteed not to die for eternity is necessarily one which will never be susceptible to sin. Both ideas are represented in the description of imperishability.

Verse 43 continues, "*it is sown in dishonor, it is raised in glory.*" "*Glory*", as a term, describes a state of worthiness or dignity. It is a state foreign to sinful man, yet is true of the resurrected body. The resurrected body will have a worthiness to exist in God's presence whereas the current sinful body of man does not. Of the sinful man, God told Moses, "*no one can see me and live.*"[23] While the indwelling Christ allows a believer to have fellowship with God's Spirit, the body of death must be yet transformed to a body of glory before it can be in God's literal presence in Heaven.

Continuing in verse 43 is the declaration "*it is raised in power.*" The

---

[22] Romans 6:23, Genesis 2:17
[23] Exodus 33:20

transliterated Greek term translated *power* in the NIV is *"dynamis,"* which infers *great power,* rather than general power. It is associated with miraculous power and is used in parallel with Christ, angels and spiritual powers in scripture.[24] This description indicates a power on a greater plain than man currently experiences. It is by definition, therefore, "supernatural" power which the resurrected body will be granted.

Lastly, in verse 44 it is recorded, *"it is sown a natural body, it is raised a spiritual body."* The concept of a spiritual body is foreign to man's experience. Humanity has long understood a defining line to exist between the physical and the spiritual realms. The body is understood as that which is physical while the soul is understood to be that which is spiritual. The eternal body of man, however, is of a different constitution. It is a spirit-body, specially designed for existence in the spiritual world of Heaven, just as the physical body man is given for earth life is designed for the physical world of earth. Some erroneously have concluded that man will not have a body in Heaven, but will instead exist in spirit only. While this is true of saints in Heaven prior to the advent of the resurrection, this text teaches clearly of the *body* being raised as a completely different essence. It is not mere spirit, but a *"spiritual body."*

The descriptions noted in this text define something difficult to grasp completely. It seems plausible, however, that the spiritual bodies man will be transformed into at the rapture will be similar, if not identical, to the body Christ received upon his resurrection. The risen Christ demonstrated characteristics which may indeed give insight into the nature of the resurrected body. Christ was able to appear into a room without using a door.[25] He also disappeared in similar fashion. Yet, the risen Christ was able to be touched by the disciples to prove that he was

---

[24] *Dynamis* is rendered "power" in 1 Corinthians 1:24 "...Christ the power of God and the wisdom of God."
[25] John 20:19

Chapter 2: The Rapture

not a ghost. He was able to eat.[26] While it is impossible to know if these characteristics were due to the nature of Christ's glorified body or his deity, these were not characteristics of Christ's body while he lived on earth, nor did his deity manifest itself in those fashions before he was raised and glorified. It seems probable that the characteristics of the risen Christ's body are akin to those which will be normative of the glorified bodies of the righteous.

The Timing of the Rapture

The timing of the rapture is an issue of great debate among students of eschatology. And, in scripture there are very difficult texts which lend fuel to that debate. The primary distinction between the pretribulational view of this event and other views is arguably the degree to which one follows a consistent literal interpretation of scripture. Views contrary to the pretribulational view at worst dismiss the literal interpretation of scripture and at best weaken it. Numerous texts, when taken literally, indicate a church which is not present during the distress of the great tribulation.

Beginning with Luke 21, the first observation to be made is that the possibility exists for one to escape the great tribulation.

> *Luke 21:34-36*
> *[34] "Be careful, or your hearts will be weighed down with dissipation, drunkenness and the anxieties of life, and that day will close on you unexpectedly like a trap. [35] For it will come upon all those who live on the face of the whole earth. [36] Be always on the watch, and pray that you may be able to escape all that is about to happen, and that you may be able to stand before the Son of Man."*

---

[26] Luke 24:39-41

"*That day*," referred to in verse 34, refers to the distress of the great tribulation in the context of Jesus' teaching. He states of that day that "*it will come upon all those who live on the face of the whole earth.*" This is an iron clad statement, using several over-kill words. Jesus' point is clear: if you live on earth, the great tribulation will come upon you and will affect you. However, Jesus does not presume in his teaching that everyone learning from his teachings will be on earth at that time. He encourages his students in verse 36 to "*pray that you may be able to escape*" all that will happen in that day. While he had just noted that there could be no escape for anyone living on the earth in that day he also inspires them to pray to somehow be able to escape this coming day. Clearly the possibility exists for someone to escape. And, if these events will fall upon everyone living on earth, then the only way to escape is to *not be on earth* when that day arrives.

Beyond the possibility of escaping the great tribulation comes the theology of Paul which indicates that one of the purposes of this season is inconsistent with the body of Christ participating in it.

> ### *1 Thessalonians 1:9-10*
> *⁹ ... They tell how you turned to God from idols to serve the living and true God, ¹⁰ and to wait for his Son from heaven, whom he raised from the dead--Jesus, who rescues us from the coming wrath.*

In this text Paul praises the church for having turned to God from idols and for their ability to "*wait for his Son from heaven…who rescues us from the coming wrath.*" The two parts of this phrase complement each other nicely in a literal interpretive method. The one whom is being waited on will rescue those who are waiting from a coming display of wrath.

Without reading the rest of the letter, one may wonder what this coming wrath refers to. It certainly cannot be the wrath of God against man's sin. Paul was writing to the church, not the lost. And, as for the church, Jesus received the wrath for her sins via his substitutionary atonement on the

Chapter 2: The Rapture

cross.[27] The coming wrath Paul must have been speaking of is the coming wrath of the great tribulation, which he articulates later in the letter.

> ***1 Thessalonians 5:1-10***
> *[1] Now, brothers, about times and dates we do not need to write to you, [2] for you know very well that the day of the Lord will come like a thief in the night. [3] While people are saying, "Peace and safety," destruction will come on them suddenly, as labor pains on a pregnant woman, and they will not escape.*
> *[4] But you, brothers, are not in darkness so that this day should surprise you like a thief. [5] You are all sons of the light and sons of the day. We do not belong to the night or to the darkness. [6] So then, let us not be like others, who are asleep, but let us be alert and self-controlled. [7] For those who sleep, sleep at night, and those who get drunk, get drunk at night. [8] But since we belong to the day, let us be self-controlled, putting on faith and love as a breastplate, and the hope of salvation as a helmet. [9] For God did not appoint us to suffer wrath but to receive salvation through our Lord Jesus Christ. [10] He died for us so that, whether we are awake or asleep, we may live together with him.*

As formerly indicated, the *day of the Lord* refers to the great tribulation in scripture; either the entire seven years generally, or specifically referencing the second coming of Christ at the end of that period. Here, Paul notes various principles related to the day of the Lord. He states that it will come when people are saying "*peace and safety,*" that it will come suddenly and that the church should be alert and expecting that day to come. It is at this point that he once again refers to the wrath he spoke of earlier.

> *[9] For God did not appoint us to suffer wrath but to*

---

[27] Romans 5:9; 8:1-4

> *receive salvation through our Lord Jesus Christ. ¹⁰ He died for us so that, whether we are awake or asleep, we may live together with him.*

Unmistakably Paul states that God did not appoint "*us*" (the church, to whom he is writing) to suffer wrath. Instead, the church is to "*receive salvation through our Lord Jesus Christ.*" He further states that "*whether we are awake or asleep, we may live together with him.*" This phrase indicates that even those who are not watching and waiting, as he is encouraging them to do, will still be able to escape this wrath, which complicates the idea of a partial rapture, popular in some circles.

It is clear from Paul's theology that God's wrath is not something intended to be poured out upon those who are saved in Christ. In Romans 1, Paul notes that God's wrath is being poured out against the ungodly,[28] but clearly in 1 Thessalonians 5 he states that the church is *not* appointed to receive God's wrath. Rather, the church is appointed to receive salvation, and to live together with Christ, who has taken her wrath upon himself.

Chapter 3 of this work will detail how the display of God's wrath is indeed a primary purpose of the great tribulation. Some who subscribe to mid or post-tribulational views argue that "*God never promised that the church would not endure tribulation.*" This is quite true. In fact, Jesus promised the church that it *would* endure tribulation.[29] "Tribulation," as a quality, is not synonymous with *the great tribulation.* Tribulation, as a general term, describes extreme difficulty, persecution and/or turmoil. The *great tribulation* is a title for a specific coming season. It is "the day of God's wrath" upon the earth.[30] The great tribulation is unique among tribulations. It is a tribulation brought about by God for his specific purposes; one of which is to demonstrate his wrath to those who refuse to acknowledge him as God. This

---

[28] Romans 1:18-20
[29] John 15:21; 16:33, Luke 21:12
[30] Romans 2:5

characteristic of the great tribulation is not one for which the church is appointed to suffer. She has acknowledged God, and his Servant, Christ. As the great tribulation is examined in this work it will be noted clearly that God's wrath is uniquely being poured out because of the unbelief and unrighteousness of those who reject him. The church categorically does not fit the profile of those at whom this wrath is aimed. Paul's point was precisely that. God did not appoint "*us*" to suffer the wrath of the day of the Lord.

A further example of God's sparing the church from the great tribulation is found in the very book which depicts so well the events of the great tribulation.

> ***Revelation 3:10***
> *[10] Since you have kept my command to endure patiently, I will also keep you from the hour of trial that is going to come upon the whole world to test those who live on the earth.*

The book of Revelation is addressed to seven churches in the province of Asia. It is these seven churches which the book was delivered to. It would have surely been read aloud in each congregation. In chapters 2 and 3, each of these churches is given a personal word from Christ in conjunction with the fullness of the remainder of Revelation's teaching. This text is taken from the embedded personal letter to the church at Philadelphia.

Revelation 3:10 appears to be a conditional statement on the surface. It states, "*Since you have kept my command to endure patiently, I will also keep you from the hour of trial that is going to come upon the whole world....*" Some have taken this statement, and other statements which sound similar, to indicate a partial rapture being taught in scripture.

The "partial rapture theory" teaches that only those who are prepared for the Lord's return will be raptured. Others will be left to endure the great tribulation. While there are several statements concerning rapture doctrines which appear conditional, the idea of a partial rapture is inconsistent with biblical teachings. Foremost, this theory divides the power of Christ's substitutionary atonement into two categories: one which saves completely and one which saves partially. Secondly, this theory creates a mystical line between the law and grace. It assumes a set of works which must be properly engaged in upon the moment of Christ's rapture of the church. Contrarily however, 1 Thessalonians 5:10 proclaims, *"whether we are awake or asleep, we may live together with him."* The rapture is a complete removal of the church, whether awake or asleep. While the church is charged to be prepared in the numerous warnings concerning the rapture event, that encouragement has to do with the preparedness of the church to receive her reward, as will be discussed in the next section.

The question then remains as to the meaning of Christ's statement to the church at Philadelphia, *"since you have kept my command...I will also keep you from the hour of trial."* Perhaps this statement is best understood in the context of another statement in the text in verse 12, *"Him who overcomes I will make a pillar in the temple of my God."*

Each of the letters to the seven churches have a similar structure. For example, each has a *"him who overcomes"* statement. And, several of the *"him who overcomes"* statements are statements that are true of the *whole* world-wide church, not just the particular church the statement was written to. To the church at Smyrna, for example, he writes *"he who overcomes will not be hurt at all by the second death."*[31] This statement is true universally of Christians, not just to those of Smyrna. Likewise, to the church at Saris he writes *"He who overcomes...I will never blot out his name from the book of life...,"* another statement which is universally true of the global church.[32] Clearly these statements are not conditional within the true church, or only part of the true church will receive salvation at all! Rather, it appears these statements are dividing lines by which the true church is separated out from the congregation to which the letter was written.

---

[31] Revelation 2:11
[32] Revelation 3:5

Chapter 2: The Rapture

As with congregations today, there were surely those within the congregations of the churches of Asia who were not truly following Christ. They attended church, but were not sincere in their faith, and were not truly believers in Christ. Yet, they would have heard the letter read to them along with the true church within their respective congregations. To that end, "*him who overcomes*" is the true disciple of Christ within the congregation. It is "*he who overcomes*" that will endure while the counterfeit disciple will fail.

Unless, then, one wants to attempt to demonstrate scripturally that only a part of the true church will enter Heaven, one must concede that this which was written to the church of Philadelphia is true for the whole church as well. Those who will keep God's command to "*endure patiently*" are indicative of the true believers within all congregations. The true church among that congregation will escape the hour of trial, the great tribulation, just as the true church within other congregations will escape it.

Consequently, the rapture of the church must be understood to occur *before* the great tribulation, or the true church will have no means by which to escape it.

The doctrine of pre-tribulationalism is simply that. The church will be raptured before the advent of the great tribulation, the great hour of trial upon the earth. Nothing more detailed can be determined from scripture concerning the timing of the rapture. It is imminent. It could occur at any moment before the great tribulation begins.

The Judgment Seat of Christ

Another event closely related to the rapture event concerns the judgment which will immediately follow it for the church. Throughout scripture, judgment follows bodily resurrection.

Concerning resurrection, scripture teaches that all who have ever lived will be resurrected at some future point prior to the eternal order.

John 5:28-29
^{28} "Do not be amazed at this, for a time is coming when all who are in their graves will hear his voice ^{29} and come out--those who have done good will rise to live, and those who have done evil will rise to be condemned.

Both the righteous and unrighteous from all of history will in fact experience a bodily resurrection at some future point. In this text, John only references the fact that all will rise. He is not speaking of one specific moment, but rather the fact that all have a time coming when they will rise. It will be later demonstrated that the coming "*time*" of one's resurrection will vary, depending on several factors. There is a resurrection for the church at the time of the rapture event. Another resurrection will exist for the Old Testament saints. Likewise for the tribulation saints, and those who have rejected Christ, the lost. Each will be resurrected at their appointed time. Thus, there are several resurrections. This text notes specifically that a "*time is coming*" for all to face that moment.

A characteristic of resurrections in scripture is that each is followed by a judgment for that resurrected group. While the rapture may not seem like a resurrection for the living believers who are raptured, it entails the essence of biblical resurrection in that the former bodies of death are transformed into new glorified bodies. The dead in Christ who are raised back to life at the rapture will experience a more common resurrection, having their "dead" physical bodies raised to life. Yet all who are raptured will next experience what all groups experience after their resurrections; a judgment. Judgment follows resurrection in each circumstance. The judgment of the church, which will follow the resurrection of the rapture event, is known as the judgment seat of Christ.

"Judgment," as a term, typically invokes thoughts of disciplinary action. Yet, one should not think in these terms concerning the judgment seat of Christ. Judgment can also be given for one's accomplishments. Olympic gymnasts are closely observed by a panel who are judging their qualities as an athlete and rewarding them accordingly. The judgment seat of Christ concerns itself with the church alone. This judgment will be for purposes of designating reward, rather than punishment to those who are in Christ.

Numerous biblical texts speak of this judgment. One general text is found in 2 Corinthians.

> ***2 Corinthians 5:10***
> *[10] For we must all appear before the judgment seat of Christ, that each one may receive what is due him for the things done while in the body, whether good or bad.*

Paul informs the church at Corinth that they will endure this very judgment. Each text concerning this judgment is written to the church, as it is a judgment concerned uniquely with the church, unlike other judgments which will be discussed later in this work. Paul states the substance of this judgment is that *"each one may receive what is due him."* On the surface, it sounds as if Jesus will offer reward *and* punishment. Paul even states people will be judged for what they've done *"whether good or bad."* Yet, Paul has already described this judgment to the church at Corinth in his earlier letter. The church already understands that this judgment will include reward rather than punishment. It does not include punishment at all. *"Whether good or bad,"* rather, indicates that some will receive rewards who have done good, and that some will *not* receive rewards who have done *"bad"*, as he had explained in his earlier letter.

> ***1 Corinthians 3:11-15***
> *[11] For no one can lay any foundation other than the one already laid, which is Jesus Christ. [12] If any man builds on this foundation using gold, silver, costly stones, wood, hay or straw, [13] his work will be shown for what it is, because the Day will bring it to light. It will be revealed with fire, and the fire will test the quality of each man's work. [14] If what he has built survives, he will receive his reward. [15] If it is burned up, he will suffer loss; he himself will be saved, but only as one escaping through the flames.*

Paul had formerly taught the church that their judgment would not be one which includes punishment. Christ himself has already received all punishment due the church by merit of his substitutionary atonement. The wages of sin have been paid. Instead, this judgment is a judgment which will determine the rewards due one from his life's work. He states in verse 12-13 that a man's work "*will be shown for what it is.*" This work will be tested by fire, and it will either endure or will burn up. Fire is used numerous times in scripture to denote a qualitative testing of one's work.[33] It is likened to the burning of gold in a kiln to purify it and remove the dross. In this case, "*if what he has built survives, he will receive his reward.*" That which burns up is removed, but that which endures the kiln will pass on. Even those who are truly in Christ who *fail to do any work* worthy of reward are not punished, but rather fail to receive any reward. Paul notes of them, "*if it is burned up, he will suffer loss; he himself will be saved, but only as one escaping through the flames.*"

Furthermore, the judgment seat of Christ is not a judgment to determine who gets into Heaven and who does not. In *all judgments,* that decision will have been made ahead of time. The judgments, instead, determine the level of reward or the level of punishment, in the case of the unrighteous judgments, that one is to receive based on one's works. Salvation is *not* according to one's works. The judgments, however, *are* according to one's works. In the case of the judgment seat of Christ, the church will be judged according to their works to determine the nature of their reward. Paul echoes this sentiment only a few paragraphs later.

> ***1 Corinthians 4:5***
> [5] *Therefore judge nothing before the appointed time; wait till the Lord comes. He will bring to light what is hidden in darkness and will expose the motives of men's hearts. At that time each will receive his praise from God.*

---

[33] Psalm 83:14-16, Lamentations 1:13, Matthew 3:11

Chapter 2: The Rapture

According to Paul, when "*the Lord comes,*" he will expose men's motives for what they have done. And, at that time each will receive his *praise* from God. He notes nothing of punishment for this judgment, but only praise and reward, or the lack thereof.

Paul also writes of this judgment in 2 Timothy.

> ***2 Timothy 4:7-8***
> *[7] I have fought the good fight, I have finished the race, I have kept the faith. [8] Now there is in store for me the crown of righteousness, which the Lord, the righteous Judge, will award to me on that day--and not only to me, but also to all who have longed for his appearing.*

Paul describes to Timothy a possible reward of this judgment, "the crown of righteousness." Other crowns are noted in scripture as rewards in this judgment, as is authority (Matthew 5:19, Mark 10:35-40) and other rewards which are not specified (Matthew 10:41-42, Luke 6:35).

In each text describing this judgment, the timing is noted to be at the moment when Christ returns. One can understand that return to refer either to his return to rapture the church or his return to establish his kingdom, what is commonly known as the "second coming." Christ's return to rapture the church is a different sort of "return" than his return to establish his kingdom. It could be likened more like a "fly by" of a plane over a runway. While Christ will appear to receive his church, he will appear in the air. Thus, he returns, but not in the same way he will return at the second coming, at which time he will actually set foot on the earth to establish his kingdom and will remain. In that light, passages which speak of Christ's return may refer to either event. Which event is being discussed must be deduced from the context.

Two passages which speak of the judgment of the church contain useful contextual information to allow the reader to know that the judgment seat of Christ will occur at the rapture rather than at the second coming. The first text can be noted in Luke 14.

> ### *Luke 14:12-14*
> *[12] Then Jesus said to his host, "When you give a luncheon or dinner, do not invite your friends, your brothers or relatives, or your rich neighbors; if you do, they may invite you back and so you will be repaid. [13] But when you give a banquet, invite the poor, the crippled, the lame, the blind, [14] and you will be blessed. Although they cannot repay you, you will be repaid at the resurrection of the righteous."*

In this text, Jesus speaks specifically of the reward his follower will receive for their acts of righteousness. This is the reward affiliated with the judgment seat of Christ. He notes the timing of this reward in verse 14, *"you will be repaid at the resurrection of the righteous."*

The resurrection of the righteous of the church age will be at the time of the rapture. As noted in 1 Thessalonians 4:16-17, *"the dead in Christ will rise first. After that, we who are still alive and are left will be caught up together with them in the clouds to meet the Lord in the air."* This resurrection of the righteous, to those who Jesus spoke to- the coming church- will occur when their bodies rise in the rapture event.

The judgment seat of Christ, then, coincides with the "coming" demonstrated by the meeting of the Lord in the air, or the rapture, when the bodies of the righteous will be raised.

Another text also identifies the rapture as the time of the judgment seat of Christ.

> ### *Luke 21:35-36*
> *[35] For it will come upon all those who live on the face of the whole earth. [36] Be always on the watch, and pray that you may be able to escape all that is about to happen, and that you may be able to stand before the Son of Man."*

Chapter 2: The Rapture

This text was referenced earlier in conjunction with the rapture event. Here, Jesus states that the end result of the rapture event is for one to "*be able to stand before the Son of Man.*" The idea of standing before Christ seems also to reference the judgment of Christ.

While a full observation of the nature of the rewards given at this time are beyond the scale of this work, it can be noted that numerous potential rewards during the judgment seat of Christ relate to the messianic kingdom. Believers at the time of rapture will be judged and rewarded by Christ. At least some measure of that reward relates to one's future position in the millennial kingdom. Some understand that the entirety of the rewards of this judgment will relate to a believer's future position in the millennial kingdom. More on the subject will be observed in chapter nine, but suffice it to say that there will be numerous positions of authority in the millennial kingdom which those of the church age will participate. That participation is closely, if not entirely, tied with the judgment seat of Christ and one's works of obedience during their lives on earth. Thus, a believer should understand today that failing to do the works of Christ for the sake of inconvenience in this life will hold ramifications of a much greater loss. The millennial kingdom will last one thousand years. That is a great deal of time for one to enjoy the rewards of his sixty or seventy years of service from this present age.

Chapter 3: The First Half of the Tribulation

Notes on the Book of Revelation

The study of the eschatology encompasses more than the study of the book of Revelation. However that book will receive a great deal of study concerning the tribulation as it contains much of what can be known of the events of this period, particularly the timing of events in many circumstances.

As established in the foreword, the author is a Biblicist, and believes that the Bible is to be interpreted via the literal interpretational method. While many biblical writings are symbolic in nature, they tell a *real* story and indicate *real* truths. Simply acknowledging that a writing is symbolic in nature does not mandate that the writing lacks a tangible truth or timeline. Revelation is a good example of this principle in action. The majority of the book of Revelation is the strict recall of a vision which the Apostle John had "*in the spirit.*"[34] While in worship, God appeared to him and told him in Revelation 1:11 to "*Write on a scroll what you see and send it to the seven churches....*" John did what he was told. He wrote what he saw and reported it as a first century man best could. Beginning with chapter four, what he saw becomes obviously symbolic in its substance. Yet, the use of symbolic language does not suggest that the subject matter was lacking in literal content. For example, one may say to a friend, "it's raining cats and dogs outside." While his language is symbolic, he states a literal truth; that "it's raining very hard." The dispensational view is one which understands that the Bible, even when using figurative presentation, teaches literal content

---

[34] Revelation 1:10

Chapter 3: The First Half of the Tribulation

and is to be interpreted factually.

The biggest question which must be answered prior to studying the book of Revelation, even within the confines of a literal interpretational method is, "how is one to interpret the symbolism in this book?" It is exceptionally shrouded, being full of metaphorical language and imagery. On the surface it appears nearly impossible to sort out.

This has led to two extremes in how the book is interpreted. One extreme is to conclude that the book is too full of symbols to be sorted. The other extreme is to hyper-translate the book, including all manners of postulation regarding the symbols being used.

Though the Bible uses symbolic language in many places, it is harmonious with its use of symbols. For instance, in most cases, a symbol in the Old Testament has the same meaning in the New Testament. There are a few exceptions, but they are clearly able to be discerned as exceptions from the standard rules of biblical interpretation.

Throughout history men have inserted meaning into the book of Revelation by using their own cultural experiences to derive meaning from the symbols used in the book. While that is a fine approach to use for reading a book of common poetry, it represents a great failure in biblical interpretation. Because God is the ultimate author of the entire Bible, the Bible is the first place one should examine in search of the meanings of the symbols used in the book of Revelation. In most cases, symbols in Revelation appear elsewhere in scripture and should be interpreted consistently with the rest of the written Word of God.

Another issue in studying the book of Revelation, in particular, is chronology. Revelation reads chronologically to a large degree, but at times it does not. Because John is being obedient to write what he sees in his vision, it seems almost as if John is seeing the images he writes about on a huge screen; on one side, an image representing certain events of a time period, then, at times, another image on another part of the screen, representing perhaps another place or time. It is important to remember that the book is recalling a literal vision which God gave to

John. And, that vision included scenes from a future world very different from what John would be able to comprehend at times. He wrote what he saw from the context of a first century man, himself not likely understanding all that was being revealed. Many times John writes "and then there was," or "and then I saw," which does not necessitate chronology in the historical timing of the events being described, only the chronology in which *he saw* them in his vision. There are times when it is clear from systematic biblical study that he is writing something from the past, such as when he sees a male child born who will "rule the nations with an iron scepter." Clearly he quotes Psalm 2, speaking of the birth and career of Christ, yet he writes this after depicting events which have historically not yet occurred.

In God's wisdom and grace, however, he has provided many other biblical passages which will help the biblical student assimilate the chronology of the book, as the greatest bulk of what is written in Revelation is also written about elsewhere in scripture.

The Purposes of the Tribulation

Scripture teaches that the great tribulation is a time of unique purpose. Understanding that purpose brings clarity out of what may otherwise seem to be a very uncharacteristic set of actions from God's hand. The idea of dispensationalism which has been described in this work is the understanding that God has unique purposes in the revelation of himself in all "seasons" of history. Today, living in the dispensation of grace, one sees God's character through the first coming of Christ. He offered grace for sinners. He was the mild-mannered lamb of God who took away the sins of the world. As this season ends, however, God will have endured the last of his patience for those who have rejected his Son. The great tribulation will be a time of strict judgment which will prepare the earth for the coming dispensation of the Kingdom, at which time Christ will rule the earth in the flesh. That preparation involves chiefly the outpouring of God's wrath against those who have rejected his Son. But, even in his wrath, the great tribulation demonstrates that God still extends grace, for all to whom his wrath is outpoured are also offered the

Chapter 3: The First Half of the Tribulation

opportunity to repent and receive salvation through his one and only offered provision: faith in Christ.

God's Judgment on those who reject him

> *1 Thessalonians 5:1-10*
> *¹ Now, brothers, about times and dates we do not need to write to you, ² for you know very well that the day of the Lord will come like a thief in the night. ³ While people are saying, "Peace and safety," destruction will come on them suddenly, as labor pains on a pregnant woman, and they will not escape.*
>
> *⁴ But you, brothers, are not in darkness so that this day should surprise you like a thief. ⁵ You are all sons of the light and sons of the day. We do not belong to the night or to the darkness. ⁶ So then, let us not be like others, who are asleep, but let us be alert and self-controlled. ⁷ For those who sleep, sleep at night, and those who get drunk, get drunk at night. ⁸ But since we belong to the day, let us be self-controlled, putting on faith and love as a breastplate, and the hope of salvation as a helmet. ⁹ For God did not appoint us to suffer wrath but to receive salvation through our Lord Jesus Christ. ¹⁰ He died for us so that, whether we are awake or asleep, we may live together with him.*

The context of this passage is "*the day of the Lord*," which always refers to the great tribulation as a whole, or at times, specifically the second coming of Christ at the very end of the great tribulation. In this text, a clear association is drawn between the day of the Lord and God's wrath. Paul's clear message to the church is that "*God did not appoint us to suffer wrath*," which informs the reader of the nature of the day of the Lord; it is a time of God's wrath.

Numerous other biblical texts echo this theme. Isaiah 13:9 reveals,

> *"See, the day of the Lord is coming*
> *--a cruel day, with wrath and fierce anger--*
> *to make the land desolate*
> *and destroy the sinners within it."*

Isaiah gives more information regarding this day of wrath, in that its ultimate fruition will be to "*destroy the sinners within*" the land. At the end of the tribulation, in fact, Jesus will extend a final judgment against all unbelievers remaining, and God will have prepared the earth for the coming of Christ's kingdom. This new kingdom will be demonstrated as this work unfolds to be a kingdom which begins on an earth containing the redeemed only. All who reject salvation by Christ will be judged in this day of wrath and will not live to enter the coming kingdom.

Revelation gives yet another picture of the wrathful purpose of the great tribulation.

> ***Revelation 14:6-7***
> *[6]"Then I saw another angel flying in midair, and he had the eternal gospel to proclaim to those who live on the earth--to every nation, tribe, language and people. [7] He said in a loud voice, "Fear God and give him glory, because the hour of his judgment has come. Worship him who made the heavens, the earth, the sea and the springs of water."*

Clearly, through the warning of an angel, the earth is informed that the *hour of [God's] judgment has come.* Interestingly, in this text is also demonstrated a foreshadowing of God's second purpose in the great tribulation in the substance of the angel's warning, "*Fear God and give him glory…worship him who made the heavens.*"

Repentance for those who will receive him

The angel's warning is a call to repentance, which invokes God's

Chapter 3: The First Half of the Tribulation

acceptance rather than his wrath.[35] This demonstrates the second purpose of the great tribulation, which is a call to repentance for those who are willing to accept Christ as their King. To fear God, to give God glory and to worship him are all actions indicative of true repentance. This call is an opportunity for even those objects of God's wrath to receive his offering of salvation. How gracious God is that even in his hour of judgment he offers an opportunity for repentance. Many will accept this call, as will be demonstrated. Many others will not, and will perish under the severity of God's wrath. However, it is not possible for one to legitimately harbor resentment toward God in the great tribulation, for while the tribulation is a time of great judgment, it is also a last offer of God's grace to those who would receive him. All who turn themselves away from God during this season will do so with the full opportunity to repent being intentionally ignored.

Zephaniah 2:3 indicates the same truth, "*Seek the LORD, all you humble of the land, you who do what he commands. Seek righteousness, seek humility; perhaps you will be sheltered on the day of the Lord's anger.*"

Zephaniah, likewise, warns the "*humble of the land*" to repent, that perhaps they may be sheltered in the great tribulation. It should be noted that many believers will also perish during the great tribulation, however. Zephaniah's prophecy is not a promise to be spared on the day of the Lord, but is rather offered as the option one has to "perhaps" be sheltered. What is certain is that no one will be spared who refuses to seek righteousness. By the end of the great tribulation, ending with Christ's judgment of the gentiles, only the righteous will remain and be allowed to enter the Kingdom. The singular hope one has to *possibly* endure the day of the Lord is to repent and receive Christ as King - *before* he comes to destroy the last of his enemies. As to those who do receive Christ, yet perish during the great tribulation, a special promise of resurrection is given to them that they may enter the kingdom as martyrs, and have an exalted place of service during the Kingdom.[36]

---

[35] Acts 3:19, Luke 13:2-3, 2 Peter 3:9

[36] Detailed in chapter nine

Unmistakably, God desires repentance rather than judgment for mankind. He makes the option to repent known through various sources, and even warns the earth with an angel in the midst of his wrath. Yet, in the day of the Lord's anger, this seven year period known as the great tribulation, either judgment or repentance *will* be established. Those who refuse to repent will face judgment and certain death.

God's desire for repentance rather than judgment is clearly demonstrated in Revelation 9:20-21.

> [20] *The rest of mankind that were not killed by these plagues still did not repent of the work of their hands; they did not stop worshiping demons, and idols of gold, silver, bronze, stone and wood--idols that cannot see or hear or walk.* [21] *Nor did they repent of their murders, their magic arts, their sexual immorality or their thefts.*

This text speaks of the Trumpet Judgments, which will be detailed later. Here John notes that the ungodly did not repent of their evil deeds, indicating once again that the opportunity indeed existed for them to do so while even in the midst of the judgments themselves. God's call to repentance is offered throughout the great tribulation, establishing repentance as the second purpose of the period.

One final very convincing clue that repentance is a purpose of the great tribulation is in Revelation 7:13-14, describing a multitude of people in white robes around the throne of Christ; each who represent converts from the tribulation.

> [13] *Then one of the elders asked me, "These in white robes--who are they, and where did they come from?"*
> [14] *I answered, "Sir, you know."*
> *And he said, "These are they who have come out of the great tribulation; they have washed their robes and made them white in the blood of the Lamb.*

Chapter 3: The First Half of the Tribulation

Clearly there will be salvation for many during the great tribulation. If repentance is not to be one of God's purposes in the tribulation, indeed the fruit of repentance would not be demonstrated in Revelation's story line concerning this period.

In conclusion, the great tribulation will essentially be a final clearing house for the whole of mankind. Those who receive Christ will find salvation, while those who do not will endure judgment unto death. Those who repent are promised a place in his kingdom on earth, either by being allowed to enter it alive, or being resurrected to serve him after the great tribulation. Those who reject him will only rise for their ultimate judgment to be carried out in a lake of fire at the end of the Kingdom.[37]

Clearly the best option for all is to accept the challenge issued by Christ in the book of Luke.

> *Luke 21:34-36*
> *[34] "Be careful, or your hearts will be weighed down with dissipation, drunkenness and the anxieties of life, and that day will close on you unexpectedly like a trap. [35] For it will come upon all those who live on the face of the whole earth. [36] Be always on the watch, and pray that you may be able to escape all that is about to happen, and that you may be able to stand before the Son of Man."*

To receive Christ now, prior to the rapture event, is without a doubt the best option for all. To wait until the time of the great tribulation subjects one to endure incredible distress and possibly death, even if one does receive Christ at that later date.

---

[37] Detailed in chapter eleven

Events of the First Half

The Beginning of The Tribulation

Several marker events are detailed in scripture which determine the dating sequence for the great tribulation. The first marker is the signing of a covenant between the Antichrist and Israel, which indicates the beginning of the seven year clock that will count down the days of the great tribulation.

Noted earlier in Daniel 9 was the "seventieth seven," or the last seven years which marks the time period of the tribulation. Daniel 9:27 states, *"*27 *He will confirm a covenant with many for one 'seven.'"* Since this "seven" describes the seven years of the tribulation, and the covenant is to endure for seven years, then clearly the seven, or the tribulation, will begin with the signing of this covenant. To that end, when calculating the start of the great tribulation, the marker event is the signing of a covenant by Antichrist. All other times referenced during the great tribulation are to be rendered from this marker.

Daniel states that this covenant will be a covenant "*with many*" for the seven year period. Daniel 9:27 continues to state that

> *'In the middle of the "seven" he will put an end to sacrifice and offering. And on a wing [of the temple] he will set up an abomination that causes desolation, until the end that is decreed is poured out on him'."*

Daniel, being a prophet of Israel, is prophesying in accordance with Israel's history. While the covenant is noted to be with "many," that many includes Israel herself, as noted in Isaiah.

> **Isaiah 28:15**
> [15] *You boast, "We have entered into a covenant with death, with the grave we have made an agreement. When an overwhelming scourge sweeps by, it cannot touch us,*

Chapter 3: The First Half of the Tribulation

for we have made a lie our refuge and falsehood our hiding place."

While Israel is part of this treaty, Daniel 9:27 demonstrates that her interests in the covenant will in fact be eliminated "*in the middle of the seven,*" as Antichrist puts an end to sacrifice (in the new Temple) and sets up an abomination.[38] From the mid-point of the tribulation, until the end of it, Antichrist will align the forces of the whole world against Israel. Thus, his covenant with Israel will be broken, yet he may continue to uphold his covenant with others of the "many."

This text also gives insight into the nature of the covenant. It is a treaty for protection. Here, Israel is noted to have entered this covenant as part of the "many," which grants her safety in the face of "*an overwhelming scourge.*" The covenant, however, is based upon a false premise, because Antichrist's true desire will be to lure Israel into a false sense of security: "*we have made a lie our refuge and falsehood our hiding place."* Thus, he will deceive Israel into a sense of security by admitting her into the bond of the covenant with himself. Then, half-way through the terms of the treaty, the promised protector will become Israel's greatest and most deadly enemy.

The Seal Judgments

Understanding the tribulation to have two purposes, the issuing of judgment and a call to repentance, gives one better insight as to the nature of the horrific judgment series which will unfold during this time. The first grouping of these series is referred to as "The Seal Judgments."

In Revelation 5, John details his vision concerning the unveiling of this series of judgments. This part of his vision begins with Christ seated on a throne, scroll in hand, sealed with seven seals. As those seals are opened in Revelation 6, the seal judgments begin on earth.

---

[38] Detailed in chapter four

Revelation 6:1-2
¹ I watched as the Lamb opened the first of the seven seals. Then I heard one of the four living creatures say in a voice like thunder, "Come!" ² I looked, and there before me was a white horse! Its rider held a bow, and he was given a crown, and he rode out as a conqueror bent on conquest.

The first seal judgment of the tribulation releases a rider on a white horse, riding out *"as a conqueror bent on conquest."* This rider holds a bow, which John understands to be indicative of this rider being a warrior. This warrior wears a crown. In New Testament Greek, there are two words translated into English as "crown," *stephanos* and *diadem*. A *diadem* is the crown of a king, while a *stephanos* is a crown that a victor of a sporting event or a military campaign would wear. The term used in Revelation 6:2 is *stephanos,* indicating that this rider fits the description of a military victor wearing a crown of conquest.

The description of this rider indicates clearly that he is the person of Antichrist for several reasons. First, he is emulating the appearance of Christ. At the end of the tribulation, another rider on a white horse, with a sword and wearing a crown will emerge. That rider will be demonstrated to be Christ himself. Antichrist will attempt to mimic the true Christ throughout the tribulation period in every way possible. His entry onto the world stage will be similar in appearance as the coming of Christ. He will attempt to present himself as the legitimate Christ, to deceive as many as possible.[39] Secondly, the whole of eschatological study indicates the conquering warrior of the great tribulation to be the person of Antichrist. Daniel 7 depicts Antichrist being a key player during the tribulation, waging war against the saints and against the earth in general.[40] Thus, the initial event of the great tribulation is the release of a rider on a white horse, emulating the coming of Christ, who will be bent on war. This rider fully describes the biblical portrait of Antichrist.

---

[39] 2 Thessalonians 2:4
[40] Daniel 7:21, 24-25; Daniel 9:26

Chapter 3: The First Half of the Tribulation

At this point in John's vision, then, he sees the first seal of the tribulation opened, and the first key player of the tribulation take to the field in conquest. Just as Daniel noted Antichrist as the one who begins the seven year tribulational timeline, John sees the inauguration of this campaign as Antichrist rides into battle. As this work unfolds, it will be clearly demonstrated that Antichrist will indeed be a warrior bent on war and that he will be the victor for a season in that pursuit. He will subdue the kings of the earth and establish himself as a counterfeit King of Kings on earth. He will succeed in acquiring leadership over the earth, but will ultimately be destroyed by Christ as the millennial kingdom is established.[41]

Alternatively is the white horse appearing in the book of Revelation, found in chapter 19.

> ***Revelation 19:11-12***
> *[11] I saw heaven standing open and there before me was a white horse, whose rider is called Faithful and True. With justice he judges and makes war. [12] His eyes are like blazing fire, and on his head are many crowns. He has a name written on him that no one knows but he himself.*

This rider on a white horse is Christ himself, returning at the end of the great tribulation. He not only rides a white horse, but wears *many crowns.* In this text, "crowns" is from the Greek *diadem,* the crowns of a king. Furthermore, when Christ comes riding on a white horse, wearing crowns, he, too, is riding out to make war.

These similarities go once again to confirm the counterfeiting work of Antichrist. He will attempt to establish his own kingdom on earth, imitating the kingdom Christ will succeed in establishing. His attempts will ultimately fail, yet it is fascinating that he looks similar in appearance to Christ himself as he rides out to begin his campaign.

---

[41] Daniel 7:22, 2 Thessalonians 2:8

Indeed, Antichrist will attempt to *be* the person of Jesus Christ, and to mimic every action of Christ in order to deceive as many as possible.

> *Matthew 24:23-24*
> *[23] At that time if anyone says to you, 'Look, here is the Christ!' or, 'There he is!' do not believe it. [24] For false Christs and false prophets will appear and perform great signs and miracles to deceive even the elect--if that were possible.*

It should be noted for clarity that the releasing of the rider on the white horse during the first seal judgment does not equate to the advent of Antichrist on earth. It is instead representative of the first judgment, which is the empowerment of the Antichrist to begin his deceptive ministry and officially begin the great tribulation. This seal, the first of the tribulation judgments, coincides with the signing of Antichrist's covenant with many. It is the authorization and formal beginning of his work during the tribulation. He will in fact have already been on earth prior to the breaking of this seal, and will have undoubtedly been active in government, becoming established and prepared to sign his covenant and begin the tribulation. Yet, the first seal is the authorization of his campaign. He is at this point released to fulfill his destiny as the enemy of Christ on earth.

The second seal invokes another horse and rider.

> *Revelation 6:3-4*
> *[3] When the Lamb opened the second seal, I heard the second living creature say, "Come!" [4] Then another horse came out, a fiery red one. Its rider was given power to take peace from the earth and to make men slay each other. To him was given a large sword.*

Complimenting the first rider, a second rider follows with the purpose of invoking warfare on the earth. He was "*given power to take peace from the earth and to make men slay each other.*" The political aspect of

Chapter 3: The First Half of the Tribulation

. . . .

Antichrist's governmental coup on earth now wanes in the wake of the second rider. At this point, no longer are actions political in nature, such as signing treaties and wooing kings, but are paranormal in nature. This rider supernaturally causes peace to be removed and invokes men to slay each other. The picture seems to be that of ensuing war on earth, yet without political interests being stipulated. The identity of this rider is not clear, but the outcome of his release is. Earth will become a place of great distress in light of the absence of peace.

I Thessalonians 5:3 states of the day of the Lord,

> *"While people are saying, "Peace and safety,"*
> *destruction will come on them suddenly, as labor pains*
> *on a pregnant woman, and they will not escape."*

This seal ends the period of peace that preceded the tribulation as men are instigated by this rider to slay each other in panic. The distress of the great tribulation is now fully underway.

A third seal reveals the third horse of the apocalypse.

> **Revelation 6:5-6**
> *⁵ When the Lamb opened the third seal, I heard the third living creature say, "Come!" I looked, and there before me was a black horse! Its rider was holding a pair of scales in his hand. ⁶ Then I heard what sounded like a voice among the four living creatures, saying, "A quart of wheat for a day's wages, and three quarts of barley for a day's wages, and do not damage the oil and the wine!"*

The results of the third horse and rider are a disruption in the earth's food supply in some manner. That disruption will bring a severe famine on the earth. Food will become so scarce that a day's wages cannot feed a family. "*A quart of wheat for a day's wages, and three quarts of barley for a day's wages*" is a sincerely desperate condition. In this circumstance, certainly a world economic collapse will ensue as people will be required to spend their entire incomes on food.

A noted ray of grace is included in the text by the admonition, "*do not damage the oil and the wine!*" Oil and wine were medicinal in the first century. To that end, one should likely understand this part of his vision to indicate the protection of medical supplies. While food will be very scarce, medical needs will still be able to be addressed at this early stage.

With peace removed and food in such shortage, it only stands to reason that death would follow as the fourth seal is broken.

> ***Revelation 6:7-8***
> *⁷ When the Lamb opened the fourth seal, I heard the voice of the fourth living creature say, "Come!" ⁸ I looked, and there before me was a pale horse! Its rider was named Death, and Hades was following close behind him. They were given power over a fourth of the earth to kill by sword, famine and plague, and by the wild beasts of the earth.*

Again, a horse and rider are released as the result of the next broken seal. In this case a pale horse, possibly indicating sickness, is ridden by a rider named Death, with Hades following close behind him. These are given power to kill one fourth of the earth "*by sword, famine and plague, and by wild beasts of the earth.*"

It appears that the four horsemen are released in rapid succession, as each appears to depend upon the other. Antichrist begins his campaign of military conquering, followed by the removal of peace, followed by famine and resulting in death. Death "*by sword*" will have begun with the second seal, "*famine*" by the third seal, and now the additional threats of "*plague*" and "*wild animal attack*" will be added. Plague, or disease, logically follows malnutrition, as does wild animal attack. When food sources on earth become scarce, it will affect not only humans, but the animal kingdom as well. It such extreme circumstances, animals which otherwise would have avoided human contact will become emboldened

Chapter 3: The First Half of the Tribulation

to attack people as a food source. Indeed, the early conditions of the tribulation on earth may well look as any one of numerous post-apocalyptic movies have depicted, with war, disease, malnutrition and wild animal attacks being commonplace in a planet that has literally been ravaged. The end result is that one-fourth of the earth is killed! While the tribulation grows in intensity as the seven years pass, it is truly a shocking blow to the earth even at its onset.

The fifth seal reveals events in Heaven rather than on earth, which the first four seals reference.

> ***Revelation 6:9-11***
> *⁹ When he opened the fifth seal, I saw under the altar the souls of those who had been slain because of the word of God and the testimony they had maintained. ¹⁰ They called out in a loud voice, "How long, Sovereign Lord, holy and true, until you judge the inhabitants of the earth and avenge our blood?" ¹¹ Then each of them was given a white robe, and they were told to wait a little longer, until the number of their fellow servants and brothers who were to be killed as they had been was completed.*

A product of Antichrist's program on earth will be the persecution of Christians. While this will be demonstrated in more detail later, clearly, there is already a great persecution against Christians at this fairly early point in the tribulation. The church, as noted in chapter two, has been raptured from the earth prior to the beginning of the tribulation. Yet, there are Christians on earth *during* the great tribulation. These believers are commonly referred to as the "tribulation saints." They are people who have received Christ after the rapture, and perhaps during the tribulation itself. There are many even in churches today who have heard the gospel of Christ, believe in Christ, but have not yielded their allegiance to him as Lord. These will undoubtedly have a quick change of heart after witnessing the rapture event. Surely there will be many during the period of false peace preceding the tribulation who will think they have time to make their commitment of faith to Christ. Yet, the rapture event and the onset of the tribulation will awaken them quickly to the fact that time is indeed short. A strong number of people will surrender their allegiance to Christ during the tribulation.

It will be demonstrated later that Antichrist will ultimately kill anyone who refuses to worship himself as Lord. This persecution is greatest during the second half of the tribulation, but is clearly also underway during the first half.

Another interesting note concerning the fifth seal is the answer to the question of these martyred saints, *"how long...until you judge the inhabitants of the earth and avenge our blood?"* The answer may take some by surprise. *"They were told to wait a little longer, until the number of their fellow servants and brothers who were to be killed...was completed."*

Clearly God has determined a number of believers who would be martyrs during the great tribulation. While this may be difficult for some to accept, it should be noted that these believers, having suffered death, will be granted a special place in the millennial kingdom because of their sacrifice.[42]

As the sixth seal is opened, attention is focused back to the earth for the unfolding of its judgment.

> ***Revelation 6:12-17***
> *[12] I watched as he opened the sixth seal. There was a great earthquake. The sun turned black like sackcloth made of goat hair, the whole moon turned blood red, [13] and the stars in the sky fell to earth, as late figs drop from a fig tree when shaken by a strong wind. [14] The sky receded like a scroll, rolling up, and every mountain and island was removed from its place. [15] Then the kings of the earth, the princes, the generals, the rich, the mighty,*

---

[42] Detailed in chapter nine

Chapter 3: The First Half of the Tribulation

> *and every slave and every free man hid in caves and among the rocks of the mountains. [16] They called to the mountains and the rocks, "Fall on us and hide us from the face of him who sits on the throne and from the wrath of the Lamb! [17] For the great day of their wrath has come, and who can stand?"*

The seventh seal will be observed momentarily to begin a new series of judgments, the trumpet judgments. To that end, the sixth seal is actually the last of this series of judgments. The last of each series of judgments during the tribulation will consistently yield various disturbances in nature to signify the end of the series. The same will be true for the coming trumpet and bowl judgments.

In this case there is a blackout of the lights of the sky. The sun will turn black and the moon blood red. Additionally, from a first century perspective John seems to indicate seeing a vast meteor shower as he notes "*the stars in the sky fell to the earth.*" It is reasonable to assume that a meteor shower in which the meteors fall "*to the earth*" will cause great damage and further chaos.

Another result of the turmoil in nature is to be a great earthquake, the likes of which will have had no historical equal. The end results of these upheavals in nature are that men will do two things; they will hide themselves, and they will acknowledge God as the source of the damage. "*They called to the mountains and the rocks, 'Fall on us and hide us from the face of him who sits on the throne and from the wrath of the Lamb!*" While it is encouraging that mankind will know from whom these events were sent, it is discouraging that man's response is the same as it was in the Garden of Eden; to hide, rather than to acknowledge his sin in the face of God's wrath. The martyrs noted of the fifth seal indicate that there are many who will indeed repent before the Lord. Yet, overwhelmingly the response of man will be to turn from God and attempt to hide themselves from him rather than to engage him as their King.

With the conclusion, then, of the seal judgments, man's condition is largely unchanged. While some are demonstrated to have been saved, the mass of mankind will endure these judgments without repentance, as will be his propensity throughout the tribulation period.

The Ministry on earth: The 144,000 Evangelists

> ### Revelation 7:1-4
> *1 After this I saw four angels standing at the four corners of the earth, holding back the four winds of the earth to prevent any wind from blowing on the land or on the sea or on any tree. 2 Then I saw another angel coming up from the east, having the seal of the living God. He called out in a loud voice to the four angels who had been given power to harm the land and the sea: 3 "Do not harm the land or the sea or the trees until we put a seal on the foreheads of the servants of our God." 4 Then I heard the number of those who were sealed: 144,000 from all the tribes of Israel.*

Immediately after the depiction of the seal judgments, an angel calls out to "*the four angels who had been given power to harm the land and the sea: 'Do not harm the land or the sea or the trees until we put a seal on the foreheads of the servant of our God.'*" The angels referenced are those who will administer the next series of judgments, the trumpet judgments. Thus, prior to the next set of judgments God will place a seal on the heads of these 144,000 to protect them from the coming judgment series. They are not assured protection from Antichrist and martyrdom, but from the events of the coming trumpet judgments.

That these will be called "*the servants of our God*" indicates their status as believers in Christ, but also pronounces their status in the great tribulation. They are servants of God. To serve God is to do his work. The two purposes of the tribulation, being judgment and a call to repentance, indicate their possible work assignments during this season. No biblical model would indicate that they will be involved in handing

Chapter 3: The First Half of the Tribulation

out judgments, since angels will be handling that particular part of God's program. They must then surely be involved in the second purpose of the great tribulation by administering a call to repentance to the citizens of earth. For this reason, this group is commonly referred to as the "144,000 evangelists" or ministers. These ministers will be protected from the coming judgments in order that they may be witnesses of the gospel, ministering to those who are willing to repent during this season.

The next few verses detail the fruit of their ministry.

> ***Revelation 7:9***
> *⁹ After this I looked and there before me was a great multitude that no one could count, from every nation, tribe, people and language, standing before the throne and in front of the Lamb. They were wearing white robes and were holding palm branches in their hands.*
>
> ***Revelation 7:13-14***
> *¹³ Then one of the elders asked me, "These in white robes--who are they, and where did they come from?" ¹⁴ I answered, "Sir, you know." And he said, "These are they who have come out of the great tribulation; they have washed their robes and made them white in the blood of the Lamb.*

Some have a tendency to confuse the 144,000 and the great multitude. Yet, plainly the 144,000 are on earth, being sealed for their protection from the trumpet judgments, while the great multitude are in Heaven *"before the throne and in front of the Lamb."* This great multitude are those who *"have come out of the great tribulation; they have washed their robes and made them white in the blood of the lamb."* Thus this great multitude appear to be the fruit of the ministry of the 144,000 evangelists. They are those who will experience salvation during the tribulation. While the preponderance of mankind will hide themselves from God during the judgments, still a multitude will exist which properly will respond to the judgments and receive salvation. Clearly the second purpose of the great tribulation and the ministry of the 144,000 will meet with an element of success.

Jesus spoke of the world-wide evangelistic endeavor of the 144,000 in Matthew 24.

> ***Matthew 24:14***
> *[14] And this gospel of the kingdom will be preached in the whole world as a testimony to all nations, and then the end will come.*

Before the end comes, the whole world will have heard the testimony of the gospel. The work of the 144,000 ministers will unmistakably be wide-spread, and will have a sizeable harvest in spite of the bulk of humanity's rejection of the gospel message. Through their work, the gospel will indeed be preached in the whole world.

Ministry on earth: The Two Witnesses

> ***Revelation 11:3-6***
> *[3] And I will give power to my two witnesses, and they will prophesy for 1,260 days, clothed in sackcloth." [4] These are the two olive trees and the two lampstands that stand before the Lord of the earth. [5] If anyone tries to harm them, fire comes from their mouths and devours their enemies. This is how anyone who wants to harm them must die. [6] These men have power to shut up the sky so that it will not rain during the time they are prophesying; and they have power to turn the waters into blood and to strike the earth with every kind of plague as often as they want.*

Another ministry element on the earth during the tribulation is the very public and visible ministry of two other servants of God.

The appearance onto the scene of the two witnesses will be dealt with

Chapter 3: The First Half of the Tribulation

later, but it can be established at this point that they are engaged in their ministry prior to their reference in Revelation 11. Their mention is one of pre-existence, as it is noted that the Lord will "*give power to my two witnesses.*" Clearly they are already on the scene and ministering at the time of this announcement as they are referred to as witnesses, a term indicating the currently-engaged practice of ministering.

The two witnesses have been considered to be Elijah and Enoch by many, primarily due to the fact that scripture teaches these two men have never died, but were taken directly into God's presence without tasting of bodily death.[43] The assertion of this theory is that Elijah and Enoch, *because* they have never died, will be sent back at this time to serve as prophets, and experience the death they avoided in their former lives.

This postulate has been formulated largely due to the teaching of Hebrews 9:27, "*it is appointed unto men to die once, and then face judgment.*" However, Hebrews 9:27 alone does not serve as a sufficient reason that these two witnesses should be Elijah and Enoch, as Hebrews 9:27 is a principle, rather than a strict rule or law. There are other examples of people who strictly did not adhere to the Hebrews 9:27 principle, such as Lazarus. Lazarus died once, was resurrected, then died again. This negates a strict legal interpretation of Hebrews, as do the resurrection and subsequent "second" death of Tabitha in the book of Acts[44] as well as others in both testaments. Additionally, if Hebrews 9:27 is a foundational rule, rather than a principle, each person who is to be raptured will break this rule as well, because they will not experience a physical death, but will be translated alive into their new glorified bodies.

Consequently, Hebrews 9:27 must be understood to be a principle. It is the established order of things, though not a firm law which cannot be evaded under the right circumstances. In the natural course, "*It is appointed unto men to die once,*" but there are exceptions clearly noted in scripture. This, then, greatly reduces the likelihood of the two

---

[43] 2 Kings 2:11, Genesis 5:24
[44] Acts 9:36-41

witnesses being Elijah and Enoch. It is as likely to be anyone, including two men who are unheard of in scripture. While it is possible that they are Elijah and Enoch, it cannot be conclusively determined by Hebrews alone.

Another scripture which is given as support for Elijah being one of the two witnesses is Malachi 4:5, *"See, I will send you the prophet Elijah before that great and dreadful day of the Lord comes."* However Jesus stated in Matthew 11:14 that Elijah had already come (in the person of John the Baptist), *"[13] For all the Prophets and the Law prophesied until John. [14] And if you are willing to accept it, he is the Elijah who was to come."*

He also states in Matthew 17:11-13, *"[11] Jesus replied, "To be sure, Elijah comes and will restore all things. [12] But I tell you, Elijah has already come, and they did not recognize him, but have done to him everything they wished. In the same way the Son of Man is going to suffer at their hands." [13] Then the disciples understood that he was talking to them about John the Baptist."*

Thus, Malachi 4:5 is not valid prophetical evidence for Elijah to be one of the two prophets, as Jesus stated clearly that this prophecy was fulfilled in the person of John the Baptist.

In conclusion, it remains unknown who they are. They are two witnesses that God will call for a specific purpose at this time. There is no biblical reason to assume that these two men are not raised up out of the tribulation itself as new converts.

The role of the two witnesses is plainly able to be gleaned from the text. The first clue is that they are called "*witnesses*," a term which the New Testament most commonly uses to refer to those who preach the gospel. These witnesses will minister the gospel then, and be a part of God's restorative opportunity in the great tribulation by their prophesying, or preaching.

Chapter 3: The First Half of the Tribulation

It is also noted in verse 5 and 6 that these men have great power given unto them. They have power to kill anyone who tries to kill them before their appointed time and to shut up the heavens so that they will yield no rain.

Their term is noted in verse 3, *"and they will prophesy for 1,260 days."* 1,260 days is 3 1/2 years by a Jewish calendar standard. The Jewish calendar is a lunar calendar, unlike a Western calendar which is calculated by the sun. While a solar calendar has a strict 365 1/4 day per year cycle, a lunar calendar has a differing number of days each year because each month is based on a lunar cycle, which varies in its length. Some years have more days and some less. Because of this, it is impossible to strictly render a year into days from the perspective of a Jewish calendar. To account for this limitation, historically a Jewish calendar, when required to be rendered by days, is rounded to a middle number. That number is 360 days. So, when Jewish "year" is spoken of in terms of days, it is noted to be 360 days. 1,260 days then, refers to 3 1/2 years from the perspective of a Jewish calendar year.

The tribulation is depicted as two 3 1/2 year periods, for a total of seven years. It will be demonstrated that there will be 3 1/2 years from the signing of Antichrist's covenant, which begins the tribulation period, to his establishing of himself in the Temple as God, exactly in the middle of the seven year period. There will then be 3 1/2 years from that moment until the return of Christ to destroy him. Revelation 11:2 notes that the witnesses will prophecy for exactly 3 1/2 years. For reasons that will be detailed later, it is known that the 3 1/2 years referred to in Revelation 11 is the *first* half of the tribulation, which demands that these two will begin their ministry at the beginning of the tribulation and that they will die in the middle of the tribulation. More on these two will be noted later, but for now it is sufficient to note their participation in the ministry of the first half of the tribulation. They are working in concert with the 144,000 witnesses as workers in God's redemptive purpose of the great tribulation.

The Counterfeit Ministry on earth: Babylon The Great Harlot

> *Revelation 17:1-6*
> *¹ One of the seven angels who had the seven bowls came and said to me, "Come, I will show you the punishment of the great prostitute, who sits on many waters. ² With her the kings of the earth committed adultery and the inhabitants of the earth were intoxicated with the wine of her adulteries."*
> *³ Then the angel carried me away in the Spirit into a desert. There I saw a woman sitting on a scarlet beast that was covered with blasphemous names and had seven heads and ten horns. ⁴ The woman was dressed in purple and scarlet, and was glittering with gold, precious stones and pearls. She held a golden cup in her hand, filled with abominable things and the filth of her adulteries. ⁵ This title was written on her forehead: MYSTERY BABYLON THE GREAT THE MOTHER OF PROSTITUTES AND OF THE ABOMINATIONS OF THE EARTH.*
> *⁶ I saw that the woman was drunk with the blood of the saints, the blood of those who bore testimony to Jesus.*

In addition to the legitimate ministry on earth, there is also a counterfeit ministry on earth; the ministry of Babylon the Great Harlot. Satan makes it his purpose in all aspects of his own tribulation agenda to attempt to counterfeit the workings of Christ. Much of that work is visible in his imitation christ, Antichrist. Yet, he also has another counterfeit entity which will work to draw seekers to himself rather than to the legitimate ministry of God's tribulation witnesses. That entity is a false church which will permeate the earth.

"*Mystery Babylon*" is called a harlot, or a prostitute. A prostitute, of course, is one who perverts sex for personal gain. Prostitution and fornication are common themes throughout the scripture, and are used in

Chapter 3: The First Half of the Tribulation

both literal and metaphorical ways. Undoubtedly, the mention of prostitution in this text is metaphorical. This prostitute sits on many waters, sits on a scarlet beast, holds a cup full of abominable things and is drunk on blood. All of the language of this text is symbolic, so it can be clearly understood that her being called a prostitute should be interpreted symbolically as well. While the language describing her is metaphorical, however, she depicts something which is very real.

Prostitution, when used symbolically in scripture, always refers spiritual deviance, particularly the worship of false gods and the turning away from the true "husband" of Israel, God, unto others. Examples of this metaphorical usage are seen in Hosea and Jeremiah.

> ***Hosea 1:2***
> *When the LORD began to speak through Hosea, the LORD said to him, "Go, take to yourself an adulterous wife and children of unfaithfulness, because the land is guilty of the vilest adultery in departing from the LORD."*
>
> ***Jeremiah 2:20***
> *Long ago you broke off your yoke and tore off your bonds;*
>   *you said, 'I will not serve you!' Indeed, on every high hill*
>   *and under every spreading tree you lay down as a prostitute.*

Also, Ezekiel 16:15-41; 23:5-44, and numerous other places note a metaphorical usage of prostitution. In each case, a metaphorical prostitute is one who "cheats" on God with a false god. Israel was known metaphorically in the Old Testament as the wife of Jehovah. Metaphorical prostitution, then, is when the metaphorical wife has an affair with another god.

In keeping with literal biblical interpretational methods, then, this Harlot represents a religion or a religious system which deviates from the Lord and gives his glory to another; a false god. In this case, Satan's own campaign entices the people of earth to follow a false god, Satan's counterfeit christ; Antichrist.

In verse two she is seen committing adultery with the kings of the earth, or the one world government which was referenced earlier. She is also seen riding the beast, with the seven heads and ten horns. This particular beast represents the one world government throughout the book of Revelation, while also referencing particularly the Antichrist in the second half of the tribulation, as Antichrist will be the undisputed power head of the world government at that time.

The fact that the prostitute has committed adultery with the beast indicates that this religious system is fully integrated and supported by the world government. Metaphorically, they are "in bed" together and a unity exists between the evil government and the evil religion. That being the case, it can furthermore be gleaned that this is a world-wide religion; in part because it is supported by a world-wide government which will rule the earth, and in part because of the statement in verse 1 that she "*sits on many waters.*"

The phrase "*many waters*" is used in scripture figuratively to represent nations, such as in Isaiah 17:13, "*The nations will rush like the rushing of many waters; But God will rebuke them and they will flee far away, And be chased like the chaff of the mountains before the wind, Like a rolling thing before the whirlwind.*"

The one-world government then, has a one-world religious system that accommodates it and is fully supported by it. That she sits on many waters indicates her truly global reach. Babylon the Great Harlot is a global mega-church of evil. As this study progresses, this church will be seen exalting the Antichrist as the true church would exalt the true Christ. This false church will be an instrument of Antichrist and the false prophet to secure his exaltation to god-status in the minds of the people of earth.

Chapter 3: The First Half of the Tribulation

It is noteworthy that this world-wide religion is very wealthy, sinful and influential, as would be expected. Verse 4 indicates, *"The woman was dressed in purple and scarlet, and was glittering with gold, precious stones and pearls. She held a golden cup in her hand, filled with abominable things and the filth of her adulteries."*

Purple and scarlet both have well established biblical metaphorical usages. Purple represents royalty, as in John 19:2, when Jesus was given a crown of thorns and a purple robe in mockery of his "King of the Jews" title. Scarlet represents sin, as noted in Isaiah 1:18, *"Come now, let us reason together," says the Lord. "Though your sins are like scarlet, they shall be as white as snow; though they are red as crimson, they shall be like wool."* Thus this false church is understood to be very sinful and corrupt, while seen as royalty, being the chosen vessel of the government and having the participation of the kings of the earth in her worship of evil.

Gold, precious stones and pearls clearly portray her great wealth. It is easy to imagine a religion with near world-wide assimilation as being extremely wealthy. This harlot is noted to be *"glittering"* with wealth. It is a clearly defining trait of her by John's observation. She literally swims in her wealth, yet is ironically supported by a world with no money for food.

Verse 4 notes that she *"held a golden cup in her hand, filled with abominable things and the filth of her adulteries."* A cup is used symbolically in scripture to note one's lot, or path, such as in Jesus' prayer at Gethsemane prior to the cross, (Matthew 26:39) *"take this cup from me."* Her lot, or path, then, is one of asserting abominations against the Lord. She is truly a counterfeit, having the systematized appearance of religion, yet being fully Satanic in nature. Satan's desire from the beginning of history was to be worshipped and to intervene on God's glory. This counterfeit church will give him that opportunity on the earth for a short season.

Verse 6 notes, *"I saw that the woman was drunk with the blood of the saints, the blood of those who bore testimony to Jesus."*

Being drunk is indicative of excess or of an uncontrolled state.[45] In this case, the excess concerns the blood of the "*saints*," a term the New Testament uses to refer to those who belong to Christ. Note that this does not refer to other uses of "sainthood," which are extra-biblical, but it refers to the Bible's own use of the term. This text clearly indicates, then, that the false church will actively persecute the saints unto their deaths. The killing of the saints of God is part of Satan's own wrath, knowing that his time is short.[46] This persecution intensifies during the second half of the tribulation, but is clearly underway during the first half, as the multitude of Revelation 7 referenced earlier indicates.

This counterfeit church helps complete Satan's imitation ministry. There now has been revealed a counterfeit father, who is Satan himself, a counterfeit son, who is Antichrist, and a counterfeit church, who will be Babylon the Great Harlot. Soon will also be revealed a counterfeit Holy Spirit to assist in Satan's own program during the great tribulation.

The Rise of Babylon (The City)

Along with the rise of the world religion is the rise of the city of that religion, the restored Babylon. Not much is given in scripture as to the development of the city, but much is said, which will be discussed in chapter 5, about the destruction of the city. The destruction of a nonexistent city demands the building of such city at some future point. In this case, Babylon, bearing the same name as the counterfeit religion of the tribulation, must be raised as a functioning city on earth.

It is unclear from scripture as to the timing of the re-emergence of the city of Babylon. It is clear, however, that the city will be well established by the mid-point of the tribulation. What can be gleaned about the city of the religion of Antichrist will be observed in this short section.

---

[45] Ephesians 5:18
[46] Revelation 12:12

Chapter 3: The First Half of the Tribulation

A city of the false religion

> **Revelation 17:18**
> [18] The woman you saw is the great city that rules over the kings of the earth."

Two things can be noted of Babylon here. First, that it is the city of the great religion of Antichrist, as it is represented by *"the woman you saw"* who is *"Mystery Babylon the Great"* as discussed earlier. Secondly, it is the headquarter city of Antichrist, as it is *"the city that rules over the kings of the earth."* Antichrist, as a literal world ruler, will require a center of operations just as any other world ruler would have need of. Babylon will be his earthly power center.

Revelation 17:13 notes of the ten kings that, "*They have one purpose and will give their power and authority to the beast.*" This is an important part of Antichrist's rise to power. While Daniel demonstrated Antichrist having power over the earth, Revelation 17 indicates that the kings of the earth will ultimately give their authority to Antichrist, who will then, in effect, be the king of the entire earth for this reason. Thus, Antichrist's role is crystal clear. He will subdue the earth and rule it.

These combined truths point to Babylon as a city of both religious and governmental importance in the tribulation. Religiously, as will be further developed later, Antichrist will exalt himself as God and the world will worship him as God. Governmentally, he will rule all as king of the world. Babylon then, as the seat of Antichrist's power, is a city that embodies both realities; the worship and governorship of Antichrist. These two ideas, themselves, are part of his great counterfeiting program.

Quoting Psalm 110, Hebrews 7 states of the legitimate Christ,

> **Hebrews 7:17**
> [17] For it is declared: "You are a priest forever, in the order of Melchizedek."

Without going into great detail, this refers to a unique aspect of Christ's rule which Antichrist will also attempt to replicate. Melchizedek was a king who was also a priest. In Judaism, kings were born of the tribe of Judah, as Christ was, while priests were born of the tribe of Levi. Christ is prophesied as a coming priest in the order of Melchizedek because he was to be both a King *and* a priest. He was a priest via his atonement, presenting his own sacrifice before God by which man's sins could be atoned. He was also born a King, who will return to establish his kingdom on earth. At the time of Christ's rule in the coming millennial kingdom, he will be God on earth and King on earth; "*a priest in the order of Melchizedek*," or a King who was made priest.

The nature of Babylon represents Antichrist's attempt to falsify Christ's characteristics of being a God-King. Antichrist will attempt to be the same. He will be the great military leader and king of earth and will later be observed also to exalt himself as God, falsely proclaiming himself as the true Christ. Thus, he will himself attempt to be a priest in the order of Melchizedek.

Babylon, the city, will purpose itself with the fruition of that ambition. Being his headquarter city, it will function as a capital city of the earth while also being the city of the worship of Antichrist. Babylon will be to Antichrist what Israel will be to the legitimate Christ in the messianic kingdom; a headquarters of both governmental and religious practice. Of its success in this quest Revelation 18:3 states, "*For all the nations have drunk the maddening wine of her adulteries. The kings of the earth committed adultery with her, and the merchants of the earth grew rich from her excessive luxuries.*"

"*The maddening wine of her adulteries*" points once again to her spiritual harlotry; she is a false religion which has "maddened" the nations by inspiring them to believe in the false Christ. Furthermore it states later in that chapter that,

> **Revelation 18:23**
> *...Your merchants were the world's great men. By your magic spell all the nations were led astray.*

Chapter 3: The First Half of the Tribulation

This *"magic spell"* of deception will convince the kings of the world of Antichrist's ability to rule and will be the demonic means by which he will convince the world of his deity.

A city of great wealth

> ### *Revelation 18:3*
> *... and the merchants of the earth grew rich from her excessive luxuries."*

Being the center of the world religion will have its perks for the city of Babylon. As the false church, Babylon the Great Harlot was demonstrated to be terrifically wealthy. Likewise will become the city which represents her.

> ### *Revelation 18:11-13*
> *[11] "The merchants of the earth will weep and mourn over her because no one buys their cargoes any more--*
> *[12] cargoes of gold, silver, precious stones and pearls; fine linen, purple, silk and scarlet cloth; every sort of citron wood, and articles of every kind made of ivory, costly wood, bronze, iron and marble; [13] cargoes of cinnamon and spice, of incense, myrrh and frankincense, of wine and olive oil, of fine flour and wheat; cattle and sheep; horses and carriages; and bodies and souls of men.*

This text refers to the coming destruction of the city, which will be detailed later. Noticeably in the text is the fact that the city is one of vast trade and industry. She is clearly a merchant city dealing in every type of commercial cargo, including the *"souls of men,"* which is an inference into her deceitful religious practices.

The city of Babylon will demonstrate some similarity to the modern day Vatican city, itself being a center of a large religious order, Catholicism. People come from around the world to see the city and to participate uniquely up close and personal in the religious celebrations and symbols tied to Catholicism. To that end, a great commerce also is associated with Vatican City. Everything from room and board to souvenirs is readily available from the central city-state of that religious order. Likewise, Babylon will clearly become a very wealthy city from the religious center which will exist there.

A city of great power

> ***Revelation 18:10***
> *"'Woe! Woe, O great city, O Babylon, city of power! In one hour your doom has come!'*

While speaking of the future destruction of the city, another attribute of it is identified. It is a city of great power. If one can imagine a city which contains the full force of the world government and a truly global religious system, then one can clearly begin to comprehend the potential for power within that context.

Worship of Antichrist will come to its peak in the middle of the tribulation. By that time, the power of Babylon will reflect the power of her figurehead.

The Seventh Seal: The Trumpet Judgments

As the seventh seal is opened a new series of judgments begins; the trumpet judgments.

> ***Revelation 8:1-5***
> *¹ When he opened the seventh seal, there was silence in heaven for about half an hour.*
> *² And I saw the seven angels who stand before God, and to them were given seven trumpets.*
> *³ Another angel, who had a golden censer, came and stood at the altar. He was given much incense to offer,*

Chapter 3: The First Half of the Tribulation

> *with the prayers of all the saints, on the golden altar before the throne. ⁴ The smoke of the incense, together with the prayers of the saints, went up before God from the angel's hand. ⁵ Then the angel took the censer, filled it with fire from the altar, and hurled it on the earth; and there came peals of thunder, rumblings, flashes of lightning and an earthquake.*

The seventh seal will bring forth seven angels who will then administer the seven trumpet judgments. Ending the seal judgments are natural disasters, as was noted earlier. In each of the three series of judgments in the book of Revelation, natural disasters and powerful upheavals in nature are experienced as the series concludes. Noted in this text are peals of thunder, rumblings, lightning and an earthquake. Indeed, the entire series of seal judgments is to be centered around great disturbances of the physical world.

The advent of the trumpet judgments appears to bring an increased vigor from the wrath of God's hand. Those who rejected the first series of seal judgments are now challenged again, but by an even more dire set of circumstances. Throughout the tribulation, the judgments appear to increasingly grow in their intensity.

> **Revelation 8:6-7**
> *"Then the seven angels who had the seven trumpets prepared to sound them. ⁷ The first angel sounded his trumpet, and there came hail and fire mixed with blood, and it was hurled down upon the earth. A third of the earth was burned up, a third of the trees were burned up, and all the green grass was burned up."*

The first angel's trumpet will bring hail and fire to the earth, mixed with blood. The end result of this plague will be that one third of the vegetation of earth will burn up. This will further frustrate the conditions of famine upon the earth introduced in the seal judgments. Now, by the great loss of plant life, the famine will be virtually guaranteed to endure. That the fire was "*mixed with blood*" indicates that death will be associated with the hail and fire storms, as would be expected from raging fires and a further reduced food supply on earth. Reminiscent of God's judgment against Sodom and Gomorrah, it will become increasingly difficult for mankind to misunderstand the judgmental purpose of these events.

The second angel's trumpet will further produce great disruptions in the natural realms.

> ***Revelation 8:8-9***
> *"The second angel sounded his trumpet, and something like a huge mountain, all ablaze, was thrown into the sea. A third of the sea turned into blood, [9] a third of the living creatures in the sea died, and a third of the ships were destroyed."*

A "*huge mountain, all ablaze*" sounds as something akin to a large meteor, as such may have been described by a first century man. This "meteor" is supernatural, however, by merit that it turns one third of the sea waters into blood. Coinciding with one-third of all ocean waters being turned into blood comes the death of one-third of all ocean life. This will be yet another incredibly difficult blow to the food supply of the earth, not to mention other natural resources associated with the sea. Additionally, this meteor causes great destruction in that one third of the sea faring ships are to be destroyed.

Some speculate concerning the blood-related judgments as to whether the blood is literal blood or a figurative representation of something else. Later, however, in one of the coming judgments, angels will comment on that very question, which will strongly lend credibility to the understanding that the blood of these judgments should be taken literally.

At this time, with one-third of the earth's vegetation and salt waters destroyed, the third angel will sound his trumpet to call judgments onto the fresh water sources.

Chapter 3: The First Half of the Tribulation

Revelation 8:10-11
"The third angel sounded his trumpet, and a great star, blazing like a torch, fell from the sky on a third of the rivers and on the springs of water-- ¹¹ *the name of the star is Wormwood. A third of the waters turned bitter, and many people died from the waters that had become bitter."*

In this judgment, one third of the fresh water rivers and streams become defiled. It is *"turned bitter"* so that people die from drinking it. The detriment of rivers and streams will certainly impact earth's drinking water supply, but will nonetheless leave the lakes, ponds and underground water sources intact. However, losing one third of the running waters will once again have a great impact on famine. Much crop irrigation depends on rivers and running streams as do water sources for various industry enterprises and municipalities. One would presume the world economy to be near the brink of collapse at this point.

This judgment is said to be carried out by a *"star."* This is obviously not a literal star, but a metaphorical use of the term. When stars are used metaphorically in scripture, most commonly they refer to angels.[47] This reference is the first of four such references in Revelation, three of which refer to angelic beings. What is unclear is if this star refers to a righteous angel or a demonic angel.

The use of the term "angel" in scripture only indicates a creature having an angelic nature. Demons are angels who joined with Satan in his fall. While this is the content of another field of theological study, it is important to reference that the term "angel" can refer to holy, "elect" angels or it can refer to unholy "fallen" angels. They all are angels. Only twice in the book of Revelation is the term "demon" used; once in chapter 9 referring to the worship of demons and once in chapter 16 referring to demons which will be discussed later. In all other references to demons in this book they are called simply "angels" or "stars" and the context informs us in some cases that they are of the demonic type.

---

[47] Isaiah 14:12,

In this case, the angel has a name, "Wormwood." Traditionally, Wormwood has been understood to be a demonic angel. Undoubtedly modern generations may have drawn that conclusion from C.S. Lewis', *The Screwtape Letters,* where a demonic character in the book is named Wormwood. Others have concluded Wormwood to be a demonic angel because of the particularly destructive and violent nature of his work. However, it should be understood that many judgments of the great tribulation will be carried out by righteous angels. It was an elect angel in Heaven which sounded the trumpet to begin this judgment. And an angel is noted to carry the judgment out. It is unclear from scripture whether this particular angel is demonic or an elect angel carrying out his Lord's requests. Many angels occupied with the oversight of events during the great tribulation will be elect, godly angels, and others will in fact be demonic angels. Both will carry out God's desires during this timeframe. While the demonic kingdom has its own agenda during the tribulation, nothing will occur outside of God's providence. To that end, the title, "the day of the Lord" should be understood to uncompromisingly demonstrate God's control being exercised by whichever means his plans are unfolded.

At the sounding of the fourth trumpet, the focus of judgment is turned away from the waters and toward the heavenly lights.

> ***Revelation 8:12***
> *"The fourth angel sounded his trumpet, and a third of the sun was struck, a third of the moon, and a third of the stars, so that a third of them turned dark. A third of the day was without light, and also a third of the night."*

The wording of this verse clearly indicates that the lights of the earth will be somehow diminished or hindered. Yet it is difficult to understand at first observation if the one-third of the day being without light indicates a change in the positioning of the heavenly bodies or if it means that the Sun is diminished in its power by one-third. The phrases "*a third of the day was without light*" and "*a third of the night,*" however, indicate the former is the case. The heavenly lights will be reduced in the hours of the day they will be permitted to shine. It may be that God will darken a

Chapter 3: The First Half of the Tribulation

certain quadrant of the night sky by some means, or it may be that he will merely prevent those bodies from reflecting light. Neither is more or less supernatural in substance.

The results of the fourth trumpet judgment are that supernaturally, the heavenly lights of earth will be diminished by one-third of their normal schedule so that the skies will be dark longer each night, and the night will have one-third of its light blacked out as well. This event will surely provide an eerie realization of the unnatural origin of these judgments.

The Woe Judgments

The "Woe Judgments" are a continuation of the Trumpet Judgments. The final three Trumpet Judgments will be so severe they are given this name by the warning of an eagle. The Woe Judgments will begin a completely new type of affliction, harsher than even the great famines which will have been experienced up to that time.

The First Woe (the fifth trumpet judgment)

> **Revelation 8:13**
> *[13] As I watched, I heard an eagle that was flying in midair call out in a loud voice: "Woe! Woe! Woe to the inhabitants of the earth, because of the trumpet blasts about to be sounded by the other three angels!"*
>
> **Revelation 9:1-12**
> *[1] The fifth angel sounded his trumpet, and I saw a star that had fallen from the sky to the earth. The star was given the key to the shaft of the Abyss. [2] When he opened the Abyss, smoke rose from it like the smoke from a gigantic furnace. The sun and sky were darkened by the smoke from the Abyss. [3] And out of the smoke locusts came down upon the earth and were given power like that of scorpions of the earth. [4] They were told not to harm the grass of the earth or any plant or tree, but only those people who did not have the seal of God on their*

foreheads. *⁵ They were not given power to kill them, but only to torture them for five months. And the agony they suffered was like that of the sting of a scorpion when it strikes a man. ⁶ During those days men will seek death, but will not find it; they will long to die, but death will elude them.*
⁷ The locusts looked like horses prepared for battle. On their heads they wore something like crowns of gold, and their faces resembled human faces. ⁸ Their hair was like women's hair, and their teeth were like lions' teeth. ⁹ They had breastplates like breastplates of iron, and the sound of their wings was like the thundering of many horses and chariots rushing into battle. ¹⁰ They had tails and stings like scorpions, and in their tails they had power to torment people for five months. ¹¹ They had as king over them the angel of the Abyss, whose name in Hebrew is Abaddon, and in Greek, Apollyon.
¹² The first woe is past; two other woes are yet to come.

The first Woe Judgment contains several specific images which must be understood to paint a very peculiar picture. The first image, is again, the metaphorical image of a star.

This "*star*," or angel, is in charge of the execution of this judgment. In this case, some deductions can be made which affirm this angel as a demonic angel rather than a righteous angel. To begin with, the angel is noted to be a star "*that had fallen from the sky to the earth.*" As John tells what he sees, he does not see an angel "falling" to the earth, but one that "*had fallen.*" John's imagery is undoubtedly of a "fallen" angel, or a demon, who had rebelled with Satan and had been cast to earth, which will be examined later in this work.

The next key image in this text is that of the Abyss itself. The term "Abyss" is a Greek term, used only eight times in the New Testament. A systematic study of the passages referencing the Abyss indicate clearly that the Abyss is a place of demonic confinement. It is unclear how long

Chapter 3: The First Half of the Tribulation

demons may be confined in the Abyss, but it is crystal clear that the Abyss is a place unique among spiritual abodes in that it is a demonic "jail" of sorts, where demons are confined to serve sentences for particular actions. Demons are demonstrated in scripture to be released from the Abyss at various times, which eliminates the assumptions of some, that the Abyss is the lake of fire. The lake of fire is eternal, while the Abyss is a temporary place of confinement.

That the Abyss is affiliated with demons is consistent throughout the New Testament. In Luke 8:30-31, when Jesus confronted "Legion," a man filled with demons, [30] *Jesus asked him, "What is your name?"*
"Legion," he replied, because many demons had gone into him.
31 And they begged him repeatedly not to order them to go into the Abyss.

Not only is the Abyss a place of demonic confinement, but it is clearly a place where Jesus has authority to send demons, and a place in which they do not desire to be.

The next key image in this text is that of the locusts which will come out of the Abyss. These locusts do not sound remotely like any natural locust found on earth today. John noted that they looked as horses, with human faces, women's hair, and wore crowns of gold. They stung with scorpion-like stings which tortured people for five months. Clearly these locusts were not literal locusts, but figurative ones, as literal locusts have none of these characteristics. Given their descriptions and the fact that they arose from the Abyss it is clear that what John is describing as the first Woe Judgment is the release of a demonic invasion upon mankind.

In this invasion, the demons were not allowed to harm the 144,000 missionaries with God's seal, but only those who refused to repent of their evil practices. The torturous attacks of these demonic beings did not kill, but brought painful stings to each person they stung, which endured for five months. Those inflicted desired to die, but were not allowed to. They were forced to live with their pain and endure the judgment to its end.

A final key image of this text is the name of the demonic angel in charge of these demons. Verse 11 states *"they had as king over them the angel of the Abyss, whose name in Hebrew is Abaddon, and in Greek, Apollyon."* Abaddon is a Hebrew term which is translated "destruction." Abaddon is also the name given in the Old Testament for the unrighteous portion of Sheol, the place of the dead. Thus, the name of the leader of this group is unconditionally associated with unrighteousness rather than righteousness. This attack clearly illustrates that the judgment purposes of the great tribulation are carried out even through the hands of God's enemies, the demonic kingdom.

The Second Woe (the sixth trumpet), as would be expected, reveals yet a further increase in the intensity of God's wrath.

> ***Revelation 9:13-21***
> *[13] The sixth angel sounded his trumpet, and I heard a voice coming from the horns of the golden altar that is before God. [14] It said to the sixth angel who had the trumpet, "Release the four angels who are bound at the great river Euphrates." [15] And the four angels who had been kept ready for this very hour and day and month and year were released to kill a third of mankind. [16] The number of the mounted troops was two hundred million. I heard their number.*
>
> *[17] The horses and riders I saw in my vision looked like this: Their breastplates were fiery red, dark blue, and yellow as sulfur. The heads of the horses resembled the heads of lions, and out of their mouths came fire, smoke and sulfur. [18] A third of mankind was killed by the three plagues of fire, smoke and sulfur that came out of their mouths. [19] The power of the horses was in their mouths and in their tails; for their tails were like snakes, having heads with which they inflict injury.*
>
> *[20] The rest of mankind that were not killed by these plagues still did not repent of the work of their hands; they did not stop worshiping demons, and idols of gold, silver, bronze, stone and wood--idols that cannot see or*

Chapter 3: The First Half of the Tribulation

hear or walk. [21] Nor did they repent of their murders, their magic arts, their sexual immorality or their thefts.

Yet another invasion follows and is noted to be led by angels. In this case, four angels who were "bound" at the Euphrates river. The fact that these angels are bound indicates that they too, are fallen, demonic angels rather than elect, righteous angels. Clearly they have sinned at some point to have been bound and held for this moment. There is no scriptural basis to believe that a righteous angel would ever have need of being bound. Being bound indicates a punitive sentence which is unwarranted by the elect angels, who are obedient in nature. However, being bound and chained is a biblically noted sentence concerning certain demonic angels in specific scenarios.[48]

These four demons will lead an army two hundred million strong. They are described as riders on horses with lion heads, snake tails and mouths which spew fire and toxic smoke. They clearly are not indicative of any natural source. To that end, all evidence concludes the second Woe Judgment to be a second demonic invasion to be released upon the earth.

Unlike the first demonic invasion, this army will be allowed to kill one-third of the inhabitants of earth. As with the seal judgments and the coming bowl judgments, the trumpet judgments intensify with each new allocation. Those who failed to repent after being tortured for five months will be given further reprimand leading to their deaths in the next judgment.

Fascinatingly, even with two hundred million demons attacking and killing mankind, verse 21 notes that man did not repent of "*their murders, their magic arts, their sexual immorality or their thefts.*" Even more incredibly, verse 20 notes that "*they did not stop worshiping demons!*"

The mention of the possibility of repentance demonstrates once again

---

[48] Jude 6, 2 Peter 2:4

that a call to repentance is always available during the great tribulation for those who are willing to accept it. Yet, sadly, even in light of the Woe Judgments, none remain who are willing at this point.

The third Woe Judgment, which is the seventh trumpet judgment, corresponds to the coming bowl judgments, and will be examined later in the timeline.

Other Events of the First Half of the Tribulation:

World War (near the middle of the tribulation)

Many wars will indeed take place during the unfolding of the tribulation. Not all of them will be studied in this work, but only certain pertinent conflicts. One such very pertinent battle is described in Daniel 11.

> ***Daniel 11:40-45***
> *[40] "At the time of the end the king of the South will engage him in battle, and the king of the North will storm out against him with chariots and cavalry and a great fleet of ships. He will invade many countries and sweep through them like a flood. [41] He will also invade the Beautiful Land. Many countries will fall, but Edom, Moab and the leaders of Ammon will be delivered from his hand. [42] He will extend his power over many countries; Egypt will not escape. [43] He will gain control of the treasures of gold and silver and all the riches of Egypt, with the Libyans and Nubians in submission. [44] But reports from the east and the north will alarm him, and he will set out in a great rage to destroy and annihilate many. [45] He will pitch his royal tents between the seas at the beautiful holy mountain. Yet he will come to his end, and no one will help him.*

The "him" of verse 40 refers to Antichrist in the context of Daniel 11.

Chapter 3: The First Half of the Tribulation

The war referred to in Daniel eleven details the establishment of Antichrist militarily. This rise to power was also observed in Daniel 7 as the "little horn" (Antichrist) uprooted three of the horns (three of the ten kings) on the great beast of Daniel's vision in that chapter. That beast was discussed earlier to represent a future one world government, and Daniel 11 details in this text one of several battles which secured Antichrist's position as the military leader on earth. As Antichrist defeats the three kingdoms he fights with in this text, he takes their power and becomes well-established for coming events in the middle of the tribulation, when he will proclaim himself as the sovereign God of the heavens and earth.

Several key observations in this text are worthy of note.

First, as Antichrist establishes his military strength, it is revealed in verse 41 that *"he will also invade the Beautiful Land."* It notes in verse 45 that he *"will pitch his royal tents between the seas at the beautiful holy mountain."* It is at this point that Antichrist breaks his covenant with Israel. The signing of the covenant was the sign of the beginning of the tribulation. His attack on Israel is the sign of his breaking of the covenant, and a sign that the middle of the tribulation has arrived. Once his power is asserted on earth, he will spend the remainder of his time, the entire second half of the tribulation, attempting to destroy Israel.

Another important observation is found in verse 41, where it states *"many countries will fall, but Edom, Moab and the leaders of Ammon will be delivered from his hand."* Antichrist will, in effect, be the king of the entire earth, as Revelation 17:13 notes that the kings of the earth *"will give their power and authority to the beast."* Yet, Daniel specifically references three ancient nations which will not fall to Antichrist; Edom, Moab, and Ammon. Edom, Moab and Ammon are East of Israel and comprise most of modern day Jordan. God's preservation of Jordan will be demonstrated later in this work to be an action of great purpose and value.

The last important note concerning this battle is that Antichrist is literally killed during the conflict.

Antichrist is killed

Concerning this reality, Daniel 11:45(b) states very simply,

"he will come to his end and no one will help him."

Revelation 13 gives more detail to this intriguing development.

> ***Rev 13:1-8***
> *[1] And the dragon stood on the shore of the sea.*
> *And I saw a beast coming out of the sea. He had ten horns and seven heads, with ten crowns on his horns, and on each head a blasphemous name. [2] The beast I saw resembled a leopard, but had feet like those of a bear and a mouth like that of a lion. The dragon gave the beast his power and his throne and great authority. [3] One of the heads of the beast seemed to have had a fatal wound, but the fatal wound had been healed. The whole world was astonished and followed the beast. [4] Men worshiped the dragon because he had given authority to the beast, and they also worshiped the beast and asked, "Who is like the beast? Who can make war against him?"*
> *[5] The beast was given a mouth to utter proud words and blasphemies and to exercise his authority for forty-two months. [6] He opened his mouth to blaspheme God, and to slander his name and his dwelling place and those who live in heaven. [7] He was given power to make war against the saints and to conquer them. And he was given authority over every tribe, people, language and nation. [8] All inhabitants of the earth will worship the beast--all whose names have not been written in the book of life belonging to the Lamb that was slain from the creation of the world.*

Verse 3 notes the nature of Antichrist's death. He had received a fatal wound to the head.

Chapter 3: The First Half of the Tribulation

> *³ One of the heads of the beast seemed to have had a fatal wound, but the fatal wound had been healed. The whole world was astonished and followed the beast.*

In this context, Antichrist begins a new chapter of his counterfeit ministry on earth. While Revelation states that the beast "*seemed to have had a fatal wound,*" one must remember that John only wrote what he saw. He saw what "*seemed*" to be a fatal wound which "*had been healed.*" Daniel, however, speaking of the same person, noted specifically that Antichrist would "*come to his end.*" Daniel depicts that what John saw was indeed one who had died. John precisely observes that this fatal head wound "*had been healed.*" Antichrist will indeed be killed in the battle for these three kingdoms. Yet, his would will be healed. One who dies, yet is later proclaimed "healed" can arrive at such a condition through only one method. Antichrist is to be killed and resurrected.

Adding to his impressive "Christ like" resume, Antichrist now has another essential attribute to flaunt in his great deception of the people of earth; a counterfeit resurrection. Just as the real Christ died and was resurrected, so Antichrist will die on a battlefield, and have his head wound "*healed,*" being resurrected to live again. Understanding Antichrist to be a mere man makes this teaching problematic. Understanding, however, Antichrist to be of a demonic/human conception allows him abilities that are inhuman and demonic in nature, such as being somehow unstopped by a physical death blow.

Verse 2 unveils yet another significant revelation of Satan's counterfeit Christ program.

> *The dragon gave the beast his power and his throne and great authority.*

Just as God gave his authority to Christ, Satan will give his authority to his false Christ, further adding to the fallacious portrayal of Antichrist as the genuine Messiah. He now will add to his false trinity and artificial church a counterfeit resurrection of a forged messiah, whom he will give his authority to, further enhancing his impersonation of deity to mankind. Very shortly, a false Holy Spirit will also be added to the counterfeit godhead, that Satan may attempt to lead his own kingdom program during the great tribulation, convincing even the elect, if that were possible, that Christ has indeed arrived on the earth in the person of Antichrist. Jesus' warning in the Olivet Discourse is now clearly understood.

> ***Matthew 24:23-26***
> *[23] At that time if anyone says to you, 'Look, here is the Christ!' or, 'There he is!' do not believe it. [24] For false Christs and false prophets will appear and perform great signs and miracles to deceive even the elect--if that were possible. [25] See, I have told you ahead of time. [26] "So if anyone tells you, 'There he is, out in the desert,' do not go out; or, 'Here he is, in the inner rooms,' do not believe it.*

Chapter 3: The First Half of the Tribulation

Chapter 4: The Middle of the Tribulation

While scripture divides the tribulation into two 3 1/2 year portions, many events occur roughly around the middle of the tribulation. Technically, the exact mid-point of the tribulation is determined in Daniel as the moment when Antichrist will break his covenant with Israel. Yet, so many occurrences are centered generally around the middle of the tribulation that it is helpful to examine these affairs categorically as mid-term events.

Death of the Two Witnesses

One such significant mid-term occurrence concerns the completion of the ministry of the two witnesses which were active throughout the first half of the tribulation.

> *Rev 11:7-14*
> *⁷ Now when they [the two witnesses] have finished their testimony, the beast that comes up from the Abyss will attack them, and overpower and kill them. ⁸ Their bodies will lie in the street of the great city, which is figuratively called Sodom and Egypt, where also their Lord was crucified. ⁹ For three and a half days men from every people, tribe, language and nation will gaze on their bodies and refuse them burial. ¹⁰ The inhabitants of the earth will gloat over them and will celebrate by sending each other gifts, because these two prophets had tormented those who live on the earth.*
> *¹¹ But after the three and a half days a breath of life from God entered them, and they stood on their feet, and terror struck those who saw them. ¹² Then they heard a loud voice from heaven saying to them, "Come up here."*

Chapter 4: The Middle of the Tribulation

> *And they went up to heaven in a cloud, while their enemies looked on.*
> *[13] At that very hour there was a severe earthquake and a tenth of the city collapsed. Seven thousand people were killed in the earthquake, and the survivors were terrified and gave glory to the God of heaven.*
> *[14] The second woe has passed; the third woe is coming soon. [brackets added]*

The "*beast that comes up from the Abyss*" referenced in this text refers once again to Antichrist. Antichrist comes up from the Abyss because he had been killed and resurrected, as noted in Daniel 11 and Revelation 13.

Once again, the Abyss is a place of confinement which is used uniquely for demonic angels. Men are never seen in scripture as being cast into the Abyss except for this singular text concerning Antichrist.[49] Death involves having one's spirit separated from the body. In Antichrist's case, being a hybrid human/demonic being, upon his death he will be sent to the Abyss rather than to Hades, where the souls of the dead of unrighteous humanity would be sent. The fact that Antichrist comes up out of the Abyss rather than coming up out of Hades demonstrates his uniquely demonically-human status. Upon Antichrist's resurrection then, his spirit will rise from the Abyss and be reunited to his body, head wound and all, that he may resume his counterfeit ministry as a resurrected false deity. At this point, Antichrist will have fulfilled a counterfeit virgin birth, death, burial and resurrection in the manner of the true Christ he seeks to impersonate.

Upon coming up out of the Abyss to resume his unholy ministry, Antichrist will kill the two witnesses as a further attempt to demonstrate his power. God had formerly not allowed anyone, including Antichrist, to kill them. Yet, at this point, their ministry complete, God will allow them to be killed for the further demonstration of his glory and power through their resurrections.

---

[49] See Chapter One, " Antichrist's Nature"

While God's glory will be demonstrated to the righteous through their resurrection, Antichrist enjoys the glory from unrighteous men through their deaths. He will have risen from the dead, killed those who could not be killed and removed those who had tormented the sinful consciences of man with their continual preaching of the truth.

Verse nine notes that "*every people, tribe, language and nation will gaze on their bodies and refuse them burial*" for three and one half days. This is a beguiling revelation in all but most modern history. At the time of the writing of Revelation, it would not seem at all plausible that "*men from every people, tribe, language and nation will gaze on their bodies.*" In fact, at no time prior to modern history would such a biblical claim seem probable at all. Yet, with the advent of satellite television and world-wide internet networking, modern news events today are regularly seen in real time on a global scale. In reality the *whole world* will witness the spectacle of the dead witnesses and will corporately glory in their demise; sending gifts to one another as if their worst enemy had been eliminated.

Verse 13 notes that after their resurrection "*they went up to heaven in a cloud, while their enemies looked on.*" As the world continues to look upon the spectacle, God will use the captured attentions of the earth to demonstrate his power over Antichrist. Antichrist will have been granted the power to kill them, but God will demonstrate the ultimate victory by resurrecting them with the entire world watching. It is hard to imagine the fear which will surely be stricken into the hearts of the wicked who will have rejoiced at the deaths of the witnesses.

It is important to note that these events will take place in Israel; specifically in Jerusalem, "*where their Lord was crucified.*" Consequently, it is at this place and point in time that a transformation begins in the hearts of Israelites. The transformation is not completed until the end of the tribulation, but it is at this moment that Israel begins to understand that the God of heaven - their God - is the God of the Christ which the two witnesses had proclaimed. Israel, who rejected Christ at his first coming, will begin to understand that Christ was indeed who he claimed to be, as is verified by their response to the earthquake

Chapter 4: The Middle of the Tribulation

which is to occur next.

Lastly, as was the case with the seal judgments, the end of the trumpet judgments will yield violent convulsions in nature. *"The second woe has passed; the third woe is coming soon,"* signifies the end of the trumpet judgments, as the seventh trumpet judgment is the beginning of the bowl judgments.

> *[13] At that very hour there was a severe earthquake and a tenth of the city collapsed. Seven thousand people were killed in the earthquake, and the survivors were terrified and gave glory to the God of heaven.*

While the world watches and gives glory to Antichrist, those on the ground in Jerusalem who survive this great quake will give glory to the God of heaven. They are *"terrified"* for good reason! At this time they will begin to realize that the God of heaven has resurrected the witnesses of the Christ they had rejected. Realizing that God was in control of the resurrection of the witnesses is tantamount to understanding that the Christ which they preached was the rightful Messiah. The preaching of the witnesses will be validated in the sight of Israel. This is the beginning of what will come to full fruition at the very end of the tribulation: the national salvation of Israel. Israel will not experience a spiritual regeneration at this point, but will at least make the right connection in their minds that the Christ which the witnesses preached has been affirmed by God to be the legitimate Messiah they had formerly rejected. They will understand that it is the God of heaven who is in charge of the events of their day; a truth the rest of the world will not be so inclined to accept.

Worship of Antichrist

Among most of the hardened remainder of humanity, the complete opposite message is perceived, as Antichrist is instead elevated as one worthy of worship.

> ***Revelation 13:3-8***
> *³ One of the heads of the beast seemed to have had a fatal wound, but the fatal wound had been healed. The whole world was astonished and followed the beast. ⁴ Men worshiped the dragon because he had given authority to the beast, and they also worshiped the beast and asked, "Who is like the beast? Who can make war against him?"*
> *⁵ The beast was given a mouth to utter proud words and blasphemies and to exercise his authority for forty-two months. ⁶ He opened his mouth to blaspheme God, and to slander his name and his dwelling place and those who live in heaven. ⁷ He was given power to make war against the saints and to conquer them. And he was given authority over every tribe, people, language and nation. ⁸ All inhabitants of the earth will worship the beast--all whose names have not been written in the book of life belonging to the Lamb that was slain from the creation of the world.*

Because of his resurrection and the killing of the two prophets who could not be killed, men will begin to worship the beast (Antichrist) and the dragon (Satan) who gave power to the beast.

It should be clarified that up until this time, references to *"the Beast"* were oriented toward the global government of earth during the great tribulation. At this point in the book of Revelation, however, allusions to *the Beast* become personified into the person of Antichrist.

> *⁴ Men worshiped the dragon because he had given authority to the beast, and they also worshiped the beast and asked, "Who is like the beast? Who can make war against him?"*

At this point, the reference to the one-world government, or the Beast, are regarded as references to that government's head figure, Antichrist. Men say *"who can make war with him?"* while speaking of the power of

Chapter 4: The Middle of the Tribulation

the Beast, formerly symbolizing the government, but now with the understanding that their government is fully in Antichrist's control. He *is* the Beast. He is the head of authority which the defiled government operates under and receives all glory from his admiring kingdom.

In response, Antichrist absorbs his worship and begins uttering "*proud words and blasphemies*" and exercises *"his authority for forty-two months."* The reference to forty-two months informs the reader that the timeline is now centered in the middle of the tribulation period, for three and one half years remain of Antichrist's authority which will be destroyed with the coming of Christ and the end of the great tribulation.

In synopsis, the very middle of the tribulation will bring a great polarization among the inhabitants of the earth. The remnant in Israel will begin to recognize the Lord God as being in control of the cataclysmic events of the day, while the bulk of the earth- "*all whose names have not been written in the book of life*" -will give glory and their full allegiance to Antichrist.

This giving of glory and allegiance to Antichrist will take the form of direct Satanic worship, as the counterfeit christ program is proven highly successful among those who remain.

> *⁴ Men worshiped the dragon because he had given authority to the beast, and they also worshiped the beast and asked, "Who is like the beast? Who can make war against him?"*

No longer satisfied to reject the Lord's discipline, men now are instigated to literally subject their worship to Satan and his illicit son.

The Abomination of Desolation

Also at this point, perhaps that very day, the abomination of desolation observed earlier in Daniel and Matthew 24 will come to its fruition as Antichrist establishes himself officially as the fallacious God on earth.

Daniel 9:25-27
²⁵ "Know and understand this: From the issuing of the decree to restore and rebuild Jerusalem until the Anointed One, the ruler, comes, there will be seven 'sevens,' and sixty-two 'sevens.' It will be rebuilt with streets and a trench, but in times of trouble. ²⁶ After the sixty-two 'sevens,' the Anointed One will be cut off and will have nothing. The people of the ruler who will come will destroy the city and the sanctuary. The end will come like a flood: War will continue until the end, and desolations have been decreed. ²⁷ He will confirm a covenant with many for one 'seven.' In the middle of the 'seven' he will put an end to sacrifice and offering. And on a wing [of the temple] he will set up an abomination that causes desolation, until the end that is decreed is poured out on him".

The last "*seven*" of Daniels "*seventy sevens*" is the time period of the great tribulation, as earlier observed. Daniel states, "*in the middle of the seven, he will put an end to sacrifice and offering.*" Thus, the timing of the abomination of desolation lines up exactly at this point, in conjunction with Antichrist's realization of the worship of earth and Israel's realization of God's sovereignty on earth. Continuing the work of this divergence, Antichrist will begin a great persecution against Israel and the active pursuit of his own worship on earth. He will at this point end the worship practices of Israel by ceasing sacrificial offerings in the temple, which Israel will have been practicing.

As noted earlier, the temple ministry will have resumed and Israel will once again have taken up their former Old Testament practices of animal sacrifices to God. It should be noted that Israel's worship in the Old Testament vein is *false* worship, even though oriented toward the true God of Israel. While Israel rejected Christ as their messiah, they do continue to presume to worship the true God of heaven even today, though not in the way he has prescribed; via faith in Christ. Christ

Chapter 4: The Middle of the Tribulation

. . . .

fulfilled the sacrificial system.[50] Yet, Israel will have resumed worship in their former vein when the Temple is rebuilt. Those worship practices will be underway in the middle of the tribulation as Antichrist is raised and begins to receive his own worship at its highest level of zeal.

Verse 27 notes, " *on a wing [of the temple] he will set up an abomination that causes desolation, until the end that is decreed is poured out on him.*" The term "wing" indicates the highest point of the temple. It is at the highest and most prominent place, visible to all, that Antichrist will set up his abomination of desolation.

At this point a theological term commonly referred to as "the rule of double reference" should be examined. Double reference is an interpretational rule for biblical prophecy in which prophetic predictions are fulfilled at differing times but are described in a singular prophetical passage as if they were a singular event. J. Dwight Pentecost says it in this way:

> *"Two events, widely separated as to the time of their fulfillment, may be brought together into the scope of one prophecy. This was done because the prophet had a message for his own day as well as for a future time.*[51]*"*

The "*abomination of desolation*" is an example of this principle. An "abomination" is defined biblically as something which is loathsome and repulsive in God's sight. It could be an action which defiles that which should be holy, for example. In 166 BC, Antiochus Epiphanes halted temple worship and sacrificed a pig on the altar of the Temple, thus fulfilling Daniel's depiction of an "*abomination that causes desolation.*" Anyone living at that time would have understood Daniel's prophecy concerning the abomination of desolation to have been fulfilled by this action. Yet, another abomination of desolation can be noted in later

---

[50] Hebrews 10:1-18

[51] J. Dwight Pentecost, *Things To Come* [Grand Rapids: Zondervan Publishing House, 1964], p. 46.

history.

In 70 AD Titus Flavius Vespasianus destroyed the temple entirely; thus for all practical purposes, ending the Jewish-Roman War and destroying Israel as a nation. Prior to the destruction of the Temple he had erected his image inside it, as would be customary of a conquering leader of his day. His image being in the Temple would have been seen as a further abomination in the eyes of Israelites, who reserved the Temple as a completely holy piece of real estate dedicated to the Lord alone.

Daniel's concept of an abomination that causes desolation fits perfectly with both actions. Antiochus Epiphanes sacrificed a pig on the altar, and Titus established his own image in the Temple. Both of these events could be understood as the fulfillment of Daniel 9. Yet a problem remains. Jesus, in Matthew 24 quotes Daniel 9 in reference to a specific future event related to the end of the age.

> *Matthew 24: 3-16 "[3] As Jesus was sitting on the Mount of Olives, the disciples came to him privately. "Tell us," they said, "when will this happen, and what will be the sign of your coming and of the end of the age?"*
> *[4] Jesus answered: "Watch out that no one deceives you. [5] For many will come in my name, claiming, 'I am the Christ,' and will deceive many. [6] You will hear of wars and rumors of wars, but see to it that you are not alarmed. Such things must happen, but the end is still to come. [7] Nation will rise against nation, and kingdom against kingdom. There will be famines and earthquakes in various places. [8] All these are the beginning of birth pains.*
> *[9] "Then you will be handed over to be persecuted and put to death, and you will be hated by all nations because of me. [10] At that time many will turn away from the faith and will betray and hate each other, [11] and many false prophets will appear and deceive many people. [12] Because of the increase of wickedness, the love of most will grow cold, [13] but he who stands firm to*

Chapter 4: The Middle of the Tribulation

> *the end will be saved. [14] And this gospel of the kingdom will be preached in the whole world as a testimony to all nations, and then the end will come.*
> *[15] "So when you see standing in the holy place 'the abomination that causes desolation,' spoken of through the prophet Daniel--let the reader understand-- [16] then let those who are in Judea flee to the mountains.*

Jesus speaks after the time of Antiochus Epiphanes' sacrifice of a pig on the alter and *before* the destruction of the Temple by Titus. For this reason, a common view of groups such as Amillennialists, is that Jesus' prophecy in Matthew 24 was completely fulfilled by Titus Flavius. Even in that view, dual fulfillment is observed. Daniel's abomination of desolation was referencing the events of both Antiochus Epiphanes and Titus. Yet, that position omits a very important part of Matthew 24, which is the context from which Jesus spoke.

In verse 3, the question asked is, "*when will this happen, and what will be the sign of your coming and of the end of the age?*" Three questions are in fact being asked in the context of this conversation. The first question is "*when will this happen?*" "*This*" refers to the immediate context in which Jesus had just informed the disciples that the temple would be utterly destroyed. His answer is "*when you see standing in the holy place 'the abomination that causes desolation,' spoken of through the prophet Daniel--let the reader understand-- then let those who are in Judea flee to the mountains.*"

What is interesting about Jesus warning is that the generation to which Jesus spoke thought they *had already historically observed* the abomination of desolation. They understood the abomination of desolation to have referred to Antiochus Epiphanes' sacrificing of a pig on the altar. And, it was. But, it was *also* a warning to the generation to which Jesus spoke, that forty years later Titus would once again put an abomination of desolation in the temple. In this case, the law of double reference is observed. The prophecy of Daniel related to two different historical events, although it was written as if it were one event. Those who had formerly observed the perceived fulfillment of prophecy observed it again in another generation; a warning which was doubly referenced and doubly effective. That warning saved the lives of countless believers in the time of Titus' destruction of Israel. When Titus placed his image in the Temple, time was still ample for those who believed Jesus' warning to flee the city and the coming destruction.

While some believe the abomination of desolation to be now fulfilled with the second advent of the prophecy to have been fulfilled in the coming of Titus, there still remains a problem which indicates a still future and final fulfillment of the abomination of desolation.

Jesus' answer to that questions asked in Matthew 24 indicate that the abomination of desolation is an event which will signal his soon return.

> ***Matthew 24:4-25***
> *[4] Jesus answered: "Watch out that no one deceives you. [5] For many will come in my name, claiming, 'I am the Christ,' and will deceive many. [6] You will hear of wars and rumors of wars, but see to it that you are not alarmed. Such things must happen, but the end is still to come. [7] Nation will rise against nation, and kingdom against kingdom. There will be famines and earthquakes in various places. [8] All these are the beginning of birth pains. [9] "Then you will be handed over to be persecuted and put to death, and you will be hated by all nations because of me. [10] At that time many will turn away from the faith and will betray and hate each other, [11] and many false prophets will appear and deceive many people. [12] Because of the increase of wickedness, the love of most will grow cold, [13] but he who stands firm to the end will be saved. [14] And this gospel of the kingdom will be preached in the whole world as a testimony to all nations, and then the end will come. [15] "So when you see standing in the holy place 'the abomination that causes desolation,' spoken of through the prophet Daniel--let the reader understand-- [16] then let those who are in Judea flee to the mountains. [17] Let no one on the roof of*

Chapter 4: The Middle of the Tribulation

> *his house go down to take anything out of the house. [18] Let no one in the field go back to get his cloak. [19] How dreadful it will be in those days for pregnant women and nursing mothers! [20] Pray that your flight will not take place in winter or on the Sabbath. [21] For then there will be great distress, unequaled from the beginning of the world until now--and never to be equaled again. [22] If those days had not been cut short, no one would survive, but for the sake of the elect those days will be shortened. [23] At that time if anyone says to you, 'Look, here is the Christ!' or, 'There he is!' do not believe it. [24] For false Christs and false prophets will appear and perform great signs and miracles to deceive even the elect--if that were possible. [25] See, I have told you ahead of time.*

In verse 14 Jesus states "*this gospel of the kingdom will be preached in the whole world as a testimony to all nations, and then the end will come.*" This portion of Jesus warning clearly are geared toward the question "*what will be the signs of the end of the age.*" As noted earlier, the end of the age refers to the end of the age which will precede the next age; the age of Jesus' kingdom, which is the coming millennial kingdom. Jesus states a sign here that the gospel will be preached to the whole world; to every nation, as will be fulfilled by the ministry of the 144,000 evangelists and the ministry of the two witnesses.

Then, immediately following this sign, Jesus states, *[15]"So when you see standing in the holy place 'the abomination that causes desolation,' spoken of through the prophet Daniel--let the reader understand-- [16] then let those who are in Judea flee to the mountains."* Here, Jesus' warning is noted to follow the preaching of the gospel to the entire world; something which was *not* fulfilled prior to the destruction of the city in 70 AD, but *will* be fulfilled prior to the coming of the millennial kingdom. Thus, once again, dual reference is observed. In this case, perhaps "triple reference" is a fair term to describe Jesus' warning, as his warning has a third, yet future observation to be *completely* fulfilled. Each warning is valid, yet each references a different manifestation of the abomination of desolation. It references Antiochus Epiphanes sacrifice of a pig on the altar of the Temple. It references Titus'

establishment of his image in the Temple; a warning to Israelites to escape the city before it's destruction in 70 AD. And, it references the coming abomination of Antichrist, who will proclaim himself to be God prior to his campaign against Israel in the coming great tribulation.

Antiochus Epiphanes nor Titus completely fulfill Daniel's prophecy. It will be finally and completely fulfilled in the last seven, when Antichrist establishes *his* abomination in the Temple.

Another scriptural reference which helps to understand the nature of Antichrist's abomination of desolation is observed in 2 Thessalonians.

> ***2 Thessalonians 2:3-4***
> *³ Don't let anyone deceive you in any way, for that day will not come until the rebellion occurs and the man of lawlessness is revealed, the man doomed to destruction.*
> *⁴ He will oppose and will exalt himself over everything that is called God or is worshiped, so that he sets himself up in God's temple, proclaiming himself to be God.*

This picture of the man of lawlessness, or the Antichrist, setting himself up in God's temple and proclaiming himself to be God is a clear depiction of what Daniel would define as an abomination, and is the final fulfillment of Jesus' warning which concerns the very end of this age. A clear description of this final reference to the abomination of desolation, along with the ministry of the false prophet is given in detail in Revelation 13.

The False Prophet

In concert with Antichrist's establishing himself to be God arrives also the advent of the false prophet onto the stage of world events. He plays a great role in the deception which instigates men to worship Antichrist. Revelation 13 gives details concerning this individual.

Chapter 4: The Middle of the Tribulation

> ***Revelation 13:11-15***
> *[11] Then I saw another beast, coming out of the earth. He had two horns like a lamb, but he spoke like a dragon. [12] He exercised all the authority of the first beast on his behalf, and made the earth and its inhabitants worship the first beast, whose fatal wound had been healed. [13] And he performed great and miraculous signs, even causing fire to come down from heaven to earth in full view of men. [14] Because of the signs he was given power to do on behalf of the first beast, he deceived the inhabitants of the earth. He ordered them to set up an image in honor of the beast who was wounded by the sword and yet lived. [15] He was given power to give breath to the image of the first beast, so that it could speak and cause all who refused to worship the image to be killed.*

This description of the false prophet reveals that "*he had two horns like a lamb, but he spoke like a dragon.*" A lamb symbolically represents Christ himself in the book of Revelation throughout. The fact that the false prophet had horns "*like a lamb*" indicates that he was presented in some way likened unto Christ. This beast appeared "Christ-like" in fashion, as if he were a legitimate Christian leader. This Christ-like appearance is fitting unto the service of Antichrist, himself attempting to imitate the legitimate Christ. The false prophet, being in the service of Antichrist, continues the charade, having the appearance of a legitimate ambassador of Christ.

While appearing Christian, however, he is noted to speak "*like a dragon.*" Just as a lamb represents Christ in Revelation, so a dragon represents Satan and his kingdom throughout. The dragon, in Revelation, refers to the one-world government of the Antichrist, or the Antichrist himself. But, Antichrist is the agent of Satan, which the dragon represents on a larger scale. While this lamb appeared as a legitimate Christian leader, his words were not the words of Christ, but of Antichrist, Satan's false messiah. Satan's character of speech are revealed throughout scripture, having qualities of lying,[52] manipulating[53] and perverting truth.[54] The general description of the false prophet, then, is one of a deceiver. He appears legitimate, like a lamb, but speaks deceitful lies on behalf of the Antichrist. He pretends to be righteous, but is in fact an agent of Satan himself.[55]

Verse 12 indicates his purpose in Satan's campaign in that *"he exercised all the authority of the first beast on his behalf."* The false prophet is an agent of Antichrist, speaking and acting on his behalf. The use of that authority was clearly aimed, however, at inspiring the inhabitants of the earth to worship Antichrist. Verse 12 stipulates that the false prophet *"made the earth and its inhabitants worship the first beast, whose fatal wound had been healed."* His role, then, was to use Antichrist's authority to inspire the earth to worship Antichrist.

All descriptions of the false prophet in this text lead one to understand that his purpose is to round out Satan's counterfeit trinity by emulating the workings of the Holy Spirit. Just as the legitimate Holy Spirit entices true believers to worship the true God through Christ, so this counterfeit Holy Spirit entices non-believers to worship Antichrist, the false Christ. There is now a counterfeit father, Satan, a counterfeit son, the Antichrist and a counterfeit holy spirit, the false prophet.

Verse 13 states that he *"performed great and miraculous signs, even causing fire to come down from heaven to earth in full view of men."* Through these signs, verse 14 reveals that he was able to deceive the inhabitants of earth. Throughout the tribulation, Satan and his agents use miracles to deceive the inhabitants of earth, further fulfilling the prophecy of 2 Thessalonians 2:9-10.

> *"The coming of the lawless one will be in accordance*

---

[52] John 8:44
[53] 2 Cor 2:11
[54] Mat 4:6
[55] 2 Cor 11:14

Chapter 4: The Middle of the Tribulation

> *with the work of Satan displayed in all kinds of counterfeit miracles, signs and wonders, [10] and in every sort of evil that deceives those who are perishing."*

Revelation 13:14-15 states,

> *He ordered them to set up an image in honor of the beast who was wounded by the sword and yet lived. [15] He was given power to give breath to the image of the first beast, so that it could speak and cause all who refused to worship the image to be killed.*

To fulfill his role as a counterfeit Holy Spirit, the false prophet will order an image of the beast to be set up that Antichrist may be worshiped through it. This is the completion of the fulfillment of the abomination of desolation of which Jesus warned.

> **Daniel 9:27**
> [27] *He will confirm a covenant with many for one 'seven.' In the middle of the 'seven' he will put an end to sacrifice and offering. And on a wing [of the temple] he will set up an abomination that causes desolation, until the end that is decreed is poured out on him".*

Daniel 9:27 notes that Antichrist will set up an image of himself, but Revelation 13:14 indicates that he does so through the false prophet, who has been given his authority and acts in his stead.

The image which was set up is confirmed in Revelation 13 to be a supernatural idol, or image, fitting perfectly the idea of an "*abomination.*" Verse 15 notes that the false prophet was given power to give "*breath*" to the image so that it could speak, and so that it could kill those who refused to worship it. The word translated "*breath*" is the Greek word *pneuma,* or "spirit." This image is not a common idol, but is indwelled by a living spirit. The lucid deduction of this language is that the image is controlled by a demonic entity itself, a spirit which causes it to speak and which brings death upon those who refuse to worship it.

2 Thessalonians 2:4 says of Antichrist, that *"he sets himself up in God's temple, proclaiming himself to be God."* The false prophet, who does the Antichrist's will, was "*given power to give breath to the image...so that it could speak.*" Thus, Antichrist's will is carried out vicariously through the false prophet.

The Mark of the Beast

Revelation 13:16-18 continues,

> *[16] He also forced everyone, small and great, rich and poor, free and slave, to receive a mark on his right hand or on his forehead, [17] so that no one could buy or sell unless he had the mark, which is the name of the beast or the number of his name.*
> *[18] This calls for wisdom. If anyone has insight, let him calculate the number of the beast, for it is man's number. His number is 666.*

Not only is there a counterfeit Father, Son, Holy Spirit, and Church, but there is a counterfeit "seal" on the heads of the disciples of the counterfeit trinity. As the Holy Spirit is the seal of disciples of Christ, so is the infamous "mark of the Beast" a seal upon the heads of the disciples of Antichrist. This mark is forced upon all on the earth by means of economic sanctions. No one is permitted to conduct business without this mark.

About the mark

This marking will be placed on the right hand or on the forehead and will be given to all who subject themselves to the Antichrist. Noticeably from verse 15, anyone who refused the mark would be refusing to worship the Beast and would be killed. Ostensibly, then, everyone within the confines of organized society will receive this mark out of necessity. It will be compulsory to have the mark in order to conduct the usual business of life and will be a death sentence to live one's life in

Chapter 4: The Middle of the Tribulation

public while *not* having the mark.

Many have presumed wild and sensational theories about what exactly this mark entails. The text, however, clearly states that this mark will serve in some way similar to a business permit which the government of Antichrist will enforce on all business transactions.

A common presumption is that this mark will somehow be connected with credit cards or banking systems. While there is nothing in the text that confirms this, there is neither anything that denies this possibility. As pure speculation, it very well could be that a magnetic strip, or something similar to the popular Mondex chip, could be implanted in such a way as to provide this mark. It *could* be that this mark will contain banking information as do current ATM cards or credit cards, as well as medical charts, etc. Yet, it cannot be known with any certainty if this will be the case or not. What *is* clear from the text is that a failure to receive the mark will serve as an utter detriment to buying or selling. Failure to receive it will result in certain death, either by the hand of Antichrist or by starvation as a result of not being able to purchase food, which will be in critically scarce supply as it is.

Interpreting the Mark

Verse 18 notes that wisdom is necessary to interpret the mark. Several clues are given which will lend themselves to the wisdom to do just that.

The first clue is that the mark is "the name of the Beast." Thus, if the mark is interpreted properly, it will yield the name of Antichrist.

Additionally, the mark is said to be "the number of the Beast," "the number of his name" and "the number of a man." It is logical that the number of the Beast is the number of a man, since Antichrist, while being a hybrid angelic/human being, will be in appearance, at least, "a man." Each other clue indicates that the number is tied to his identity. The number "is 666."

With wisdom, then, using the number 666 one can confirm the identity of

Antichrist, since it is the "*number of his name*," which is the biggest clue of the text.

John, being Jewish, would almost certainly have understood "*the number of his name*" to indicate a numerical value which would be obtained from the spelling of Antichrist's name.

Hebrew letters are inherently assigned numerical values. John, being Jewish, would have known this, of course, and would have assumed that much of his readership would know this truth. By merit of each letter having a numerical value, the value of a word, or "*the number of his name*," can be determined by calculating the sum represented by each letter in the word. Thus, the sum of the values of each letter in Antichrist's name will equal 666.

It is difficult to put this phenomenon into practice when spelling words (or names) from other languages due to the fact that the Hebrew alphabet does not align with other alphabets perfectly. But, any name could be transliterated into Hebrew, theoretically, and the "*number of his name*" obtained. This statement, then, indicates that the name of Antichrist, if spelled out in Hebrew letters, would equal 666, "*the number of his name.*"

Many names can numerically equal 666 in Hebrew, however, so it is impossible to determine this name in advance. But, when the time comes, and one exhibits the qualities of Antichrist described in scripture, his name can in fact be calculated by those with the intelligence to accurately do so. (v.18- *If anyone has insight, let him calculate the number of the beast*)

It should be noted that commonly all manners of persons are accused of having the number of the Beast as their name. A simple query of an internet search engine will yield hundreds of world leaders being inaccurately "demonstrated" to be Antichrist by merit of creative and sometimes downright humorous numerological devices. John would not have entertained any understanding for the "*number of his name*" other

Chapter 4: The Middle of the Tribulation

than the direct correlation of the Hebrew alphabet. There are 22 letters in the Hebrew alphabet. The numbers associated with them, in order, are 1, 2, 3, 4, 5, 6, 7, 8, 9, 10, 20, 30, 40, 50, 60, 70, 80, 90, 100, 200, 300, and 400. Using only transliterated *Hebrew* letters and simple addition then, one can associate a name with "*the number*" of one's name. Jesus' Hebrew number was 749. The author's name uses letters which are not available in the Hebrew alphabet and must be omitted. To the best of his limited knowledge, his number is 587. The dynamics of this system demand that there surely exist numerous people whose names will equal 666. They are certainly not *all* the Antichrist! The purposes of the inclusion of the number of his name are demonstrated in the text, that "*If anyone has insight, let him calculate the number of the beast.*"

At the time Antichrist arrives on the scene of history, enough information should be available to affirm one who necessarily meets the numerous other criteria to be the Antichrist. Yet, when that time does arrive, one who has insight will be able to positively confirm the identity of Antichrist using this method, assuming he meets all other criteria.

The Breaking of the Seven Year Covenant

The defining event by which the exact middle of the tribulation is calculated is the breaking of the seven year covenant. Daniel 9:27 states,

> *²⁷ He will confirm a covenant with many for one 'seven.' In the middle of the 'seven' he will put an end to sacrifice and offering. And on a wing [of the temple] he will set up an abomination that causes desolation, until the end that is decreed is poured out on him."*

As Daniel's seventy sevens were discussed earlier, this covenant was noted as one which Antichrist will make with Israel. Daniel's book was written to Israel, so when he writes that Antichrist will "*confirm a covenant with many,*" he speaks necessarily of Israel, though other nations may also be involved. Likewise, the breaking of that covenant is shown to impact Israel specifically, by Antichrist halting sacrifices in the

Temple, which affirms that the covenant is a covenant specifically involving Israel.

The text determines that the covenant will be broken in the middle of the "seven" - or at the mid-point of the tribulation. The breaking of the covenant- at least as far as it concerns Israel- then, is the event which centers directly in the middle of the tribulation.

Daniel 11:40-45 details Antichrist's war with the three kings he will overturn as was noted in chapter 1. Verse 41 says *"he will also invade the beautiful land,"* which is Israel. The invasion of Israel is certainly an act of aggression which will render the covenant null and void. The nature of the covenant is not expressed as to its content in Daniel 9, but it is certainly logical to conclude that any covenant would have to be broken for one to invade and make war with a nation he had formerly made a covenant with. Isaiah 28 does give specific analysis of the covenant content, however, to demonstrate specifically that an act of aggression would halt it. This invasion of Antichrist in Daniel is in conjunction with his annulment of his treaty with Israel. He will invade Israel, cease sacrifices in the temple and establish himself as God in Israel's temple. It is the author's opinion that these events will happen in rapid succession, initiating the mid-point of the tribulation perhaps all within a day or days.

Isaiah 28:15-18 demonstrates more fully the nature of this covenant.

> *[15] You boast, "We have entered into a covenant with death,*
> *with the grave we have made an agreement.*
> *When an overwhelming scourge sweeps by,*
> *it cannot touch us,*
> *for we have made a lie our refuge*
> *and falsehood our hiding place."*
> *[16] So this is what the Sovereign LORD says:*
> *"See, I lay a stone in Zion, a tested stone,*
> *a precious cornerstone for a sure foundation;*
> *the one who trusts will never be dismayed.*

Chapter 4: The Middle of the Tribulation

> *17 I will make justice the measuring line*
> *and righteousness the plumb line;*
> *hail will sweep away your refuge, the lie,*
> *and water will overflow your hiding place.*
> *18 Your covenant with death will be annulled;*
> *your agreement with the grave will not stand.*
> *When the overwhelming scourge sweeps by,*
> *you will be beaten down by it.*

It is clear that Israel will enter into this covenant for the purposes of assuring her safety in the very volatile political system of the world in that time. It is also plain in the text that God will be angry for her having rejected the "stone" he provided for her safety (Christ) and having instead made a covenant with "death" (Antichrist). Israel, having rejected her legitimate King, will have fallen into the very trap Satan has set with the advent of Antichrist. She will have turned to the false christ for her protection rather than the true Christ, her rightful King.

God informs Israel in verse 18 that she will indeed fall and that her covenant with death will be annulled. Indeed, Antichrist will plunder Israel and Jesus' warning from Matthew 24 (below) will clearly be understood.

The breaking of this covenant is best understood from what will transpire after Antichrist's invasion of Israel; notably his unrelenting persecution of Israel from that point onward until the return of Christ. It is painfully obvious that Satan's plans for Antichrist's covenant with Israel were always for her destruction; by luring her into a sense of false security with the rising star of the world government promising her safety.

The Persecution of the Jews

In conjunction with Antichrist's breaking of the treaty, then, he will begin an assault on the nation with a formidable vengeance.

Matthew 24:15-28 gives insight into this persecution.[56]

> [15] "So when you see standing in the holy place 'the abomination that causes desolation,' spoken of through the prophet Daniel--let the reader understand-- [16] then let those who are in Judea flee to the mountains. [17] Let no one on the roof of his house go down to take anything out of the house. [18] Let no one in the field go back to get his cloak. [19] How dreadful it will be in those days for pregnant women and nursing mothers! [20] Pray that your flight will not take place in winter or on the Sabbath. [21] For then there will be great distress, unequaled from the beginning of the world until now--and never to be equaled again. [22] If those days had not been cut short, no one would survive, but for the sake of the elect those days will be shortened. [23] At that time if anyone says to you, 'Look, here is the Christ!' or, 'There he is!' do not believe it. [24] For false Christs and false prophets will appear and perform great signs and miracles to deceive even the elect--if that were possible. [25] See, I have told you ahead of time.
>
> [26] "So if anyone tells you, 'There he is, out in the desert,' do not go out; or, 'Here he is, in the inner rooms,' do not believe it. [27] For as lightning that comes from the east is visible even in the west, so will be the coming of the Son of Man. [28] Wherever there is a carcass, there the vultures will gather.

As was noted earlier, this text is Jesus' response to the question *"what will be the sign of your coming and of the end of the age?" (Matthew 24:3)*

The warning to Israelite believers is that at the moment of the abomination of desolation, or Antichrist's establishing himself as God in

---

[56] See parallel passages also in Mark 13 and Luke 17

Chapter 4: The Middle of the Tribulation

the temple, they are to take immediate flight out of the country. They are not to turn back for their coat or to take anything out of their homes. They are simply to go quickly out of the city. They are also told to pray that this event does not happen in the winter or on the Sabbath.

In Israel, on the Sabbath there is no public transportation available. The Arabs took advantage of this knowledge in the Yom Kippur War of 1973. By attacking on Yom Kippur, a Holy day, it was very difficult to get Israeli forces to the battle lines.

In the Winter, their path to the mountains in the East, where Jesus tells them to go, will be treacherous due to flash floods. Israel receives almost all of its rain in the Winter months, which create flash floods in the numerous small valleys throughout the mountainous region. Their path through the mountains would take them through dry river beds which could instantly fill with water during these months due to these floods.

While Israel as a whole would fail to consider the words of Christ in Matthew, being that she has rejected him as her King, there is a growing remnant of believers in Israel, particularly beginning at this mid-point of the tribulation. Some, who *do* trust Christ, will heed his words. Those elect will find protection from his warning, while the disobedient will remain in the city for a national purging which will be detailed later in this work.

Revelation 12 gives more detail about this flight of Israel.

> ***Revelation 12:1-6***
> *¹ A great and wondrous sign appeared in heaven: a woman clothed with the sun, with the moon under her feet and a crown of twelve stars on her head. ² She was pregnant and cried out in pain as she was about to give birth. ³ Then another sign appeared in heaven: an enormous red dragon with seven heads and ten horns and seven crowns on his heads. ⁴ His tail swept a third of the stars out of the sky and flung them to the earth. The*

> *dragon stood in front of the woman who was about to give birth, so that he might devour her child the moment it was born. ⁵ She gave birth to a son, a male child, who will rule all the nations with an iron scepter. And her child was snatched up to God and to his throne. ⁶ The woman fled into the desert to a place prepared for her by God, where she might be taken care of for 1,260 days.*

The vision of Revelation 12 is a picture from world history. It is important to remember that the visions of the book of Revelation are of what John *saw* in his vision, and not necessarily a literal time-line of human history. His visions at times may reflect things from ancient history and at times reveal a contextual process of a future timeline. The timing of what John saw is deciphered from the context.

John sees a woman "*clothed with the sun, with the moon under her feet, and a crown of twelve stars on her head.*" While many have presumed all manners of speculation concerning this part of John's vision, such speculation is unnecessary, for the details of this vision are mentioned elsewhere in scripture. When the Bible uses symbolic language which was used elsewhere in scripture, one should seek no additional interpretation from the secondary reference in most cases, but should understand the use of symbolism to be consistent with former references. In this case, the interpretation of the symbols describing the woman is clearly seen from the book of Genesis, where the sun, moon and twelve stars are explained.

> ***Genesis 37:9-11***
> *⁹ Then he had another dream, and he told it to his brothers. "Listen," he said, "I had another dream, and this time the sun and moon and eleven stars were bowing down to me." ¹⁰ When he told his father as well as his brothers, his father rebuked him and said, "What is this dream you had? Will your mother and I and your brothers actually come and bow down to the ground before you?" ¹¹ His brothers were jealous of him, but his father kept the matter in mind.*

Chapter 4: The Middle of the Tribulation

Genesis 37 details a dream of Joseph. Verse 10 is clear as to the substance of the symbolism regarding the sun, moon and twelve stars. Explained in the text is that Joseph's father and mother are who are referred to as the "sun and moon." His father, Jacob, explain the symbolism plainly, *"will your mother and I and your brothers actually come and bow down to the ground before you?"* Clearly the heavenly bodies in the dream represented Jacob's family. The sun and moon are his parents, while the twelve stars are the twelve sons.

Joseph is one of the twelve stars, with the other eleven bowing to him in his dream being his brothers. Jacob was later renamed "Israel" and is the father of the nation of Israel, with his sons being the heads of the twelve tribes of Israel.

This woman clothed in the sun, with the moon under her feet and a crown of twelve stars on her head, represents the fullness of Jacob's family; the nation of Israel. Every family member from the earlier use of the symbol is represented in John's vision.

The nation of Israel, then, is about to give birth to a son in John's vision. Israel's "*son,*" "*who will rule all the nations with an iron scepter*" can be none other than Jesus. The same language is used in Psalm 2 concerning Messiah.

> **Psalm 2:6-9**
> ⁶ *"I have installed my King on Zion, my holy hill."* ⁷ *I will proclaim the decree of the Lord: He said to me, "You are my Son; today I have become your Father.* ⁸ *Ask of me, and I will make the nations your inheritance, the ends of the earth your possession.* ⁹ *You will rule them with an iron scepter; you will dash them to pieces like pottery."*

The son, or Christ, is "*snatched up to God and to his throne,*" which, of course, depicts Jesus' historical resurrection and ascension.

As noted earlier, the term "*dragon*" is almost always symbolic of Satan throughout scripture. Yet, in Revelation is revealed a dragon, who is also representative of Satan, but more specifically, the government of Antichrist, to whom Satan gave his authority. This dragon of Revelation 12 is described in the similar terms to those which the one-world government of Daniel is described. It has seven heads, ten horns, and seven crowns on his heads.

In verse 4, prior to the time the woman was to give birth, the dragon and one-third of the *"stars"* are swept out of the sky. Once again, stars, when used symbolically in scripture, almost always represent angels unless another interpretation is given. One exception is Joseph's dream, as was just mentioned. However, the exception in the use of the metaphorical stars was explained in the text which used it.

Understanding stars to be representative of angels, then, these stars would refer the demonic hosts who followed Satan in his rebellion against God prior to the creation of man.

Satan Pursues Israel

Verse 4 notes the dragon is seeking to devour the child when he is born. This attempt to destroy the person and ministry of Christ is seen throughout the New Testament. Satan attempted to kill Jesus at birth using Herod's decree to kill young Israeli males. He attempted to get Jesus to worship him in Matthew 4 and he attempted to discredit Jesus throughout his ministry. Satan additionally had attempted to kill Jesus many times before his appointed time, as is demonstrated in this minihistory lesson of Revelation 12.

In the end, Satan failed at that mission. Though Jesus was crucified, he was killed within the perfect timing and completion of the ministry which the Father had intended. He then was resurrected and *"snatched up"* to the Father. It is at this point that the persecution of Israel is identified. V6 says, *"The woman fled into the desert to a place prepared for her by God, where she might be taken care of for 1,260 days."* This is a key part of this text in indicating the persecution of Israel which Jesus warned about in Matthew 24:9. The woman (Israel) flees (the dragon) for 1,260 days (3 ½ years). This timeline refers to the second

Chapter 4: The Middle of the Tribulation

half of the tribulation, when as Jesus warned, Israel should flee upon the observation of the abomination of desolation to a place "*prepared for her by God.*" Those in Israel who will heed Christ's warning will be spared in that special location.

Next in Revelation 12 is detailed a war in Heaven.

> **Revelation 12:7-9**
> ⁷ *And there was war in heaven. Michael and his angels fought against the dragon, and the dragon and his angels fought back.* ⁸ *But he was not strong enough, and they lost their place in heaven.* ⁹ *The great dragon was hurled down--that ancient serpent called the devil, or Satan, who leads the whole world astray. He was hurled to the earth, and his angels with him.*

The conclusion of this war is that Satan is hurled to the earth. As to the timing of this war, some believe this to be a reference backward historically to Satan's original ousting from Heaven, some believe he returns to Heaven at this time in history to make war and some believe that Satan's abode was uniquely in the heavenly realms rather than earth prior to this event.

The key distinction between views is the interpretation of the term "heaven." Heaven, translated from the Greek term *ouranos,* can refer to the sky, outer space, or Heaven proper; God's home. If *ouranos* refers to Heaven proper in this text, then it would make sense to consider this a historical reference to Satan's fall, for at some distance past time he was in fact removed from Heaven proper because of his sin.[57] If, however, *ouranos* refers to the skies and/or outer space, then the text would indicate that Satan is to be relegated to the physical earth for the remainder of history. As such, the text would be understood to be saying "there was a war *in the skies"* and Satan and his angels lost their place, being hurled to the earth, no longer allowed to enter the skies, or

---

[57] Ezekiel 28:16

heavens.

This is the most logical explanation, because the continuation of the text uses this "grounding" of the dragon as an excuse for him to pursue the woman. This response does not fit the idea of the war in heaven being relegated to distant history, but rather a new event which is tied into the story.

Revelation 12 continues the timeline, indicating that the dragon's realization of his bondage to earth led him to pursue Israel and increase persecution against her.

> ***Revelation 12:13-17***
> [13] *When the dragon saw that he had been hurled to the earth, he pursued the woman who had given birth to the male child.* [14] *The woman was given the two wings of a great eagle, so that she might fly to the place prepared for her in the desert, where she would be taken care of for a time, times and half a time, out of the serpent's reach.* [15] *Then from his mouth the serpent spewed water like a river, to overtake the woman and sweep her away with the torrent.* [16] *But the earth helped the woman by opening its mouth and swallowing the river that the dragon had spewed out of his mouth.* [17] *Then the dragon was enraged at the woman and went off to make war against the rest of her offspring--those who obey God's commandments and hold to the testimony of Jesus.*

At this point in John's vision, the dragon, having lost the opportunity to devour the child and being confined to the earth now pursues the woman (Israel) to make war with her and to destroy her. In the tribulation, Satan's desire is the utter destruction of Israel, as the people of Christ and God's chosen nation to reveal himself to the world.

Consequently, it should be one's understanding that Satan's persecution of Israel, like other events in the tribulation, are at God's pleasure and purpose. It will be demonstrated in chapter six that Israel is in fact being

Chapter 4: The Middle of the Tribulation

subject to God's own program. His desire is to purge Israel and prepare her to call on her King. Once again, these days are called "the day of the Lord" in scripture rather than the day of Satan. While Satan will have his own agenda, that agenda is being allowed only insomuch as it accomplishes God's own purposes; for it is *his* day. Satan's deception of the nations is part of God's own wrath being poured out upon the earth. His persecution of Israel plays a key role in God's purging of Israel of those who will refuse their King.

Thus, it is important to note the irony that some Jews will continue to follow Antichrist, but it is also pertinent to note that Israel gave glory to God at the resurrection of the two witnesses. There is the beginning of a polarization in Israel at this time, and some are turning to Christ and trusting him as their legitimate King. These are the ones who will listen to Jesus' words in Matthew 24 and will flee to the place where God will provide refuge for them. The remainder will endure a purging which will turn even more to their King while destroying those who refuse to repent. The great persecution against Israel is now beginning to peak with the control of the world's governments firmly in Satan's hands. He will attempt to literally destroy Israel in its entirety, yet will fail, as God's purging program in Israel will complete and one third of the remaining nation will be saved. Chapter six will observe this process in detail.

Israel's Flight

As to the flight of Israel, several statements are made which point to a special provision for those who *do* trust Christ and who listen to his warning to flee the country. Verse 14 notes,

> *"the woman was given the two wings of a great eagle, so that she might fly to the place prepared for her in the desert, where she would be taken care of for a time, times and half a time, out of the serpent's reach."*

"Time, times and half a time" refer to the remaining three and one half years of the tribulation. Thus, the elect of Israel who flee at the middle of the tribulation will be protected for the entirety of the remaining tribulation season. The location of this prepared place is foreshadowed in Daniel's prophecy. Daniel 11:41, describing Antichrist's mid-tribulational attack on Israel, states,

> *"he will also invade the Beautiful Land. Many countries will fall, but Edom, Moab and the leaders of Ammon will be delivered from his hand."*

Edom, Moab and Ammon are spared from Antichrist's domination. They are not conquered, but are delivered from Antichrist. Effectively, the entire world is controlled by Antichrist, yet he is unable to establish a stronghold in these three ancient lands. Jesus tells Israel in Matthew 24 to flee to the mountains when the abomination of desolation is observed. The clear point of Jesus' warning is for his followers to get out of the country. To flee to the mountains, in pursuit of leaving the country, will send his followers East, toward Jordan, the nearest exit from the country. In Jordan exist all three of the ancient tribal areas of Edom, Moab and Ammon.

Likewise, Revelation 12 states that the woman will flee to the wilderness. Specifically, she will flee to a place "*prepared*" for her. It is now clear that God will spare Edom, Moab and Ammon from Antichrist's authority because he has directed the elect of Israel to flee there to be protected from the pursuit of the dragon during Antichrist's war on Israel. Once again, God issues special protection concerning his elect. While there will be Christian martyrs during the tribulation, there are also numerous events which particularly will protect the saints from God's wrath. The rapture removes the church before God's program of wrath begins. The 144,000 ministers are sealed for their protection during the trumpet judgments. The demons invading during the first woe judgment (or the fifth trumpet judgment) were only allowed to harm the lost. And in Israel, those who were prepared to trust Christ will heed his warning to exit the country and be spared from Antichrist's war. They will be protected in Jordan, out of Antichrist's reach.

Chapter 4: The Middle of the Tribulation

Chapter 5: The Second Half of the Tribulation

Continuing in the understanding that the great tribulation is the *day of the Lord,* rather than the "day of Satan," the judgments of the second half have in some cases a uniquely demonic influence. Yet, it is clear that the tribulation is God's wrath being poured out on earth, and God's grace being offered through that wrath as a last opportunity for people to accept his salvation offer through Christ. He remains in control throughout all events of this great and dreadful day of the Lord.

However, it becomes increasingly clear through any study of eschatology that Satan has his own program's agenda in play as well. But Satan is allowed to conduct his program only within the parameters of God's control. God has foretold his permission for Satan's actions by the very fact of the inclusion of Satan's work in the prophetic writings. God is warning the readers of prophetic literature that Satan will be given an opportunity during the great tribulation to attempt his own program and bring great destruction of his own. This warning, and God's allowing of Satan's great campaign of deception demonstrates God's two-fold purpose in the tribulation. He is calling sinners to repentance, yet exercising immediate judgment on the earth in the process. Those who will hear the voice of God should attentively heed the warnings of scripture that Satan will be conducting a very successful crusade in deception, attempting to proclaim his own false messiah as the King of Kings.

The second half of the great tribulation seems to carry a heavier burden for those who choose to continue to reject God's call to repentance. While repentance is observed in the second half of the tribulation, it seems more centered around Israel than the Gentile nations, while the repentance noticed in the first half seems largely Gentile oriented. Corporately, though, those who reject the gospel message of the witnesses and 144,000 evangelists will endure more severe judgment in

Chapter 5: The Second Half of the Tribulation

the second half. They will also appear to be yet more determined to be rebellious in clinging to their sin.

In the first half, six of the seven trumpet judgments were observed. It appears that the seventh trumpet judgment will occur in the second half. The seventh trumpet judgment, like the seventh seal judgment, will be a series of new judgments: the bowl judgments.

The First Six Bowl Judgments

The first Bowl Judgment:

> ***Revelation 16:1-2***
> *¹ Then I heard a loud voice from the temple saying to the seven angels, "Go, pour out the seven bowls of God's wrath on the earth."*
> *² The first angel went and poured out his bowl on the land, and ugly and painful sores broke out on the people who had the mark of the beast and worshiped his image.*

The first bowl judgment is pointed solely at those who have received the mark of the Beast. Yet again, a judgment is given which only affects people *"who had the mark of the beast and worshiped his image."* This fact continues to lend understanding to the inhabitants of earth that God is in control of these severe events. He has drawn a line between those who have pledged themselves to Antichrist and those who have not. This judgment demonstrates God's wrathful purpose in the tribulation. He will pour this judgment only upon those who have clearly rejected his grace.

Yet, the purpose of redemption is also observed in this judgment, as God protects all of those who have *not* taken the mark of the Beast. Those who have not received the mark will not only include *Christians*, but also those who are not believers, yet have chosen to not receive the mark and pledge their allegiance to Antichrist. This could most simply be understood as an "undecided" group. To these who have not affirmatively sworn their loyalty to Antichrist, God will continue to demonstrate his grace and give them incentive to follow him rather than Antichrist by merit of sparing them from this very painful judgment.

The nature of this judgment is that they will receive *"ugly and painful sores"* which sounds as something akin to skin ulcers or perhaps some sort of skin disease. The fact that the sores are described as *"ugly"* indicates that they are clearly visible, which will help people to properly discern that only those with the mark of the Beast are afflicted with this plague.

The second Bowl Judgment:

> ***Revelation 16:3***
> *³ The second angel poured out his bowl on the sea, and it turned into blood like that of a dead man, and every living thing in the sea died.*

In the second Trumpet Judgment, one-third of the salt water is destroyed. In this, the second Bowl Judgment, the remainder of the sea will be turned to blood, and every living thing in the sea will die.

The question was posed in chapter three, "is this literal or figurative blood?" Arguments can be made either way, of course. On one hand, one must remember that in the book of Revelation, John is simply following the instructions given to him in Revelation 1:11, "*Write on a scroll what you see and send it to the seven churches.*" John is writing what he sees. He is not attempting to explain things nor to give commentary. An argument for the blood being figurative is that fact. John sees blood, so he reports it. And, John writes down everything he sees from the lens of a first century man. Perhaps some things he sees are beyond his first century world-view, such as the ability of the entire world to observe the deaths of the two witnesses, or to discern between

Chapter 5: The Second Half of the Tribulation

literal blood or another phenomenon. While such things are not incredible to us, they very well may have seemed so to John. He faithfully reports what he sees. In this figurative view, the blood could be a red tide or some other sort of global environmental disaster of unknown origins.

On the other hand is the author's view, is that the blood is literal. While the arguments for figurative blood are valid, a further clue to the nature of this blood is given in the report concerning the third trumpet judgment, which will be discussed shortly.

The end result of the seas turning to blood is exceptionally clear in the text, however. All life in the sea will die. Whether literal or figurative, this blood which John reports will bring upon the earth the most formidable judgment perhaps that has been revealed up to this point; an utterly dead oceanic system. It is hard to imagine a world with absolutely no sea life available. The destruction of one third of all sea life in the second trumpet judgment would have severely affected the lives of millions. But the destruction of all sea life in the second bowl judgment will be catastrophic. All sources of food and commerce related to the sea will be immediately eliminated.

Jean-Michel Cousteau's "Ocean Futures Society" reported in 2005 that oceanic income was well over $40 Billion per year *in California alone*, accounting for some 480,000 jobs.[58] A world-wide oceanic catastrophe would further devastate the global economy and create food shortages of extreme magnitudes.

The third Bowl Judgment:

Revelation 16:4-7

---

[58] http://www.sfgate.com/cgi-bin/article.cgi?f=/n/a/2005/07/23/financial/f213532D37.DTL&hw=ocean&sn=002&sc=972

> *⁴ The third angel poured out his bowl on the rivers and springs of water, and they became blood. ⁵ Then I heard the angel in charge of the waters say:*
> *"You are just in these judgments,*
> *   you who are and who were, the Holy One,*
> *   because you have so judged;*
> *⁶ for they have shed the blood of your saints and prophets,*
> *   and you have given them blood to drink as they deserve."*
> *⁷ And I heard the altar respond:*
> *"Yes, Lord God Almighty,*
> *   true and just are your judgments."*

Just as a similarity exists between the second trumpet judgment and the second bowl judgment, so one exists between the third trumpet and bowl judgments. It seems in several cases that the bowl judgments will complete the work begun in the trumpet judgments. In the third Trumpet Judgment, one-third of the fresh water streams were destroyed, while in the third Bowl Judgment, all remaining rivers and streams of fresh water are turned to blood. At this point, all seawater, and all moving freshwater streams are utterly destroyed. It seems incomprehensible that the earth could continue to sustain life in such circumstances, but life will be sustained. Even with the great magnitude of destroyed waters, there will still be fresh water sources on the earth in the underground water table and still bodies of water, such as lakes and ponds.

This continuation of the blood judgments brings a declaration of an angel which helps to establish the purpose of the unique nature of the blood judgments, and also confirms that the blood of these judgments is literal in nature rather than figurative. The angel states in verse 6 that God's judgments are just,

> *⁶ for they have shed the blood of your saints and prophets, and you have given them blood to drink as they deserve."*

Chapter 5: The Second Half of the Tribulation

When interpreting a text, an important distinction to make is that terms in that text will be used either literally or figuratively *throughout* the text. Clearly, the angel proclaims a literal shedding of the blood of the saints, as during the tribulation much bloodshed against the saints will be administered. This angel then speaks of the return of that literal blood to the earth, *"you have given them blood to drink as they deserve."*

In the end, a debate over the literal or figurative blood is without serious consequence. The results are the same. And, it is no more miraculous for God to turn the seas, streams and rivers of earth to literal blood than it is to turn them into some other concoction which this blood may figuratively represent. Either way, God has caused it, and the results will be absolutely devastating.

The fourth Bowl Judgment:

> **Revelation 16:8-9**
> *⁸ The fourth angel poured out his bowl on the sun, and the sun was given power to scorch people with fire.*
> *⁹ They were seared by the intense heat and they cursed the name of God, who had control over these plagues, but they refused to repent and glorify him.*

The fourth Trumpet Judgment destroyed one-third of the light source of the sun. The fourth Bowl Judgment will cause the sun to have intense heat that will *"scorch people with fire."* While this judgment affects people's bodies directly, the assurance of protection of the saints of God on earth is not specifically given as it was concerning the painful sores of the first bowl. Indeed, numerous of the tribulation judgments will affect everyone who lives on earth in some way. Everyone will be impacted by the lack of food, water and surely by the intense heat of the sun as well.

Ironically, in the intensity of the bowl judgments, men demonstrate themselves to be fully aware of their source. *"They cursed the name of God, who had control over these plagues, but they refused to repent and glorify him."* Rather than to recognize the *purpose* of judgment when it is given and repent, as Israel began to do after the resurrection of the two witnesses, man will utterly recognize God's judgment and *refuse* to repent after the fourth bowl judgment.

The fifth Bowl Judgment:

> **Revelation 16:10-11**
> [10] *The fifth angel poured out his bowl on the throne of the beast, and his kingdom was plunged into darkness. Men gnawed their tongues in agony* [11] *and cursed the God of heaven because of their pains and their sores, but they refused to repent of what they had done.*

The fifth Trumpet Judgment brought complete darkness to the earth for a period of time. Similarly, the fifth Bowl Judgment will bring complete darkness, but that darkness will be limited to the kingdom of the Beast. The kingdom of the Beast, or Antichrist, includes the entire world other than Edom, Moab and Ammon (or modern day Jordan) where God is protecting the elect of Israel who fled the abomination of desolation.

Yet again, an utter refusal to repent is man's response. Amid total darkness, with intense pain from sores and the burns of the recently scorching sun, starving and with limited water resources, man continues to obstinately reject the opportunity to repent in light of God's judgment. The suggestion that men refused to repent is also indicative that the possibility existed for them to do so. Clearly they will have the *opportunity* to give glory to God and repent, but they will flatly refuse.

The Sixth Bowl Judgment

The sixth and seventh bowl judgments are uniquely tied to the time period of the Battle of Armageddon, and will be discussed in the next chapter.

Chapter 5: The Second Half of the Tribulation

The Fall of Babylon

As was earlier demonstrated, the rise of "Babylon the Great Harlot," the one-world religion of Antichrist, also will give rise to a great city of the same name, which will be the headquarters of the religion and government of Antichrist. While the inhabitants of this great city and the religion and government it represents will have served Antichrist wholeheartedly, scripture teaches that he will not return their support.

Babylon is abandoned by the Antichrist

> ***Revelation 17:15-18***
> *[15] Then the angel said to me, "The waters you saw, where the prostitute sits, are peoples, multitudes, nations and languages. [16] The beast and the ten horns you saw will hate the prostitute. They will bring her to ruin and leave her naked; they will eat her flesh and burn her with fire. [17] For God has put it into their hearts to accomplish his purpose by agreeing to give the beast their power to rule, until God's words are fulfilled. [18] The woman you saw is the great city that rules over the kings of the earth."*

His purposes for her finished, Antichrist demonstrates his hatred for the harlot and *"leaves her naked."* The idea of nakedness indicates his leaving of her exposed and without protection. Isaiah 13 speaks of God's pending destruction of Babylon, which will result in an eternal desolation of the city, never to be lived in again. Isaiah 13 mirrors Revelation 17 also in the proclamation of demonic haunts being relegated to living there, which will be examined later in this work.

God will purpose of himself to destroy the great city, yet Antichrist will even participate himself by burning and abandoning the city ahead of God's coming judgment upon it. It may seem incredulous that Antichrist *"hates"* those who worshipped him during the great tribulation, but it shouldn't. Satan hates everyone. His counterfeit son will emulate his master's attitude. Satan is a user, and has been so from the beginning.

He is utterly without the capacity of relationship or honor. Babylon The Great Harlot, though she worshipped him, only served his purposes and his base desires. Now, finished with her, he will destroy her, as is his nature to do. He is without compassion or concern. He shares loyalty with no one; even those who serve him to their deaths.

Verse 16 notes that *"they will eat her flesh and burn her with fire."* It seems to fit into the time-line that this will happen as Antichrist heads to Armageddon. At this point his purposes for the one-world religion, along with all of its riches, are over because all that remains for him to do is fight against Israel, particularly the final battle against Israel, and her King.

To that end, a gap seems to appear in Revelation concerning Antichrist's campaign. He is shown in the middle of the tribulation in Jerusalem beginning his persecution of Israel, while in this text he is exiting Babylon for the final time, leaving it in ruins. Clearly he has returned at some point prior to his final assault on Israel, the Battle of Armageddon, which will be covered in chapters six and seven.

> ***Revelation 18:9-10***
> [9] *"When the kings of the earth who committed adultery with her and shared her luxury see the smoke of her burning, they will weep and mourn over her.* [10] *Terrified at her torment, they will stand far off and cry: "'Woe! Woe, O great city, O Babylon, city of power! In one hour your doom has come!'*

While Antichrist sheds no tears for Babylon, the other kings of the earth will mourn for her loss. They lived the "good" life there, as much as that will be possible during the great tribulation, with riches and luxury at their disposal. Her destruction will be the end of their comfort in a world which affords so very little of it in light of God's continuing judgments.

The destruction of the city will be sudden, happening in *"one hour,"* in a single day.

Chapter 5: The Second Half of the Tribulation . . . .

Chapter 6: The Battle of Armageddon

Setting of the Stage: the Assembling of the Armies

> **Revelation 16:12-16**
> *12 The sixth angel poured out his bowl on the great river Euphrates, and its water was dried up to prepare the way for the kings from the East. 13 Then I saw three evil spirits that looked like frogs; they came out of the mouth of the dragon, out of the mouth of the beast and out of the mouth of the false prophet. 14 They are spirits of demons performing miraculous signs, and they go out to the kings of the whole world, to gather them for the battle on the great day of God Almighty.*
> *15 "Behold, I come like a thief! Blessed is he who stays awake and keeps his clothes with him, so that he may not go naked and be shamefully exposed."*
> *16 Then they gathered the kings together to the place that in Hebrew is called Armageddon.*

In verse 14, the kings of "*the whole world*" are summoned to battle. The place of the battle is noted in verse 16 as "*Armageddon*" in Hebrew. "Armageddon" is a compilation of two Hebrew words which reference Megiddo, a plains area North and West of Jerusalem, in Israel. Meggido was a strategic city at the western end of the Valley of Jezreel, guarding the Meggido pass into Israel's largest valley. Note that the battle does not happen in this location uniquely, but it is here that the armies will gather their forces. To that end, the battle of Armageddon would perhaps more accurately be known as the "battle of Jerusalem," for it is Jerusalem and its surrounding areas which scripture describes as being under attack during this series of assaults.

For all of the kings of the earth to gather their armies, the kings of the east will have to negotiate the Euphrates river. Verse 12 notes the effects of the sixth bowl judgment, which is the drying out of the Euphrates river

Chapter 6: The Battle of Armageddon

to make the passage of the kings of the east easier. The Euphrates cuts the Middle East in half, coming from Turkey, through Syria and Iraq where it empties into the Persian Gulf. All nations joining the assembly from east of that location will then have a dry river bed crossing in the southern portion of Iraq.

At first glance, having a bowl judgment to assist in the gathering of the evil kings of the earth against Israel seems ironic. God is clearly aiding the enemies of his people in accessing their target. Yet, when one understands the outcome of this battle, this preparation of the path of the kings of the east is best understood as leading lambs to their own slaughter, in judgment. Before being slaughtered, however, they will also inflict great injury against Israel, in keeping with God's purposes of refining Israel in preparation for the coming of Christ's Kingdom. This preparation of the Euphrates brings both parties together for their respective judgments by making the path easier to traverse for the armies of the east.

Evil spirits are noted in verse 13 who will perform miraculous signs to entice the kings of the earth to join Antichrist in the final battle. *"Evil spirits"* is a common biblical reference to fallen angels, or demons. Throughout the tribulation demonic activity will keep the kings of the earth in subjection to Antichrist and deluded into his service. This final series of battles is no exception.

Verse 14 notes the purpose of their gathering is *"to gather them for battle on the great day of God Almighty."* The "day of the Lord" has been planned from the beginning. They are there by God's design, and with God's purposes at hand, even in the midst of Satan's own agenda, that Christ may return and make a mockery of the Antichrist, destroying him forever. The reference to *"the great day of God Almighty"* is an example of a "day of the Lord" reference specifically targeting the very *end* point of the tribulation. While all "day of the Lord" references point to the tribulation period, some, such as this one, point to a specific point in the great tribulation, the very moment of the return of Christ.

Antichrist's purposes in the Battle of Armageddon

The short "world-history" noted in Revelation 12 tells the source of Satan's hatred for Israel.

> **Revelation 12:13-17**
> "When the dragon saw that he had been hurled to the earth, he pursued the woman who had given birth to the male child. [14] The woman was given the two wings of a great eagle, so that she might fly to the place prepared for her in the desert, where she would be taken care of for a time, times and half a time, out of the serpent's reach. [15] Then from his mouth the serpent spewed water like a river, to overtake the woman and sweep her away with the torrent. [16] But the earth helped the woman by opening its mouth and swallowing the river that the dragon had spewed out of his mouth. [17] Then the dragon was enraged at the woman and went off to make war against the rest of her offspring--those who obey God's commandments and hold to the testimony of Jesus."

Israel is the chosen people of God's revelation of himself to mankind. Israel is the people of Abraham, through whom God made his covenant to provide a blessing to the world. Israel is the family of the very advent of Christ himself. The woman who gave birth to the male son is Satan's arch enemy, for this Son lived to redeem mankind to God and destroy Satan's work of deception which he began in the Garden of Eden. Satan has made it his personal career to usurp God's authority and deem himself "*like the most high.*"[59] Israel represents God's own program for the redemption of mankind through Christ, which makes her Satan's bitter enemy. Furthermore, Satan knows scripture. He quoted it to Eve and to Christ, distorting it in his attempts to deceive them.[60] Knowing scripture, he also knows that his final hour approaches. Revelation 12:12 states, "*...he is filled with fury because he knows that his time is short.*"

---

[59] Isaiah 14:14
[60] Genesis 3:1, Matthew 4:3,6

Chapter 6: The Battle of Armageddon

His war on Israel will be his last attempt of vengeance against his enemy before he is bound for the duration of Christ's millennial kingdom.

In Revelation 12, when the Dragon was unable to kill the child (Jesus) of the woman (Israel) he then pursued the woman herself. In verse 13 he pursues her and in verse 17 he "*went off to make war with the rest of her offspring*" after she fled to the wilderness.

Clearly the remnant who listened to Jesus' warning in Matthew 24 have fled to the place provided for them, which was demonstrated to be Edom, Ammon and Moab, the "*place prepared for her in the dessert.*" Upon his discovery that this remnant is now out being protected in Jordan, Satan will pursue "*the rest of her offspring - those who obey God's commandments and hold to the testimony of Jesus.*" However, it will be made clear in the next chapter that Antichrist also has armies attempting to destroy the remnant of Jewish believers in Edom, as well, although Rev. 12 informs us that they will be "*out of the serpent's reach.*"

Antichrist had already begun war with Israel when he annulled his covenant with them in the middle of the tribulation. He now returns with the kings of the world fully supporting him in an attempt to completely eradicate the nation.

Psalm 2 more precisely prophesies Satan's interests in Israel in the Battle of Armageddon. While he is noted to be angry because "*he knows his time is short,*" his focus on Israel is demonstrated to have a peculiar purpose associated with it.

> **Psalms 2:1-6**
> *¹Why do the nations conspire and the peoples plot in vain?*
> *² The kings of the earth take their stand and the rulers gather together*
> *against the LORD and against his Anointed One.*
> *³ "Let us break their chains," they say, "and throw off their fetters."*
> *⁴ The One enthroned in heaven laughs; the Lord scoffs*

at them.
⁵ Then he rebukes them in his anger and terrifies them in his wrath, saying,
⁶ "I have installed my King on Zion, my holy hill."

The first observation of Psalm 2 is that the stand of the kings of earth is against "*the LORD and against his Anointed One.*" Satan's interest in Israel is due to the fact that she is the chosen tool of the Lord to reveal the Anointed One. His thoughts are clearly stated; "*Let us break their chains,*" they say, "*and throw off their fetters.*" The destruction of Israel is seen by Satan, via the kings of the earth, as a means to rid the world of God's interests in it. If there is no Israel, they postulate, then God will have no reason to contend for the earth, nor will Christ have an interest in a coming kingdom to rule; for his subjects will have been removed. God's promise to Israel concerning this coming kingdom was made to David through what is known as the Davidic covenant. In this covenant God promised a King for Israel who would sit David's throne for eternity.

Isaiah 9 sketches God's promises concerning this coming King.

Isaiah 9:2
² The people walking in darkness have seen a great light; on those living in the land of the shadow of death a light has dawned.

Isaiah 9:6-7
⁶ For to us a child is born, to us a son is given, and the government will be on his shoulders. And he will be called Wonderful Counselor, Mighty God, Everlasting Father, Prince of Peace. ⁷ Of the increase of his government and peace there will be no end. He will reign on David's throne and over his kingdom, establishing and upholding it with justice and righteousness from that time on and forever. The zeal of the Lord Almighty will accomplish this.

Chapter 6: The Battle of Armageddon

A King is prophesied as coming to rule on David's throne, "*upholding it with justice and righteousness from that time on and forever.*" While the literality of this promise will be discussed in Chapter 8, the substance of this promise is particularly destructive to Satan's career. Righteousness, peace and justice are contrary to Satan's character and his own plans to establish himself "*like the most high.*" A coming kingdom of righteousness is clearly a kingdom which Satan is to have no part.

The essence of Satan's campaign, according to Psalm 2, is that if there is no Israel, there are no people of the promise to rule. If there is no kingdom, the King will have nothing to return to rule. The destruction of Israel is seen as a means to rid the world of God's interest and to break the cords that hold him in the world.

In Psalm 2:5-6, God laughs at them and rebukes them.

> *⁵ Then he rebukes them in his anger and terrifies them in his wrath, saying,*
> *⁶ "I have installed my King on Zion, my holy hill."*

God states defiantly, "*I have installed my King on Zion.*" Spoken as already completed, his plans will come to fruition in spite of any and all resistance.

The First Wave

Zechariah 12-14 portrays the events of the Battle of Armageddon through several reiterating views.

> **Zechariah 12:1-3**
> ¹*This is the word of the LORD concerning Israel. The LORD, who stretches out the heavens, who lays the foundation of the earth, and who forms the spirit of man within him, declares:* ² *"I am going to make Jerusalem a cup that sends all the surrounding peoples reeling. Judah will be besieged as well as Jerusalem.* ³ *On that*

> *day, when all the nations of the earth are gathered against her, I will make Jerusalem an immovable rock for all the nations. All who try to move it will injure themselves.*

Zechariah prophesies specifically of this battle being "*on that day when all the nations of the earth are gathered against her.*" This statement refers to a historical event which has never occurred and must be understood to align with the final gathering of the nations against Israel at Armageddon. There has been no time when all of the nations of earth have gathered against Israel formerly in history. *Some* nations have gathered against Israel historically, but never *all*. Only once in history will "*all the nations of the earth*" be ever gathered against Israel; the coming Battle of Armageddon, as noted in Revelation 16.

The reason the battle is divided into separate "waves" in this work is that it is clear from scripture that there are parts of the battle where God gives Israel strength, yet parts of the battle where she is overrun. The division into separate offensives highlights the purposes of each phase of this battle, though it should not be construed to necessarily indicate that there are different attacks, separated by a period of time. That assumption is unclear in scripture, and should not be gleaned from the author's presentation.

With that understanding, what will be referred to as the "first wave" in this work is that portion of the battle in which God himself will once again enter the battle on Israel's behalf, similar to what he will have done in the Gog-Magog war. However, the results will not be the same. In the Gog-Magog war, God will completely destroy the offending armies in an immediate display of his power. In the Battle of Armageddon, God's hand is in control the entire time, yet he chooses not to immediately destroy the armies of Antichrist in the first wave, but waits a period of time for a specific purpose to come to pass. That purpose is the purging of Israel of those who are unwilling to call on their King to save them. Just as will be the case for all of humanity during the tribulation, even Israel will be purged of those who are unwilling to repent and call upon Christ.

Chapter 6: The Battle of Armageddon

God states in verse 2 of the first wave, "*I am going to make Jerusalem a cup that sends all the surrounding peoples reeling.*" He notes in verse 3, "*I will make Jerusalem an immovable rock for all the nations.*" The picture given is one of an utter inability to infiltrate Jerusalem or to bring any harm to the city from what amounts to the summary military might of the entire world. While stated simply, the picture is an impressive one, indeed. All manner of military might are targeted, from all nations on earth, at one city; yet without making any headway whatsoever. He states also in verse 3 that "*all who try to move it will injure themselves.*" It appears that the attempts to inflict military on Jerusalem will actually backfire and cause damage on the attackers themselves. While it is unclear how this will occur, in some way the weapons of attack, be they missiles, artillery or bombs, will bring injury on the armies of Antichrist instead. It will be tantamount to a gun that fires backwards, and will have a serious impact on the morale of the armies of Antichrist.

Zechariah 12:4-9
⁴On that day I will strike every horse with panic and its rider with madness," declares the LORD. "I will keep a watchful eye over the house of Judah, but I will blind all the horses of the nations. ⁵ Then the leaders of Judah will say in their hearts, 'The people of Jerusalem are strong, because the LORD Almighty is their God.'

⁶ "On that day I will make the leaders of Judah like a firepot in a woodpile, like a flaming torch among sheaves. They will consume right and left all the surrounding peoples, but Jerusalem will remain intact in her place.

⁷ "The LORD will save the dwellings of Judah first, so that the honor of the house of David and of Jerusalem's inhabitants may not be greater than that of Judah. ⁸ On that day the LORD will shield those who live in Jerusalem, so that the feeblest among them will be like David, and the house of David will be like God, like the Angel of the LORD going before them. ⁹ On that day I will set out to destroy all the nations that attack Jerusalem.

Verse 4 notes panicking horses and riders struck with madness. One would expect the Lord to use language which those he spoke to would understand. Just as in Ezekiel's account of the Gog-Magog war, weaponry known to Ezekiel was used, so in Zechariah's account, weaponry known to Zechariah is used. It is unclear for certain if the "*horses*" refer to a method of navigating the terrain, or if they are referencing actual implements of war. However, the horses "*panicking*" and being "*blinded*" certainly presents a portrait of their failure to traverse their intended terrain properly, but rather erratically and haphazardly. This could be a description of modern weapons of war, having been confused by the Lord in their navigational abilities so that they are "*panicked*;" unable to reach their target. Also noted are riders struck with madness, which could refer to the operators of such equipment crazed by the lack of ability to control their weaponry. What is most certain about the predicament is God's utter manipulation of the horses and riders to the loss of control of their operators.

The picture is one of ultimate chaos. With weapons backfiring on their handlers and implements of war incapable of meaningful navigation, God confuses the war making ability of the nations so that Jerusalem will stand "*in her place*" while Judah is "*like a firepot in a woodpile,*" or "*a flaming torch among sheaves.*" With the war making abilities of the surrounding armies obstructed, Judah will have an unhampered ability to wreak her own damage against her enemy. She will "*consume right and left all the surrounding peoples,*" while Jerusalem will be an "*immovable rock*" and will not be penetrated by the armies of Antichrist in this first wave. Israel will decidedly have the advantage against the armies of Antichrist during the first wave of this battle.

Of the inhabitants of Israel it is stated that "*the feeblest among them will be like David,*" indicating that God will supernaturally give even the weak, lame and incapable of war the ability to fight in this battle. To compare the weak with the strength of David is perhaps the strongest metaphor an Israelite could humanly imagine. David was the mightiest and most celebrated king in Israel's history; a formidable enemy for any army which opposed him.

Chapter 6: The Battle of Armageddon

Lastly is noted, "*on that day I will set out to destroy the armies all the nations that attack Jerusalem.*" Clearly the end is near. God has purposed himself to destroy all the nations of the earth who are attacking his people; which, of course, represents the entire world, minus modern day Jordan. The end is clearly near. Christ will soon be coming, but not yet; for there is still a very key fulfillment of prophecy which must be accomplished before the King will return. Israel must call upon her Messiah. Christ, whom she rejected upon his first coming, must be received and welcomed prior to his second coming.

The Second Wave

Zechariah, like many prophetic writings, tells the events of the Battle of Armageddon in bits and pieces. In chapters 12-14 he tells the story three times, yet with varying degrees of detail in each instance. He begins telling the beginning and end of the story in chapter twelve, then speaks specifically at the end of chapter twelve and in chapter thirteen of the national salvation of Israel. Then, in chapter fourteen he seems to give the entire chronology again, with more detail than given originally. The events are all present, but the orchestration of the order must be interpreted by the reader.

Clearly, the original push is a devastating defeat to the armies of Antichrist. Yet, chapter fourteen gives more information that lends to an understanding of a secondary offensive, which serves to break down Israel to a point where she is finally - as a whole - ready and willing to bow her knee and call upon her coming King.

> ***Zechariah 14:2***
> ²*I will gather all the nations to Jerusalem to fight against it; the city will be captured, the houses ransacked, and the women raped. Half of the city will go into exile, but the rest of the people will not be taken from the city.*

"The city will be captured," in verse two is clearly distinct from the results of the first offensive. The reasons God allows this sudden change in the balance of the battle will be clear in the next section which speaks to Israel's national regeneration. Skipping backward in the text slightly, however, Zechariah 13:8 informs that two thirds of the inhabitants of Israel will die prior to the division of Jerusalem into halves noted in chapter fourteen.

> *[8] In the whole land," declares the LORD,*
>   *"two-thirds will be struck down and perish;*
>   *yet one-third will be left in it.*

By the end of the battle, only one-third of the entire nation will survive, and one half of the city of Jerusalem will go into exile, or will somehow escape the city.

Of the remaining half of Jerusalem, Zechariah 14:2 notes that houses are ransacked and women are raped. Clearly the battle has transformed greatly toward the advantage of Antichrist and Israel receives significant damage, with only one-third surviving overall. The remaining one-third, however, will be transformed through this process and will make the choice Israel had failed to make prior to that point.

The Salvation of Israel

God's purging of Israel

Zechariah 13 fills in other gaps in the story, namely the depiction of the national salvation of Israel.

> ***Zechariah 13:1-6***
> *[1]"On that day a fountain will be opened to the house of David and the inhabitants of Jerusalem, to cleanse them from sin and impurity.*

Chapter 6: The Battle of Armageddon

> ²"On that day, I will banish the names of the idols from the land, and they will be remembered no more," declares the LORD Almighty. "I will remove both the prophets and the spirit of impurity from the land. ³And if anyone still prophesies, his father and mother, to whom he was born, will say to him, 'You must die, because you have told lies in the LORD's name.' When he prophesies, his own parents will stab him.
> ⁴"On that day every prophet will be ashamed of his prophetic vision. He will not put on a prophet's garment of hair in order to deceive. ⁵He will say, 'I am not a prophet. I am a farmer; the land has been my livelihood since my youth.' ⁶If someone asks him, 'What are these wounds on your body?' he will answer, 'The wounds I was given at the house of my friends.'

Verse one notes that a cleansing begins during the Battle of Armageddon in Israel. Verse 2 states, "*On that day, I will banish the names of the idols from the land,*" picturing Israel making a decisive effort to seek God's will as a nation once again and to turn wholly to their God and away from idolatry. God says in verse 2 that he will remove all memory of Israel's idolatry, indicating his forgiveness being granted to the nation. He states "*I will remove both the prophets and the spirit of impurity from the land.*"

"*The prophets*" refers to the false prophets in Israel, who have propagated the idolatry spoken of in the text. Of those false prophets, he states, "*if anyone still prophesies, his father and mother...will say to him 'You must die, because you have told lies in the LORD's name.'*" Clearly repentance is gripping Israel, as they turn from every form of idolatry and shift their attention fully to the Lord their God. Israel is noted in the middle of the tribulation to have begun a revival, yet at this point- the very end of the tribulation - they have utterly resigned all traces of their idols and are putting their full faith in the Lord, alone. Verse 4 notes, "*On that day every prophet will be ashamed of his prophetic vision,*" indicating that even the prophets themselves are ashamed, a sign of sincere repentance.

God promises salvation to the one-third who live past this second offensive.

> ***Zechariah 13:7-9***
> *7 "Awake, O sword, against my shepherd,*
> *against the man who is close to me!"*
> *declares the LORD Almighty.*
> *"Strike the shepherd,*
> *and the sheep will be scattered,*
> *and I will turn my hand against the little ones.*
> *8 In the whole land," declares the LORD,*
> *"two-thirds will be struck down and perish;*
> *yet one-third will be left in it.*
> *9 This third I will bring into the fire;*
> *I will refine them like silver*
> *and test them like gold.*
> *They will call on my name*
> *and I will answer them;*
> *I will say, 'They are my people,'*
> *and they will say, 'The LORD is our God.'"*

The one-third who remain will be brought "*into the fire*" and refined "*like silver*." These phrases refer to spiritual regeneration and sanctification, which can only be fulfilled in the person of Jesus Christ.[61] The picture of Zechariah 13 is not the picture of Israel returning to Old Testament sincerity, but a picture of Israel accepting salvation in the King they had formerly rejected as a nation.

Israel Calls on Christ

Hosea 5 speaks of Israel's continued unfaithfulness to God and of God's departure from them at that time. Yet, he also makes a prophecy as to his return to them at a future time.

---

[61] Acts 4:10-12

Chapter 6: The Battle of Armageddon

> ***Hosea 5:14-15***
> *14 For I will be like a lion to Ephraim,*
>   *like a great lion to Judah.*
> *I will tear them to pieces and go away;*
>   *I will carry them off, with no one to rescue them.*
> *15 Then I will go back to my place*
>   *until they admit their guilt.*
> *And they will seek my face;*
>   *in their misery they will earnestly seek me."*

One of the great questions concerning the Battle of Armageddon is "why did God demonstrate his control so effectively in the first wave, then allow Israel to be torn to pieces in the second wave?" Hosea indicates precisely God's intentions: to "*go back to my place until they admit their guilt.*" While Hosea had a word for his own day, he also has a word for Israeli history in general: God will not come to the aid of those who refuse to worship him on his own terms.

Hosea 5:9 notes, *"⁹ Ephraim will be laid waste on the day of reckoning. Among the tribes of Israel I proclaim what is certain."*

Just as in Hosea's day, Israel is once again laid waste and God waits for them to call on him. God's distance from Israel (and all of humanity) throughout scripture has always had one solution: repentance.

While the Israel of Hosea's day were distant from the Lord, her greatest historical sin was the rejection of her savior and King, Christ, and her utter refusal to acknowledge the hundreds of prophecies which demonstrated him to be her promised Messiah. In these final moments of the tribulation, Israel is finally repentant, not only to the Lord God they once knew well, but to his chosen servant, Israel's King, Jesus. At this point they are truly prepared to repent and call on the very one they had formerly rejected.

> ***Zechariah 12:9-14***
> *⁹ On that day I will set out to destroy all the nations that attack Jerusalem. ¹⁰ "And I will pour out on the house of*

> *David and the inhabitants of Jerusalem a spirit of grace and supplication. They will look on me, the one they have pierced, and they will mourn for him as one mourns for an only child, and grieve bitterly for him as one grieves for a firstborn son. ¹¹ On that day the weeping in Jerusalem will be great, like the weeping of Hadad Rimmon in the plain of Megiddo. ¹² The land will mourn, each clan by itself, with their wives by themselves: the clan of the house of David and their wives, the clan of the house of Nathan and their wives, ¹³ the clan of the house of Levi and their wives, the clan of Shimei and their wives, ¹⁴ and all the rest of the clans and their wives.*

Prior to the Lord's promise to "*set out to destroy*" the nations waging war against them, it is essential that Israel truly repents of her greatest sin and calls upon the King whom God had sent to them prior and they had rejected.

Verse 10 records the attitude which leads to Israel's final conversion, "*And I will pour out on the house of David and the inhabitants of Jerusalem a spirit of grace and supplication.*

The Holy Spirit, necessary for salvation,[62] is poured out on all of Israel – a "*spirit of grace and supplication,*" or prayer. In that moment, Israel repents of her sin of the past two thousand years. Israel calls on Christ, her true King.

Verse 10 notes, "*They will look on me, the one they have pierced, and they will mourn for him as one mourns for an only child, and grieve bitterly for him as one grieves for a firstborn son.*"

That Israel will call on "*the one they have pierced*" is a fascinating statement to be found in the Old Testament book of Zechariah. Written

---

[62] Titus 3:5, 1 Corinthians 12:3, Hebrews 10:15-16

Chapter 6: The Battle of Armageddon

over 500 years before the crucifixion of Christ, and arguably hundreds of years prior to the very invention of Roman crucifixion, this text illuminates Zechariah's prophetic vision, clearly pointing to Jesus Christ as the Lord whom they will call out to.

The fulfillment of Israel's call upon Christ is a fundamental event which absolutely must precede the coming of Christ to their rescue. The second coming of Christ is uniquely tied to the completion of the work of his first coming. At his first coming, Israel rejected her King, claiming Christ did his miracles by means of the works of Satan, rather than through God's power.[63]

In Matthew 12, Jesus performed an exceptionally unique miracle in the presence of Israel's religious leaders. He healed a blind and mute demon possessed man. The way a demoniac had traditionally been delivered by a Jewish priest was that the demon's name was first obtained by asking. The possessed person would answer. If the person was mute, however, tradition held that he could not be delivered, because he could not speak the demon's name. It was a widely held and known Jewish tradition *that only the Messiah* would be able to deliver a mute from demon possession.

When Jesus delivered the blind mute from a demon, the response of the people reflected this view.

> **Matthew 12:23**
> [23] *All the people were astonished and said, "Could this be the Son of David?"*

This question indicates their understanding that this healing was the work of Messiah. The people saw the evidence they needed to put their faith in Christ as their King. Yet, the Pharisees quickly took control of the situation!

---

[63] Matthew 12:24

> **Matthew 12:24**
> ^{24} But when the Pharisees heard this, they said, "It is only by Beelzebub, the prince of demons, that this fellow drives out demons."

The Pharisees proclamation was that Jesus was demon possessed himself! Rather than acknowledge the clear signs Jesus gave them, they formally and publicly rejected him, to which Jesus responded concerning the very misunderstood pronouncement of the unpardonable sin.

> **Matthew 12:31-32**
> ^{31} And so I tell you, every sin and blasphemy will be forgiven men, but the blasphemy against the Spirit will not be forgiven. ^{32} Anyone who speaks a word against the Son of Man will be forgiven, but anyone who speaks against the Holy Spirit will not be forgiven, either in this age or in the age to come.

Throughout Jesus' ministry on earth Israel's religious rulers sought to discredit him at every opportunity, in spite of numerous miracles which proclaimed him to be the coming King and Messiah. While some individual Jews put their faith in Christ as their Messiah, as a whole, Israel had rejected her delivered promise. Jesus laments this fact in Matthew 23, as he completes his public ministry in Jerusalem, and leaves the city.

> **Matthew 23:37-39**
> ^{37} "O Jerusalem, Jerusalem, you who kill the prophets and stone those sent to you, how often I have longed to gather your children together, as a hen gathers her chicks under her wings, but you were not willing. ^{38} Look, your house is left to you desolate. ^{39} For I tell you, you will not see me again until you say, 'Blessed is he who comes in the name of the Lord.'"

Note Jesus' prophecy, "*you will not see me again until you say, 'Blessed*

Chapter 6: The Battle of Armageddon

is he who comes in the name of the Lord,'" a phrase coming from Psalm 118:

> **Psalm 118:22-26**
> ²² *The stone the builders rejected has become the capstone;* ²³ *the Lord has done this, and it is marvelous in our eyes.* ²⁴ *This is the day the Lord has made; let us rejoice and be glad in it.* ²⁵ *O Lord, save us; O Lord, grant us success.* ²⁶ *Blessed is he who comes in the name of the Lord. From the house of the Lord we bless you.*

"*Blessed is he who comes in the name of the Lord*" is the statement of the rejected stone becoming the capstone. It is the statement of recognition that Jesus was indeed the coming Messiah. In short, Jesus informed Israel that he would return when this statement was proclaimed.

Until then, Jesus would return to the father and wait for that proclamation. Jesus' statement, "*you will not see me again until you say, 'Blessed is he who comes in the name of the Lord,'*" is the same sentiment as God's statement in Hosea 5:15:

> *Then I will go back to my place*
> *until they admit their guilt.*
> *And they will seek my face;*
> *in their misery they will earnestly seek me."*

Jesus concludes his ministry, then tells the details of his second coming in Matthew 24-25 and is crucified in chapter 27. His ministry is complete, but for Israel's future repentance and his return to take up his throne as King at his second coming, *at a future date when Israel calls on him as King.*

The intermediary time, known as "the time of the Gentiles" has transpired from those moments to the present. Jesus extended his kingdom to others, as noted in his parable in Matthew 21.

THE RETURN OF THE KING: A Prophetic Timeline of End time Events

Matthew 21:33-45 (NIV)
^{33} *"Listen to another parable: There was a landowner who planted a vineyard. He put a wall around it, dug a winepress in it and built a watchtower. Then he rented the vineyard to some farmers and went away on a journey. ^{34} When the harvest time approached, he sent his servants to the tenants to collect his fruit. ^{35} "The tenants seized his servants; they beat one, killed another, and stoned a third. ^{36} Then he sent other servants to them, more than the first time, and the tenants treated them the same way. ^{37} Last of all, he sent his son to them. 'They will respect my son,' he said. ^{38} "But when the tenants saw the son, they said to each other, 'This is the heir. Come, let's kill him and take his inheritance.' ^{39} So they took him and threw him out of the vineyard and killed him. ^{40} "Therefore, when the owner of the vineyard comes, what will he do to those tenants?" ^{41} "He will bring those wretches to a wretched end," they replied, "and he will rent the vineyard to other tenants, who will give him his share of the crop at harvest time." ^{42} Jesus said to them, "Have you never read in the Scriptures: "'The stone the builders rejected has become the capstone; the Lord has done this, and it is marvelous in our eyes'? ^{43} "Therefore I tell you that the kingdom of God will be taken away from you and given to a people who will produce its fruit. ^{44} He who falls on this stone will be broken to pieces, but he on whom it falls will be crushed." ^{45} When the chief priests and the Pharisees heard Jesus' parables, they knew he was talking about them.*

Jesus proclaimed the taking of the kingdom from Israel and the giving of it to other tenants *"who will produce its fruit,"* the gentiles. At the time of the writing of this work, it is the Gentile nations who produce the ministry of the Kingdom of Christ.[64] There certainly are Messianic Jews,

---

[64] See also the parable of the Wedding Banquet: Matthew 22:1-14

Chapter 6: The Battle of Armageddon

those of Jewish descent who have claimed Christ as their Messiah and Lord. And, Messianic Christians do a phenomenal work of ministry in the earth. Yet, as a whole, Israel has continued to reject Christ as her King. When the time of Christ's return comes, however, he will be fully accepted by the Jews, and will establish himself firmly as King. The only prophecy necessary to be fulfilled at this point in the timeline of this work, is for Israel to call, "*blessed is he who comes in the name of the Lord.*" Israel must call on her King.

For the nation to call on her King requires that Israel affirm him as he is; the Messiah, Son of God and King of Kings. Israel must have a Christian conversion, which is precisely what scripture declares will occur. All Israel will be redeemed as believers in Christ.

Concerning the salvation of Israel, scripture teaches it to be a *full restoration*. *All* of Israel will be saved, rather than the handful of believing Jews which exists today. Paul states,

> **Romans 11:25-27** *[25] I do not want you to be ignorant of this mystery, brothers, so that you may not be conceited: Israel has experienced a hardening in part until the full number of the Gentiles has come in. [26] And so all Israel will be saved, as it is written:*
> *"The deliverer will come from Zion;*
>   *he will turn godlessness away from Jacob.*
> *[27] And this is my covenant with them*
>   *when I take away their sins."*

Paul designates two important details concerning Israel's final salvation. First, he establishes that the time of the Gentiles is a calculated time, a time enduring until "*the full number of the Gentiles has come in.*" Clearly, by God's grace the current historical season is an opportunity for as many Gentiles to find salvation in Christ as God has apportioned. Gentiles will have the opportunity to be saved even during the tribulation, for their numbers are still coming in up to the point of Israel's salvation. Secondly, he states unconditionally that "*all Israel will be saved*" when that time arrives. In order for all of Israel to be saved, however, all Israel must be *willing* to repent and experience that salvation.

Ezekiel 20 speaks volumes to the process whereby "*all*" Israel is saved, by means of the removal of those who will refuse to be brought into the bond of the new covenant with Christ.

> ***Ezekiel 20:34-38***
> *[34] I will bring you from the nations and gather you from the countries where you have been scattered--with a mighty hand and an outstretched arm and with outpoured wrath. [35] I will bring you into the desert of the nations and there, face to face, I will execute judgment upon you. [36] As I judged your fathers in the desert of the land of Egypt, so I will judge you, declares the Sovereign LORD. [37] I will take note of you as you pass under my rod, and I will bring you into the bond of the covenant. [38] I will purge you of those who revolt and rebel against me. Although I will bring them out of the land where they are living, yet they will not enter the land of Israel. Then you will know that I am the LORD.*

In this text, God speaks through Ezekiel the events described thus far, giving a full explanation of the destruction of two-thirds of Israel during the Battle of Armageddon.

First is noted the bringing back together of Israel as a nation, observed historically in 1948, "*I will bring you from the nations and gather you from the countries where you have been scattered.*"

Next is noted a separation of Israel through judgment. "*I will bring you into the desert of the nations and there, face to face, I will execute judgment upon you.*" The "*desert of the nations*" refers to the desert where the nations will be gathered, rather than a desert belonging to other nations. It references the Battle of Armageddon, where the nations of the earth are gathered as noted in Revelation 16.

Chapter 6: The Battle of Armageddon

Lastly, God specifies the criteria of the judgment, *"³⁷ I will take note of you as you pass under my rod, and I will bring you into the bond of the covenant. ³⁸ I will purge you of those who revolt and rebel against me."* Those who are prepared to enter the bond of the covenant with Christ to which God is calling Israel will be spared. Those who revolt and continue to rebel against the Lord will be delivered to their enemies in this judgment. It is noted that the rebellious and the obedient alike will be gathered, but only the obedient will "*enter the land of Israel*," which in the context of eschatology refers to the kingdom of Israel in the millennial kingdom, which the returning King will rule over, rather than the pre-millennial Israel, which exists today.

Unmistakably, God's program will bring Israel to a very clear and final moment of decision. Jews will stand or fall based on their willingness to submit to God's program through Christ. That moment is currently observed in the timeline; the calling on Christ noted in Zechariah 12-13 at the conclusion of the Battle of Armageddon. It is this moment history has waited for. Israel will experience a full regeneration among those who live to the end of that battle. She will call on her King and he will answer.

Joel speaks of this event in chapter two of his prophecy.

> ### Joel 2:28-32
> *²⁸ 'And afterward, I will pour out my Spirit on all people.*
> *Your sons and daughters will prophesy, your old men will dream dreams,*
>   *your young men will see visions.*
> *²⁹ Even on my servants, both men and women, I will pour out my Spirit in those days.*
> *³⁰ I will show wonders in the heavens and on the earth, blood and fire and billows of smoke.*
> *³¹ The sun will be turned to darkness and the moon to blood*
>   *before the coming of the great and dreadful day of the Lord.*

> *[32] And everyone who calls on the name of the LORD will be saved;*
> *for on Mount Zion and in Jerusalem there will be deliverance,*
> *as the LORD has said, among the survivors whom the LORD calls.*

Joel 2 demonstrates God's spirit being poured prior to the *"day of the Lord."* The use of *"day of the Lord"* in this text is the second and most specific use of the phrase, pointing specifically to the final event of the tribulation; the return of Christ. Before that day comes, Joel stipulates in verse 32 that there will be deliverance *"among the survivors,"* once again indicating some who will not survive the Battle of Armageddon, who will not experience deliverance.

The national salvation of Israel is not an isolated theme in scripture. It is an essential event which must precede the return of Christ.

Now, with that event being complete, the King will return and fulfill the remainder of Zechariah's prophecy in Zechariah 14:3 *"Then the LORD will go out and fight against those nations, as he fights in the day of battle."*

Chapter 6: The Battle of Armageddon

Chapter 7: The Return of the King

Having called on her King, the Lord promises that he will answer Israel's call. Zechariah speaks clearly concerning the one-third who will survive the battle.

> ***Zechariah 13:9***
> *⁹ This third I will bring into the fire; I will refine them like silver and test them like gold. They will call on my name and I will answer them; I will say, 'They are my people,' and they will say, 'The LORD is our God.'"*

It is promised that this one-third will be refined, that they will call on the Lord and that he "*will answer them; I will say, 'they are my people,' and they will say, 'The LORD is our God.'*"

Jesus will return to "*fight against those nations, as he fights in the day of battle.*" He will do this as he does all things, in a calculated and orderly fashion, though with unfathomable force and destruction.

The Route

The most basic of revelations concerning the route Jesus will take when he returns to rescue Israel from Antichrist is found in the Olivet Discourse.

Jesus, in Matthew 24, warns the disciples not to believe reports that he has already come. He informs them that his coming will be seen by all.

> ***Matthew 24:26-27***
> *²⁶ "So if anyone tells you, 'There he is, out in the desert,' do not go out; or, 'Here he is, in the inner rooms,' do not believe it. ²⁷ For as lightning that comes from the east is visible even in the west, so will be the coming of the Son*

Chapter 7: The Return of the King

of Man.

Jesus' warning appears to be aimed at those who heeded his earlier warning and have escaped the city; going into hiding. As discussed earlier, the appointed hiding place "*in the wilderness*" is in Edom, or modern day Jordan. In Matthew 24 Jesus warns them not to believe any story that Jesus has arrived, apparently because Antichrist may invent such a story to draw the elect of Israel out of Edom, causing them to think Christ has returned and that the battle is over. In the course of that warning, Jesus states that "*just a lightning coming from the east is visible even in the west, so will be the coming of the Son of Man.*"

The substance of his statement is that he will in fact come from the east, just as lightning coming from the east is visible even in the west. Those who see him coming, then, will be west of him as he returns.

Because his warning is given to those who believe, each of which will end up in Edom, it can be understood that even in Edom one would look eastward to see Christ's return. He will come from the east, at the very least, from the perspective of those to whom he is warning. To that end, Christ's landfall, so to speak, will be east of Edom.

The continuing path of his return is also noted in his warning, in the next verse.

Matthew 24:28 (NIV)
[28] *Wherever there is a carcass, there the vultures will gather.*

Just as a carcass is that which would draw a vulture to it, so there is an objective which draws Christ. In short, Christ will appear East of Edom, and be drawn toward his target, which is the conglomerate armies of Antichrist. It will shortly be demonstrated that Antichrist's armies are not only in Israel, but also attempting to assault Edom for the Jewish remnant in protection there. He will appear East of Edom, then, travel toward his targets, beginning with Edom itself, to destroy the armies of

Antichrist accumulated nearby, then progress toward Israel to finish the task and eliminate the entirety of the forces of evil.

Micah paints a portrait of the coming of Christ over Edom.

> ***Micah 2:12-13 (KJV)*** *[12] I will surely assemble, O Jacob, all of thee; I will surely gather the remnant of Israel; I will put them together as the sheep of Bozrah, as the flock in the midst of their fold: they shall make great noise by reason of the multitude of men. [13] The breaker is come up before them: they have broken up, and have passed through the gate, and are gone out by it: and their king shall pass before them, and the LORD on the head of them.*

This text is rendered in KJV because the NIV translators replaced the literal interpretation *"sheep of Bozrah"* (Heb. *tsone-*[sheep] *bosra-*[Bozrah]) with a symbolic interpretation which reads *"sheep in a pen"* in the NIV. In the context of this study, understanding that Israel *literally* had been protected in Bozrah requires one to accept a literal interpretation for "Bozrah" as Micah's intended prophecy, although the reference to sheep holds the biblically typical metaphorical understanding as the disciples of Christ. Micah's metaphorical language spoke of Israel as sheep, but the location was literal; they are the sheep of a literal Bozrah.

The ancient city of Bozrah is located in Edom, or southern Jordan. Micah 2 indicates that as Christ comes to the battle, those in Edom fall in behind him and follow him as he finishes the battle. Verse 13 notes, *"their king shall pass before them,"* which supports that the return of Christ begins somewhere (eastward) prior to Bozrah, since he passes overhead before they follow.

Isaiah demonstrates the actual fighting of Christ's wrath beginning in Bozrah, in Edom, where the remnant have been protected.

Chapter 7: The Return of the King

> ***Isaiah 63:1-4*** *¹ Who is this coming from Edom,*
> *from Bozrah, with his garments stained crimson?*
> *Who is this, robed in splendor,*
> *   striding forward in the greatness of his strength?*
> *"It is I, speaking in righteousness, mighty to save."*
> *² Why are your garments red,*
> *   like those of one treading the winepress?*
> *³ "I have trodden the winepress alone;*
> *   from the nations no one was with me.*
> *I trampled them in my anger*
> *   and trod them down in my wrath;*
> *their blood spattered my garments,*
> *   and I stained all my clothing.*
> *⁴ For the day of vengeance was in my heart,*
> *   and the year of my redemption has come.*

Isaiah, being a Jewish prophet, speaks presumably as one who is viewing from Israel. He sees one, "*coming from Edom, from Bozrah.*" In this case, it is Isaiah who in the West who sees the coming of Christ from the East in his vision. This text does not indicate whether Christ had appeared elsewhere first, only that he is seen coming from Bozrah. But, Jesus indication of vultures being drawn to carcasses suggests that Christ probably will begin the actual battle in Bozrah, as Bozrah will be the farthest westerly location where armies of Antichrist will be gathered. There is no biblical inference to the armies of Antichrist being at any locations other than in Bozrah and in Israel, though it is possible that the armies of Antichrist will be distributed throughout that region, perhaps engaged in sending troops from one location to the other.

In this text, it is inescapably clear that the battle has been underway at the point in time when Isaiah sees Christ coming. His garments are "*stained crimson,*" indicated to stem from his assault on the armies, as "*their blood spattered my garments.*" It again becomes clear that Antichrist has troops which have attempted to reach the remnant in Edom. Coming from Bozrah, Christ's robes are already stained red from the blood of the battle. While Bozrah is a place of protection, Antichrist has still attempted to reach the remnant being held there, and has continued to attempt to draw them from their position of safety by his false claims of Christ having already come.

Christ Finishes The Battle

> ### *Revelation 19:11-16*
> *[11] I saw heaven standing open and there before me was a white horse, whose rider is called Faithful and True. With justice he judges and makes war. [12] His eyes are like blazing fire, and on his head are many crowns. He has a name written on him that no one knows but he himself. [13] He is dressed in a robe dipped in blood, and his name is the Word of God. [14] The armies of heaven were following him, riding on white horses and dressed in fine linen, white and clean. [15] Out of his mouth comes a sharp sword with which to strike down the nations. "He will rule them with an iron scepter." He treads the winepress of the fury of the wrath of God Almighty. [16] On his robe and on his thigh he has this name written: KING OF KINGS AND LORD OF LORDS.*

Once again is a rider seen coming on a white horse. In the beginning of the tribulation, Antichrist rode out on a white horse, "*bent on conquest.*"[65] He was, of course, emulating what Christ was going to do at this future moment. Unlike the first rider, this rider exhibits the qualities of the true King. He is "*called Faithful and True,*" rather than being a mass deceiver as Antichrist will be. "*With justice he judges and makes war.*" Antichrist waged war, but in *injustice,* he made war against those who refused to worship him. Christ's war is just. It is carried out against God's enemies who are attempting to destroy his subjects; Israel.

John's vision continues, "*[12] His eyes are like blazing fire, and on his head are many crowns. He has a name written on him that no one knows but he himself. [13] He is dressed in a robe dipped in blood, and his name is the

---

[65] Revelation 6:2

Chapter 7: The Return of the King

Word of God." This portrait of Christ is clearly one very unlike what one learned about in Vacation Bible School! Contrary to the Jesus of the Dispensation of Grace, at this point will be seen a Jesus who is described in language indicative of vengeance and wrath, the first objective of the great tribulation, and the only objective remaining at this point in the timeline. The moment for repentance has passed for all, and Jesus will ride out in destruction for the great day of the wrath of God.

Unlike the crown Antichrist will wear, this rider wears many crowns. "*Crowns*" in this text is translated from the Greek term *diadem*, as opposed to the *stephanos* crown observed upon Antichrist's head at the beginning of the tribulation. A *stephanos* is the crown of royalty. It is not the crown of a military victor, as Antichrist's crown will be, but of a true King; *the* true King, returning to his nation who have called to him.

John also affirms the wrathful purposes of the coming King. He notes, "*he is dressed in a robe dipped in blood.*" John, of course, writing only what he sees, describes a robe "*dipped in blood.*" However, Isaiah 63:3 explains that what John is seeing is a robe that was previously stained with blood from the battle this rider had been engaged in, as he declared, "*their blood spattered my garments, and I stained all my clothing.*"

The "*armies of heaven*" are seen following this rider, but will not participate in the battle, as noted in Isaiah 63:3, "*I have trodden the winepress alone.*" The term "*armies of Heaven*" refer to angelic armies. Jesus had formerly noted his angels would be present with him when he returns.

> **Matthew 25:31**
> *³¹ "When the Son of Man comes in his glory, and all the angels with him, he will sit on his throne in heavenly glory.*

Included with these angelic armies of Heaven, however, will also be the raptured saints, as noted in 1 Thessalonians 4:17, "*After that, we who are still alive and are left will be caught up together with them in the clouds to meet the Lord in the air. And so we will be with the Lord forever.*"

From the moment of the rapture, wherever Christ goes, the church will go. This will include the Battle of Armageddon, the judgments, the final millennial kingdom on earth and eternity in Heaven.

A final captivating revelation from this text is found in the statement, *"out of his mouth comes a sharp sword with which to strike down the nations."* The sword coming out of his mouth is not indicative of a literal sword, of course, but a figurative one. One holds a literal sword in one's hands. This sword is not held at all, but *"comes out of his mouth."* The nature of this sword is revealed in the books of Ephesians,

> **Ephesians 6:17**
> *17 Take the helmet of salvation and the sword of the Spirit, which is the word of God.*

and Hebrews.

> **Hebrews 4:12**
> *12 For the word of God is living and active. Sharper than any double-edged sword, it penetrates even to dividing soul and spirit, joints and marrow; it judges the thoughts and attitudes of the heart.*

The imagery of a sharp sword coming out of the mouth of Christ draws its meaning, as most other metaphors in Revelation do, from earlier scriptural references. Revelation 19:15 notes the sword is that with which Christ will *"strike down the nations."* Thus, the battle is won by the power of Christ in the same manner as the very creation: His word will be spoken, and it's power will produce his spoken will. Paul describes this event identically in his letter to the church at Thessalonica.

> **2 Thessalonians 2:8**
> *8 And then the lawless one will be revealed, whom the Lord Jesus will overthrow with the breath of his mouth and destroy by the splendor of his coming.*

Chapter 7: The Return of the King

The symbolic sword does not indicate a symbolic battle, however. The battle Jesus will undertake will be very literal. It will involve factual bloodshed, yet will be waged with nothing more than the breath of his mouth. The power of his spoken word will destroy, just as it created. The end result is that he will tread "*the winepress of the fury of the wrath of God Almighty*" in a battle of great bloodshed. This fascinating picture is that of a victorious Christ, riding into battle, and plainly *speaking* destruction on the armies of Antichrist. As he speaks, they are literally and violently destroyed in a very bloody battle.

May the reader never sing "The Battle Hymn of the Republic" quite the same again! The images of Christ in Isaiah and Revelation treading a winepress are exceptionally graphic and violent. It is so with significant cause, indicating the incredible power and finality of God's vengeance. The first purpose of the great tribulation is complete. This act of Christ's destruction of the armies of Antichrist begins the final fulfillment of the campaign of *the great and dreadful day of the Lord*, which ends in utter destruction and judgment upon the armies of the nations. God's wrath, indeed, paints an ugly, ugly picture. Woe to those on whom it falls.

> **Nahum 1:2**
> *² The LORD is a jealous and avenging God; the LORD takes vengeance and is filled with wrath. The LORD takes vengeance on his foes and maintains his wrath against his enemies.*

The Process

While some of the process of the battle has already been portrayed, more is noted in scripture concerning the advance of the battle. Revelation notes the call of birds of prey to feed on the flesh of kings.

> **Revelation 19:17-18**
> *¹⁷ And I saw an angel standing in the sun, who cried in a loud voice to all the birds flying in midair, "Come, gather together for the great supper of God, ¹⁸ so that*

> *you may eat the flesh of kings, generals, and mighty men, of horses and their riders, and the flesh of all people, free and slave, small and great."*

This call once again affirms the *literal* slaying of the armies of Antichrist. As Christ proceeds from Edom into Israel, he slaughters violently all who are affiliated with the armies of Antichrist. As they die in their places they are cleansed from the earth by birds of prey.

Zechariah speaks of the actual process of their destruction in very specific terms.

> ***Zechariah 14:12-13***
> [12] *This is the plague with which the LORD will strike all the nations that fought against Jerusalem: Their flesh will rot while they are still standing on their feet, their eyes will rot in their sockets, and their tongues will rot in their mouths.* [13] *On that day men will be stricken by the LORD with great panic. Each man will seize the hand of another, and they will attack each other.*

This is a continuation of Zechariah's discourse on the Battle of Armageddon. In this text, we see a vivid picture of how Christ's word destroys his enemies. Verse 12 notes, *"Their flesh will rot while they are still standing on their feet, their eyes will rot in their sockets, and their tongues will rot in their mouths."* The picture is one of instantaneous and hideous death. It also appears to be a painful death, though the text does not specifically reference pain. Yet, the immediate rotting of flesh from one's body certainly gives the inference of great pain, but definitely invokes a vast panic of those nearby who see what is coming.

Verse 13 notes men will be stricken with panic, seizing the hands of others and attacking each other. The fact that men will have time to respond by seizing each other indicates that this battle is moving at a calculated pace, rather than its being an instantaneous global act, such as the rapture event. Just as Isaiah saw the Lord Jesus coming at a

Chapter 7: The Return of the King

calculated pace, with his robes stained, so it appears people will have an opportunity to witness those before them fall and respond in panic before their own demise meets them. The lightning in the east will be visible to those in the west in the path of the coming destruction. The deaths of those who fall under Christ's sword is instantaneous, yet others will have time to see it and respond in panic. This will be an utterly horrifying event to those who will quickly come to realize that their weapons and military strength have absolutely no recourse upon their almighty enemy.

Revelation's account continues to give specific insight into the fates of the Antichrist and the false prophet.

> ***Revelation 19:19-21***
> *[19] Then I saw the beast and the kings of the earth and their armies gathered together to make war against the rider on the horse and his army. [20] But the beast was captured, and with him the false prophet who had performed the miraculous signs on his behalf. With these signs he had deluded those who had received the mark of the beast and worshiped his image. The two of them were thrown alive into the fiery lake of burning sulfur. [21] The rest of them were killed with the sword that came out of the mouth of the rider on the horse, and all the birds gorged themselves on their flesh.*

This text portrays the assault to be limited between the armies of Antichrist and Christ himself. The non-military of the earth are not involved in the specific judgment of Christ at this time, but will be judged later in a different manner very shortly. At this point, the concern is focused on the elimination of the threat against Israel, and the destruction of those who engage her in battle, as noted in Zechariah:

> ***Zechariah 14:3***
> *[3] Then the LORD will go out and fight against those nations, as he fights in the day of battle.*

Zechariah's account concerns itself with the armies gathered against

Israel, as does Revelation. To that end, "*the nations*" noted here are representatively present armies of those nations, and the destruction is limited to the fighting men.

Key to the armies, of course, are their supreme leaders, the Antichrist and the false prophet. Revelation 19:20 states that both of these men are captured and thrown alive into the lake of fire. It is at this point that the lake of fire, or Hell, as it is commonly thought of in English, is officially opened for business, in a manner of speaking. It will be demonstrated later in this work that unbelievers who die currently do not go to the lake of fire, but to Hades, a holding place for the dead. Their judgment into eternal conditions will be detailed in chapter eleven of this work. All who will enter the lake of fire will be preceded by the false prophet and Antichrist, the first to be administered the eternal punishment of God's wrath against sin.

Unlike men, the Antichrist and the False Prophet are noted to be "*cast alive*" into the lake of fire. This text is another strong signal indicating the demonic conception and nature of Antichrist, as well as the demonic nature of the false prophet. Angelic beings do not die, as do human bodies. For them to be literally killed in this battle would be contrary to their natures. The fact that everyone in the battle is demonstrated to be killed, except for these two and Satan himself, indicates again their angelic natures. They are captured rather than killed, and cast alive into the lake of fire rather than being physically killed with the rest of their armies.

The end of the battle

The battle is demonstrated to begin at Bozrah, but it will end outside of eastern Jerusalem, at the Valley of Jehoshaphat. An examination of the Valley of Jehoshaphat will be examined momentarily, but the book of Zechariah demonstrates the location of this valley.

> ***Zechariah 14:3-4***
> *³ Then the LORD will go out and fight against those*

Chapter 7: The Return of the King

> *nations, as he fights in the day of battle. ⁴ On that day his feet will stand on the Mount of Olives, east of Jerusalem, and the Mount of Olives will be split in two from east to west, forming a great valley, with half of the mountain moving north and half moving south.*

Immediately after the fighting noted in verse 3, the LORD sets his feet on the Mount of Olives. The Mount of Olives is immediately outside of the eastern gate to the ancient Temple, and most assuredly the coming Temple which will be functioning during the tribulation. At the point Christ establishes himself on the Mount of Olives, the fighting is over, and all military personnel are completely destroyed. As he sets his foot on the mountain, it will split into two parts, creating a great valley. The "*split*" is determined to create an east to west void, leaving a large valley between the two halves of the mountain on the north and the south. This revelation will be very pertinent in the coming sections.

In conclusion, the Battle of Armageddon seems to make a sweep which will begin in Edom, southeast of Israel, and ending immediately east of the Temple, in eastern Israel. Though Christ's coming is seen as coming from the east, the actual battle with have a north-western directional progression as Christ destroys the armies of Antichrist in a sweeping motion from Edom to the Valley of Jehoshaphat.

The Seventh Bowl Judgment

> *Revelation 16:17-21*
> *¹⁷ The seventh angel poured out his bowl into the air, and out of the temple came a loud voice from the throne, saying, "It is done!" ¹⁸ Then there came flashes of lightning, rumblings, peals of thunder and a severe earthquake. No earthquake like it has ever occurred since man has been on earth, so tremendous was the quake. ¹⁹ The great city split into three parts, and the cities of the nations collapsed. God remembered Babylon the Great and gave her the cup filled with the wine of the fury of his wrath. ²⁰ Every island fled away*

> *and the mountains could not be found. [21] From the sky huge hailstones of about a hundred pounds each fell upon men. And they cursed God on account of the plague of hail, because the plague was so terrible.*

With the completion of the Battle of Armageddon comes the seventh bowl judgment and final proclamation, "*It is done!*"

Although the armies are destroyed, there are still non-military citizens on the earth who have endured the great tribulation, righteous and unrighteous alike. These will shortly be given a judgment to determine their pending status in Christ's kingdom.

It should be noted that contextually, in the book of Revelation, this announcement and judgment seem to follow the gathering of the armies to Armageddon. Yet, in Revelation 17, John is shown retrospectively events which describe the destruction of Babylon. The loud voice from the throne saying, "*It is done!*," speaks to the completion of God's program of wrath. Some of the events following are John being shown the punishment brought upon the prostitute. It should be remembered that the book of Revelation is a compilation of visions, not each of which is shown in consecutive time.

Upon completion of this announcement, the final bowl judgment proceeds much like the final judgment of each observed series, with upheavals in nature. The earth reacts with a severe earthquake, rumblings and thunder. Jerusalem will split into three parts from the earthquake, cities will collapse, Islands will sink and mountains leveled. Lastly, one hundred pound hailstones will fall on some of the men who remain.

Revisiting Zechariah's account of the end of the battle may shed some light on the effects of this earthquake.

> **Zechariah 14:3-4**
> *[3] Then the LORD will go out and fight against those*

nations, as he fights in the day of battle. ⁴ On that day his feet will stand on the Mount of Olives, east of Jerusalem, and the Mount of Olives will be split in two from east to west, forming a great valley, with half of the mountain moving north and half moving south.

It appears that the splitting of the Mount of Olives may very well be in conjunction with the earthquake of the seventh bowl judgment. As these events happen at the same rough time, it is feasible that Christ sets his foot on the Mount of Olives as the earthquake erupts, causing the splitting of the mountain into a great valley. Revelation 16 notes mountains which could not be found, and Zechariah notes the splitting of the Mount of Olives.

This new valley appears to be the very location of the Valley of Jehoshaphat mentioned in the book of Joel, where the judgment of the Gentiles will occur.

The Judgment of the Gentiles

Those who remain on earth who are not of the armies of Antichrist and who were not destroyed in the Battle of Armageddon are now subject to a judgment as one of the first tasks of Christ's official kingdom on earth.

Joel speaks of this judgment, and the Valley of Jehoshaphat, where this sentencing is to occur.

> ***Joel 3:1-2***
> *¹'In those days and at that time,*
> *when I restore the fortunes of Judah and Jerusalem,*
> *²I will gather all nations*
>   *and bring them down to the Valley of Jehoshaphat.*
> *There I will enter into judgment against them*
>   *concerning my inheritance, my people Israel,*
> *for they scattered my people among the nations*
>   *and divided up my land.*

The book of Joel is a book concerning the coming "*day of the Lord.*" It details the demonic invasions of Revelation 9 and other events related to the great tribulation. The context of Joel 3 is immediately following the national Salvation of Israel and God's destruction of the armies who would war against her in the "*day of the Lord.*"[66]

Joel 3:1-2 tell details concerning what is known as "*the Judgment of the Gentiles.*"

Joel begins by stating the timing of this judgment as being, "*In those days and at that time, when I restore the fortunes of Judah and Jerusalem.*" In the context of eschatology, and the book of Joel, this restoration refers to the time of Israel's national salvation; when she calls on Christ to rescue her and receives him as her King. Christ, having finished the battle of Armageddon, is now in the process of restoring the fortunes of Judah and Jerusalem by means of the coming millennial kingdom.

Next, he depicts who is affected by the judgment. Verse 2 notes "*I will gather all nations,*" which sounds, at first, like a gathering of every nation on earth. Yet, verse 2 also notes this judgment is "*concerning my inheritance, my people Israel.*" He is gathering, then, all *other* nations of the earth "*concerning*" Israel. Israel, herself, is excluded from this judgment for two reasons. First, she is excluded because the purpose of the judgment is how other nations have treated her. It is "*concerning*" her. Secondly, she is excluded because she has participated in a national regeneration, and all of Israel has been saved. Israel has already had her pre-millennial judgment, with all who were not prepared to welcome her King having been killed by the sword of Antichrist in the second attack of the Battle of Armageddon. Her judgment was a separate item from the judgment described by Joel. The judgment of the Gentiles is concerned with a separation of those who served the Lord and those who did not, by merit of how they treated Israel during the tribulation.

---

[66] Joel 2

Chapter 7: The Return of the King

Joel also describes the nature of the actions being judged. The Lord says in verse 2, "*they scattered my people among the nations and divided up my land.*" Joel 3:3 continues,

> **Joel 3:3**
> *³ They cast lots for my people and traded boys for prostitutes; they sold girls for wine that they might drink.*

Clearly, these acts are the substance of what God means when he says this judgment is "*concerning*" Israel. It is a judgment concerning how Israel was treated within the context of the great tribulation, when all the world was against her. Clearly, during the tribulation, Jews will be treated as commodities, being exchanged for luxuries as common household items. God will execute judgment upon all who did such things at this time.

Lastly, Joel 3 speaks as to the location of the judgment. Joel 3:2 states, "*I will gather all nations and bring them down to the Valley of Jehoshaphat.*"

The Valley of Jehoshaphat is mentioned in the Bible only here, in the book of Joel. Additionally, according to the Midrash, there is no historical place which was officially named the Valley of Jehoshaphat, though many have accurately identified the location and called it such "unofficially." In fact, many in ancient Jewish tradition denied the literality of the valley, as it did not historically exist. Indeed, it was a place to come into existence at a future time.

"Jehoshaphat," as a term, is a combination of two Hebrew terms, *yhwh* (Jehovah) - or God, and *shapat* - or "judge." The "Valley of" Jehoshaphat, then, is literally "the valley where God will judge." In the context of Joel, the Valley of Jehoshaphat is an unidentified location where God will execute the judgments he is ordering. Paradoxically, historical references have dubbed the Kidron Valley area east of the temple "the Valley of Jehoshaphat" since the fourth century. Their postulates are well founded in scripture, as this is precisely where the Valley of Jehoshaphat - or the valley where God will judge - will be

226

located.

Zechariah has already established the creation of this valley.

> **Zechariah 14:4**
> [4] *On that day his feet will stand on the Mount of Olives, east of Jerusalem, and the Mount of Olives will be split in two from east to west, forming a great valley, with half of the mountain moving north and half moving south.*

The splitting in-two of the Mount of Olives, east of the temple compound, will create a new valley, never before known to humanity. It will be east of the temple, which fits well into Jesus' description of this judgment, which will be examined next. It is clear from Zechariah and Matthew 25 that this newly created valley is to be the location of "the valley where God will judge" the Gentile nations.

The Grouping

Matthew 25 is a very commonly misunderstood an improperly preached text due to people attempting to understand it outside of its proper context. It is important to note that Jesus is still speaking the Olivet Discourse. He is still answering the questions asked earlier,

> **Matthew 24:3**
> [3] *"...Tell us," they said, "when will this happen, and what will be the sign of your coming and of the end of the age?"*

Jesus details the answers to their questions through chapter 24, then tells two parables in Matthew 25, followed by the text above, detailing a judgment which will come upon his return; none other than the judgment of the Gentiles.

The timing is clear:

Chapter 7: The Return of the King

> [31] "When the Son of Man comes in his glory, and all the angels with him, he will sit on his throne in heavenly glory.

"*When the Son of Man comes in his glory, and all the angels with him,*" is precisely the setting of the judgment of the Gentiles. It is the next event in the timeline of eschatology.

The first grouping of this judgment is seen in verses 31-40. It is the separation of the righteous.

> Matthew 25:31-40
> [31] *"When the Son of Man comes in his glory, and all the angels with him, he will sit on his throne in heavenly glory.* [32] *All the nations will be gathered before him, and he will separate the people one from another as a shepherd separates the sheep from the goats.* [33] *He will put the sheep on his right and the goats on his left.*
> [34] *"Then the King will say to those on his right, 'Come, you who are blessed by my Father; take your inheritance, the kingdom prepared for you since the creation of the world.* [35] *For I was hungry and you gave me something to eat, I was thirsty and you gave me something to drink, I was a stranger and you invited me in,* [36] *I needed clothes and you clothed me, I was sick and you looked after me, I was in prison and you came to visit me.'*
> [37] *"Then the righteous will answer him, 'Lord, when did we see you hungry and feed you, or thirsty and give you something to drink?* [38] *When did we see you a stranger and invite you in, or needing clothes and clothe you?* [39] *When did we see you sick or in prison and go to visit you?'*
> [40] *"The King will reply, 'I tell you the truth, whatever you did for one of the least of these brothers of mine, you did for me.'*

Understanding that Jesus speaks of a judgment immediately after his coming as King certainly changes the context of what he has to say.

Verse 31 notes that, "*He will sit on his throne.*" Jesus' throne would almost certainly be in the Temple, as he is the coming God-King. The temple will be immediately to the west of the newly created valley, giving him a birds-eye view of his subject.

Verse 32 notes, "*All the nations will be gathered before him.*" This valley will be enormous; large enough for millions to gather before Christ. The majority of earth will have been destroyed at this point. There will presumably no longer be "billions" to gather here, but could certainly be a substantial number of people none-the-less.

Verse 32 also states that he will separate mankind "*as a shepherd separates the sheep from the goats.*" He first separates out the righteous, or the sheep, then the unrighteous, or the goats.

Verse 34 relays his message to the righteous, "*Come, you who are blessed by my Father; take your inheritance.*" The inheritance is not Heaven, as some have mistakenly presumed, but admission into Jesus messianic kingdom; his now pending one-thousand year reign of peace on earth.

Continuing, Matthew next depicts the separation of the unrighteous.

> ***Matthew 25:41-45***
> [41] *"Then he will say to those on his left, 'Depart from me, you who are cursed, into the eternal fire prepared for the devil and his angels.* [42] *For I was hungry and you gave me nothing to eat, I was thirsty and you gave me nothing to drink,* [43] *I was a stranger and you did not invite me in, I needed clothes and you did not clothe me, I was sick and in prison and you did not look after me.'*
> [44] *"They also will answer, 'Lord, when did we see you hungry or thirsty or a stranger or needing clothes or sick*

Chapter 7: The Return of the King

> *or in prison, and did not help you?'*
> *⁴⁵ "He will reply, 'I tell you the truth, whatever you did not do for one of the least of these, you did not do for me.'*
> *⁴⁶ "Then they will go away to eternal punishment, but the righteous to eternal life."*

Verse 41 speaks the fate of the unrighteous, as they are told, "*Depart from me, you who are cursed.*" Their "curse" is eternal, as they are sent into "*eternal fire prepared for the devil and his angels.*"

The grouping of the judgment of the Gentiles, then, is a grouping of great extremes. The righteous will gain entrance into Jesus' coming millennial kingdom. The unrighteous will be cast immediately into the lake of fire.

The Substance of His Judgment: Treatment of Israel

A necessary and fundamental understanding of Matthew 25 being in relation to the return of Christ is essential for one to properly understand the substance of Jesus' judgment. The context, historically, will be immediately after the great tribulation. To that end, his judgments concerning how people treated Israel must also be understood contextually to refer to that season. It is a judgment uniquely aimed at survivors of the tribulation. This text does not refer to a judgment of all mankind. The judgment of all remaining mankind will be observed in chapter 11 of this work, and is detailed in Revelation 20 in the Bible. The Great White Throne judgment of Revelation 20 is separate from what Jesus speaks of in Matthew 25, having almost no similarity whatsoever. Matthew 25 should be understood wholly in light of its context, as a judgment concluding the preparations for Jesus' millennial kingdom.

The substance of the judgment of the Gentiles is singular. It deals specifically with how people treated Israel during the tribulation. One should be careful not to read a "works salvation" into the message of the judgment of the Gentiles, however. The text states that this judgment will separate the "*righteous*" from the "*wicked*." One's righteousness or wickedness is not determined by works, but by one's allegiance to the King of Kings. The righteous will have acted righteously toward Israel, in knowledge of their King. Verse 37 states, "*then the righteous will answer him,*" in light of his having granted them entry into the Kingdom. Clearly, his judgment is not merely a works based judgment, but rather a works-based litmus test of sorts, which will rightly divide the "*righteous*" from the unrighteous. The Bible has never affirmed a works-based salvation, nor is one implied in this text. Rather, one's works are indicative of one's true status as a servant of Christ. Those who are truly followers of Christ will be able to be determined by merit of their relationship with his people, Israel. A true servant of Christ will not mistreat his chosen people, but rather will serve to protect and encourage them during the tribulation.

As to their treatment of Israel, Jesus states in verse 35 of the righteous,

> *[35] For I was hungry and you gave me something to eat, I was thirsty and you gave me something to drink, I was a stranger and you invited me in, [36] I needed clothes and you clothed me, I was sick and you looked after me, I was in prison and you came to visit me.'*

Similarly, he speaks of the unrighteous in verse 42,

> *[42] For I was hungry and you gave me nothing to eat, I was thirsty and you gave me nothing to drink, [43] I was a stranger and you did not invite me in, I needed clothes and you did not clothe me, I was sick and in prison and you did not look after me.'*

In both cases, those judged ask the question, "*when did we*" do these things? Clearly, neither the righteous nor the unrighteous had seen *Jesus* in need. They are equally misunderstanding Jesus' correlation of himself to his people, Israel. Yet, his response clears up the issue:

> "The King will reply, 'I tell you the truth, whatever you

Chapter 7: The Return of the King

> *did (or didn't do) for one of the least of these brothers of mine, you did for me.'*
> *(parenthesis added)*

The substance of the judgment of the Gentiles, then, is what one did, or did not do, unto "*these brothers of mine,*" Israel. Let one not forget that Jesus is the son and coming King of Israel. Let one not forget that Jesus was Jewish! The great tribulation entailed a great blow to Jesus' chosen people. Israel is the family of the promised son of Abraham, Jesus. Israel is the people of the Messiah! How one treated Israel is of great personal interest to Jesus, and will become a litmus test which will separate the righteous from the unrighteous at the judgment of the Gentiles.

During the great tribulation, one would have had an opportunity to support Israel in some way, or to turn against her. One would have the opportunity to share in Antichrist's hatred for her, or to protect, serve and assist her plight; to see her hungry and give her something to eat, to see her wandering and invite her in, to see her in need of clothing and clothe her, to see her sick and look after her or to see her in prison and come to visit.

Dear, church, understand that God is not through with Israel. She *is the people* of God's promises; some of which have not yet come to pass, but will indeed. Let all who think it wise to mistreat God's chosen people hear the words of Christ, and demonstrate repentance before the King arrives.

At this point in the timeline, all is now prepared for Christ to continue with the establishment of his kingdom. The King has returned and his enemies have been destroyed. The time is at hand when the King will officially take his throne, and the earth will rebuild under new management.

Chapter 8: Prophecies Concerning The Messianic kingdom

It is the belief of some groups that the idea of a messianic kingdom (or "millennial kingdom" - a literal one-thousand year reign of Christ on earth) is a product of the book of Revelation only. This belief frequently stems from the idea that the book of Revelation is metaphorical in its content and should not be taken literally. Thus, some reject the idea of a literal messianic kingdom on earth because of their lack of literal understanding of the book of Revelation. Amillennialism, for example, teaches that the one thousand year reign of Christ referenced in Revelation 20 is a figurative kingdom which began upon Christ's resurrection. However, even outside of the book of Revelation there are many biblical prophesies that can only literally be fulfilled at a future date; specifically, a date incorporating a *literal* millennial reign of Christ. The understanding that a literal millennial kingdom provides a biblical explanation for prophecies which otherwise must be explained away should lend much credibility to the literal interpretation of the one thousand year kingdom in the book of Revelation.

This chapter will demonstrate from writings *other* than the book of Revelation that the millennial kingdom noted in Revelation refers to a literal kingdom of Christ upon the earth rather than a figurative one. The basis for this position is the numerous Old Testament prophesies that remain unfulfilled in their entirety, which can *only* be fulfilled in the context of a millennial kingdom, such as a prophecy concerning a literal coming King in Israel.

Chapter 8: Prophecies Concerning The Messianic kingdom

Isaiah 9:6-7
⁶ *For to us a child is born,*
  to us a son is given,
  and the government will be on his shoulders.
And he will be called
  Wonderful Counselor, Mighty God,
  Everlasting Father, Prince of Peace.
⁷ *Of the increase of his government and peace*
  there will be no end.
He will reign on David's throne
  and over his kingdom,
establishing and upholding it
  with justice and righteousness
  from that time on and forever.
The zeal of the LORD Almighty
  will accomplish this.

While this text has rightly been interpreted as a messianic prophecy, or a prophecy concerning the coming of Messiah, what is missed by many is the observation that this prophecy has not yet been fulfilled in its entirety. It cannot be literally fulfilled outside of an earthly kingdom of Christ. While Christ did come as Messiah, he has not fully done so in the manner described in this, and numerous other texts.

Verse 6 notes particularly that, "*the government will be on his shoulders*." Many properly maintain that Christ has established his kingship and that he rules the universe from the father's right hand in Heaven. While this assertion is certainly valid, it does not do justice to the language used in Isaiah concerning the nature of the unique kingdom prophesied. Christ's spiritual kingdom is not a *complete* fulfillment of the text. Specifically, "*the government*" is referenced to be on his shoulders. And, by reading the text as a whole, the government is further stipulated to refer to a human, earthly government; specifically the government of David, Israel's most glorious and celebrated king. Christ, throughout the whole of human history, has not had a governmental position of any kind. While he was exalted to the father's right hand, this position could not be rightly understood to be a governmental position within the kingdom of David. In the millennium however, he will be an absolute monarch of a literal earthly kingdom from a throne in Israel; David's throne. The government *"shall be on his shoulder."* Isaiah, a Jewish prophet writing to a Jewish audience, specifically references that *"unto us"* a child is born and *"to us"* a son is given. The "us" in the text is Isaiah and his people; Israel. Surely Christ was born unto Israel. He was born unto a literal Israel, not a spiritual one. To that end, in keeping with the literal understanding of Israel in the text, one must also understand a literal government to be referred to. Specifically, *"the government"* refers to the government *of literal Israel* which is referenced in the text.

Verse 7 notes, *"of the increase of his government and peace there will be no end."* This government is demonstrated further to be the same government as that of David, who was a literal Israeli king. *"Upon the throne of David"* specifies the same throne as that of the historical king. Jesus, the universally understood *"child"* of this prophecy, has not sat upon David's throne in any capacity nor for any amount of time at this point in history. There has, in fact, been an end to that which was formerly understood as the fulfillment of this prophecy. David's throne has been vacant for thousands of years. Israel today is *not* a monarchy and does *not* have an heir of David upon a throne in rule of the nation, yet the text indicates his kingdom will be on David's throne, for all time thereafter.

To that end, considering this text literally throughout, this prophecy has not been fulfilled. Yet it shall be in the millennial kingdom, when Christ, David's human offspring, will take his throne forever over Israel.

David's throne was not a metaphorical throne in scripture, but a tangible one. This literal, tangible throne is the very throne the prophecy notes that Christ will rule over. Verse 7 states, *"He will reign on David's throne and over his kingdom."* Since when was Christ's sitting at the right hand of God equated with the throne of David? Truly, Jesus rules over the universe even now, but not from the throne of David in Israel. The prophecy does not speak of a breadth of government which *includes* the former throne of David. It speaks of a literal rule *from* the very throne of David. For this prophecy to be fulfilled, then, Christ must

Chapter 8: Prophecies Concerning The Messianic kingdom

return physically and establish himself as king over David's throne in Israel.

Jeremiah also speaks very tangibly concerning a coming literal descendant of David for an eternal reign.

> ***Jeremiah 33:14-21***
> *14 "'The days are coming,' declares the LORD, 'when I will fulfill the gracious promise I made to the house of Israel and to the house of Judah. 15 "'In those days and at that time I will make a righteous Branch sprout from David's line; he will do what is just and right in the land. 16 In those days Judah will be saved and Jerusalem will live in safety. This is the name by which it will be called: The LORD Our Righteousness.' 17 For this is what the LORD says: 'David will never fail to have a man to sit on the throne of the house of Israel, 18 nor will the priests, who are Levites, ever fail to have a man to stand before me continually to offer burnt offerings, to burn grain offerings and to present sacrifices.'"*
> *19 The word of the LORD came to Jeremiah: 20 "This is what the LORD says: 'If you can break my covenant with the day and my covenant with the night, so that day and night no longer come at their appointed time, 21 then my covenant with David my servant--and my covenant with the Levites who are priests ministering before me--can be broken and David will no longer have a descendant to reign on his throne.*

God's covenant to David, known as the Davidic covenant, is outlined in this text.

In verse 15, a coming *"righteous Branch"* is noted to sprout from David's line who will do what is just and right. This righteous branch is understood universally, among all differing eschatological views, to refer to a *literal* descendant; Christ. Christ was a historical descendant of David through his mother Mary. Yet, many of those who interpret verse

15 literally must quickly change to a metaphorical interpretation for verse 17 if they are to presume a literal kingdom is not referred to, for verse 17 states, *"David will never fail to have a man to sit on the throne of the house of Israel."* If the offspring is literal, then the kingdom must also be understood literally. Jeremiah speaks of a literal offspring of David who will sit on the literal throne of David's government; the *"throne of the house of Israel."*

Verse 18 continues and speaks of a tangible priestly office which will not *"ever fail to have a man to stand before me"* and give daily offerings.

Here, one should note that the substance of these offerings should not be equated with a return to the sacrificial system of the Old Testament. The final sacrifice for sins has been offered by Christ, and there will never be a return to a substitutionary atonement system outside of Christ. Yet, there will be a new variety of Temple worship which will exist in the millennial kingdom. The nature of that system and these offerings will be discussed in chapter nine.

It is the author's unconditional conclusion that without a literal millennial kingdom, the promises concerning the Davidic covenant would have been broken by God. While some promises of God are conditional, being promised under certain circumstances, this particular promise is not. In fact, God gives an utterly uncompromising certainty as to the unconditional nature of his promise in verses 20-21:

> *'If you can break my covenant with the day and my covenant with the night, so that day and night no longer come at their appointed time, ^{21} then my covenant with David my servant--and my covenant with the Levites who are priests ministering before me--can be broken and David will no longer have a descendant to reign on his throne.*

Or, stated another way, "unless someone can make the day and night cease" God promises that his covenant with David will not be broken.

Chapter 8: Prophecies Concerning The Messianic kingdom

Clearly, this is not exemplary of a conditional covenant, but an unconditional one. God speaks clearly what *he will do*.

For thousands of years, Israel has had *none* of these promises in a literal form. The starting point of this promise must be understood to refer to a future date. The literal interpretation of Revelation 20 provides the only biblical source of a historical fulfillment of these prophetic texts.

Even further clarification can be found in Luke 1, as an angel prophesies to Mary concerning her coming child.

> *Luke 1:30-33*
> *30 But the angel said to her, "Do not be afraid, Mary, you have found favor with God. 31 You will be with child and give birth to a son, and you are to give him the name Jesus. 32 He will be great and will be called the Son of the Most High. The Lord God will give him the throne of his father David, 33 and he will reign over the house of Jacob forever; his kingdom will never end."*

God reiterates the Davidic covenant in his promise to Mary, spoken through an angel.

Her son will be given the throne of David. He will reign over Israel forever. His kingdom shall never end.

The only way to escape the reality of a literal coming kingdom of Christ from this series of texts is to use a symbolic interpretation of David's throne in each of them. In such cases, it is commonly claimed that the throne of David is spiritualized, his reign over Israel is a spiritual Israel (the church) and that his kingdom refers to the kingdom of Heaven rather than a literal earthly kingdom. Yet, those who hold to this position must come to terms with heaven being equated to "*David's throne*" in these texts, which has no biblical legitimacy. Heaven is God's throne, not David's. For one to be given David's throne, one must be understood to be given a literal throne because David's throne was tangible and historical.

The first rule of biblical interpretation once again comes into necessary consideration. That rule states roughly, "When the literal sense of scripture makes sense, seek no other sense, but take every word at its literal meaning." Understandably, there are times when the literal sense does *not* make sense, such as when a metaphor is clearly used. For example, when Jesus said, "you are the light of the world," a plain literal sense does not make sense.[67] Surely Jesus is not saying that his disciples are *literal* "lights," but is making a figurative point. The context clearly indicates that he is being figurative, because he speaks to his disciples rather than a group of candles.

Yet, there are no immediate contextual reasons that the "throne of David" prophesies must be metaphorized. They are simply stated truths in a very natural and factual discourse. Thus, the literal interpretation of the above texts should serve as one's only interpretation. The throne of David is literal. It is the throne of kingship over Israel. The reign of David over Israel is historical and factual. This future King will indeed be a governmental ruler. The kingdom is understood as literal in scripture. To that end, the millennial kingdom, or the messianic kingdom, will be the literal fulfillment of prophecy.

Another area of scripture demanding a literal millennial kingdom is that area which describes the land which was promised to Abraham's descendants. Once again, the literal sense of the text makes common sense. It is not clearly metaphorical, but refers to literal real estate.

Originally, the Lord stated to Abraham,

> **Genesis 15:18-21**
> [18] ... *"To your descendants I give this land, from the river of Egypt to the great river, the Euphrates--* [19] *the land of the Kenites, Kenizzites, Kadmonites,* [20] *Hittites, Perizzites, Rephaites,* [21] *Amorites, Canaanites,*

---

[67] Matthew 5:14

Chapter 8: Prophecies Concerning The Messianic kingdom

Girgashites and Jebusites."

Once again an unconditional promise is noted, *"to your descendants I give this land."* Indeed, God did give vast real estate to Israel. No one quibbles over the fact that God's statement was referring to literal lands. Yet, the specific boundaries noted in the text do not equate to the boundaries settled by Israel at any point in history. The boundaries, stated as being *"from the river of Egypt to the great river, the Euphrates,"* are somewhat debatable, especially in light of which river is referred to in Egypt. Yet, the Euphrates is clearly known and universally understood as the eastern boundary of this covenant land. Without unnecessary debate over the western boundary, Israel has never in her history occupied the land which is described. The nearest portion of the Euphrates river is hundreds of miles from its closest portion of historical Israel. Since the promise is unconditional, it must be understood to be a yet unrealized prophecy, or one must understand a symbolic interpretation by which the prophesy should mean something else. However, since Israel *did in fact* receive a land allotment from the Lord, one should understand a literal land description was being given in the text. To spiritualize it is to be unfaithful to the common sense reading of the text.

Still another necessary observation from Old Testament texts which require a future millennial kingdom are the numerous texts which speak of a way of life which simply does not, and cannot exist on the earth outside of a fundamental change on the earth. Part of that fundamental change requires the seat of the earth's legal system to flow from Israel, as noted in Isaiah 2.

> ### Isaiah 2:2-4
> *² In the last days the mountain of the LORD's temple will be established as chief among the mountains; it will be raised above the hills, and all nations will stream to it. ³ Many peoples will come and say, "Come, let us go up to the mountain of the LORD, to the house of the God of Jacob. He will teach us his ways, so that we may walk in his paths." The law will go out from Zion, the word of*

> *the LORD from Jerusalem. ⁴ He will judge between the nations and will settle disputes for many peoples. They will beat their swords into plowshares and their spears into pruning hooks. Nation will not take up sword against nation, nor will they train for war anymore.*

Isaiah speaks in chapter two of a world that is virtually inconceivable outside of a literal millennial reign, with Christ himself as King. Clearly, the "*last days*" are referenced as the timing when "*all nations will stream*" to the mountain of the Lord's temple. And, in this future world, (as "*the last days*" certainly reflect no past world) "*the law will go out from Zion,*" or Israel, and the Lord himself will "*judge between the nations and will settle disputes for many people.*"

If this text speaks not of a millennial kingdom of the Lord Christ upon the earth, precisely what does it speak of? One cannot argue that it speaks of Heaven as a "spiritualized" kingdom. How will disputes exist in Heaven where there is no sin nature from which a dispute must originate? And, how can it be the earth which the Lord will settle disputes unless indeed the Lord is the King on earth? Indeed he will. And, under what other circumstance could it possibly be stated on earth that nations would no longer train for war, unless all nations are unified under a singular righteous King? Clearly Isaiah 2 speaks also of a situation that can only refer to a literal millennial reign.

Isaiah 11 speaks of a wolf lying with a lamb and a calf, lion and yearling together with a small child leading them. It speaks of infants playing with snakes and no harm coming to them. These attributes, all concerning a life on this earth unknown to anyone since Adam and Eve, clearly depict a new Kingdom on earth, where indeed things are uniquely changed on a fundamental level. Changes of such profundity have never been observed within the parameters of a human government, regardless of how charitable. Isaiah speaks of changes in the very conduct of nature itself, which insist on deistic intervention into the very nature of life on earth as it is known.

More attributes concerning the millennial kingdom will be observed in

Chapter 8: Prophecies Concerning The Messianic kingdom

chapter nine. As for this chapter, let it be understood that there are numerous scenarios in scripture which can only be fulfilled in a literal millennial kingdom. When Christ returns, he will return as King of Israel, and the earth. Israel will in fact be the capital city of the entire earth. Jesus, the King, will settle disputes from the literal throne of his father David. And, the God-King will change the very makeup of nature, so that even the wild animals will submit to his authority.

Chapter 9: The messianic kingdom

The Gap

Some dispensationalists refer to a gap which exists near the beginning of the messianic kingdom. Indeed, such a gap does appear in scripture in the sense that there is a season of preparation at the beginning of the millennial kingdom in which certain events appear to take place. The text which indicates such a gap is found in Daniel's observation of the very end of the tribulational time table. Seventy five days beyond the seven year tribulation period are noted in Daniel 12.

> **Daniel 12:11-13**
> [11] *"From the time that the daily sacrifice is abolished and the abomination that causes desolation is set up, there will be 1,290 days.* [12] *Blessed is the one who waits for and reaches the end of the 1,335 days.*
> [13] *"As for you, go your way till the end. You will rest, and then at the end of the days you will rise to receive your allotted inheritance."*

1,260 days is 3 ½ years if based on a 360-day Jewish calendar year. One understands each half of the tribulation to be 1,260 days because of Daniel's articulation of the last seven years; one half before the abomination of desolation, and one half afterward. Yet, in this text Daniel references well beyond 1,260 days. He speaks of 1,290 days after then abomination of desolation, then 1,335 days as key event dates.

Clearly, there are several unique dates set, each detailing a different event. Some contend that the millennial reign will not begin until 75 days after Christ returns. While the 75 day period does exist, this author leans toward the reign of Christ beginning the moment he appears east of

Chapter 9: The messianic kingdom

Bozrah. At that time he is the conqueror, and the undisputed King. Thus, logistically speaking, his reign has begun. He will impressively demonstrate himself to be the undeniable King. The text does not indicate the 1,335 days in conjunction with the reign of Christ beginning, but rather in conjunction with the time before a special blessing is to be observed. Likewise, it is not stated that the reign of Christ will fail to begin until after the 1,290 days. The rendering of the two additional dates have nothing to do with the beginning date of Christ's reign, but other events entirely.

Daniel notes 1,290 days as the duration period of the abomination of desolation. This is a full 30 days beyond the official end of the great tribulation, and consequently, 30 days beyond the return of Christ to destroy the armies of Antichrist and end the season of God's wrath. No reason is given as to why the abomination remains for an additional thirty days, but Daniel subsequently notes, *"Blessed is the one who waits for and reaches the end of the 1,335 days,"* which is yet another full 45 days later, or 75 days in total after the end of the tribulation.

The blessing for those who endure the additional 45 days (or the extra 75 days, total) is able to be determined from the context, however. The next verse states, *"¹³As for you, go your way till the end. You will rest, and then at the end of the days you will rise to receive your allotted inheritance."*

Daniel is being informed that he will be resurrected at this time to receive this blessing. *"At the end of the days you will rise to receive your allotted inheritance."* The *"end of the days"* refers to the days specifically referenced in the discourse, the 1,335 days, at which time a special blessing is promised. Thus, it appears that the First Resurrection (which will be studied shortly) will conclude on the 75th day of the Millennial reign. Daniel will be part of that resurrection group, as the Old Testament saints will be a part of the first resurrection. And, it will be a special blessing to last until that day, for reasons which will be discussed shortly.

This work will teach from the perspective of the millennial reign of

Christ beginning with His return at Bozrah. No clear biblical teaching warrants this seventy five day period to interfere with the beginning point of the millennial kingdom of Christ. It is merely an interval of time from the end of the tribulation to the time of the First Resurrection. Yet, in the author's position there arise difficulties in the time table when computing the one thousand year reign of Christ, which will be dealt with shortly as well.

Jesus Judges His Enemies

Immediately upon Christ's return in power, Jesus' first orders of business will deal with the handing out of judgments to his enemies. The judgments upon Antichrist and the False Prophet were discharged at the end of the tribulation upon their being hurled alive into the Lake of Fire. The judgment of the Armies of Antichrist occurred upon their being slain by the breath of Christ's word in the Battle of Armageddon. The judgment of the non-military personnel who remained, or "The Judgment of the Gentiles," resulted in their being sorted into "righteous" and "wicked" categories: the righteous entering the millennial kingdom and the wicked being escorted into eternal punishment; being killed and sent into the lake of fire after the Beast and the False Prophet.

One area that was not dealt with earlier is the judgment of Satan and the demonic realm.

Satan is bound for 1,000 years

Another one thousand year term is referenced specifically in Revelation 20, in parallel with the one thousand year reign of Christ on earth. It is the one thousand year binding of Satan in the Abyss.

> ***Revelation 20:1-3***
> *[1] And I saw an angel coming down out of heaven, having the key to the Abyss and holding in his hand a great chain. [2] He seized the dragon, that ancient serpent, who is the devil, or Satan, and bound him for a thousand*

Chapter 9: The messianic kingdom

years. ³ He threw him into the Abyss, and locked and sealed it over him, to keep him from deceiving the nations anymore until the thousand years were ended. After that, he must be set free for a short time.

As noted earlier, the Abyss is a place for the temporary confinement of demons, or fallen angels. Satan is not commonly referred to as a demon, but he is of the same essence; he is a fallen Angel. To be precise, he is a fallen cherub,[68] the highest ranking of all angelic types. Thus, he is noted to be bound in the place of temporary demonic confinement, the Abyss. It is the logical location for misplaced evil angelic spirits to be sentenced.

The term of his sentence is 1,000 years, exactly mirroring the time period of the millennial kingdom of Christ. During the millennial reign, then, Satan will not be allowed on the earth, but will be completely out of the world picture, being locked in the Abyss for the entire period. It is specifically noted in this text that his sentence in the Abyss is "*to keep him from deceiving the nations anymore until the thousand years are ended.*" One of the glorious characteristics of the millennial reign of Christ will be the utter absence of Satanic influence on the earth. Man will continue to struggle with sin, as he will still be born with a sin nature- even in the millennial kingdom. Yet, Satan's influence over man's sinful state will not exist. Consequently, temptation will exist from the sphere of one's own sinful nature, but will not be influenced directly by satanic powers. This fact alone will lend a peace to the millennial kingdom which has not been observed on earth since the early days of the Garden of Eden.

Verse 3 notes that the angel, after throwing Satan into the Abyss, "*locked and sealed it over him*" for the duration of the one thousand year period. Satan is therefore alone in the Abyss, without his demonic hordes. He is in effect, placed in solitary confinement for the entire one thousand year sentence. He will not be allowed to deceive the nations during Christ's reign as he has done throughout history.

---

[68] Ezekiel 28:14

Yet, the demonic realms, not being placed in the Abyss, are demonstrated in scripture to be held in confinement in other locations.

The Confinement of Demons

Scripture prophesies of two desolate places on the earth during the future millennial kingdom. These locations are Babylon and Edom; both of which have had numerous biblical judgments pronounced against them throughout history for their evil deeds, particularly against Israel. Among these numerous judgments are those which specifically note their futures to be of strict desolation from human inhabitance.

Isaiah 13 contains one such prophecy against Babylon.

> ***Isaiah 13:9***
> [9] *See, the day of the Lord is coming*
> *--a cruel day, with wrath and fierce anger--*
> *to make the land desolate*
> *and destroy the sinners within it.*

Clearly, this is a "day of the Lord" prophecy, detailing Babylon's destruction during the great tribulation, as has been demonstrated in this study. The day of the Lord did make the land desolate. Babylon was burned with fire. Interestingly, however, the text continues with a unique prophecy concerning Babylon's fate after her destruction.

> ***Isaiah 13:19-22***
> [19] *Babylon, the jewel of kingdoms, the glory of the Babylonians' pride, will be overthrown by God like Sodom and Gomorrah.* [20] *She will never be inhabited or lived in through all generations; no Arab will pitch his tent there, no shepherd will rest his flocks there.* [21] *But desert creatures will lie there, jackals will fill her houses; there the owls will dwell, and there the wild goats will leap about.* [22] *Hyenas will howl in her strongholds, jackals in her luxurious palaces. Her time*

Chapter 9: The messianic kingdom

is at hand, and her days will not be prolonged.

Verse 20 notes of her desolation, that "*she will never be inhabited or lived in through all generations.*" To be desolate inherently indicates that no human will live there. Yet, beyond the peculiar judgment of desolation, one also sees in Revelation the impossibility of human habitation in Babylon at this time due to the nature of her destruction.

> **Revelation 19:1-3**
> ¹ *After this I heard what sounded like the roar of a great multitude in heaven shouting:*
> *"Hallelujah! Salvation and glory and power belong to our God,*
> ² *for true and just are his judgments. He has condemned the great prostitute who corrupted the earth by her adulteries. He has avenged on her the blood of his servants."*
> ³ *And again they shouted: "Hallelujah!*
> *The smoke from her goes up for ever and ever."*

"*The smoke from her goes up for ever and ever*" is indicative of a barren, burning land. As the proverb goes, where there is smoke there is fire. A land which smokes forever is therefore a land which has some source of permanent burning.

Jeremiah also comments on Babylon's fate in chapter 51.

> *Jeremiah 51:43*
> *Her towns will be desolate,*
> *a dry and desert land, a land where no one lives,*
> *through which no man travels.*

Conceding that Babylon is to be a "*dry and desert land*" once again indicates a land which is utterly barren. However, Isaiah 13 continues in its text to tell a part of the story which observes that while it is to be desolate of human habitation, some manner of creatures will in fact live in this barren and burning land.

> **Isaiah 13:21-22**
> ²But desert creatures will lie there, jackals will fill her houses; there the owls will dwell, and there the wild goats will leap about.
> ²² Hyenas will howl in her strongholds, jackals in her luxurious palaces.

The obvious question one may ask is, "*how can creatures live in a land that is desert, dry, and burning?*" The description of a dry, desert, burning and smoking land is the picture of a land without vegetation to support any normal sort of wildlife.

Further examination of the Hebrew language demonstrates that these creatures are not of a natural origin, however.

In verse 21, "*desert creatures*" is rendered from the Hebrew term, *si*, which literally translates, "desert beasts."[69] "*Wild goats*" is Hebrew *sair*, literally translated, "goat demons,[70]" and "*jackals*" in verse 22 comes from the Hebrew term *tannin*, which literally translates, "dragons[71]". The KJV translates this word "dragons," opting for the more literal terminology.

The other terms translated "*owls*" and "*hyenas*" are very non-descript creatures in the Hebrew language. In every case, the language used to describe the creatures in this text are *not* normal creatures. They are not described in typical "animal" terms, but in nondescript, other-world creaturely terms instead. They live in a place that is burning, dry, and uninhabitable, and several of the terms literally denote demonic forms, such as the *sair* and *tannin*.

While it may seem an awkward step to take Isaiah literally in his

---

[69] Strong's Greek & Hebrew Dictionary, (H6723)
[70] Vines Expository Dictionary of Old and New Testament Words, "sair", Strongs (H8163)
[71] Strong's Greek & Hebrew Dictionary (H8565)

Chapter 9: The messianic kingdom

descriptions of the life forms of fallen Babylon, Revelation is much less conservative in its use of terms. Revelation 18:2 explains more clearly what is recorded in Isaiah 13.

> *"Fallen! Fallen is Babylon the Great!*
> *She has become a home for demons*
> *and a haunt for every evil spirit,*
> *a haunt for every unclean and detestable bird.*

The destroyed Babylon "*has become a home for demons*" and "*a haunt for every evil spirit.*" Understanding clearly from Revelation, one can faithfully render Isaiah's text more literally and understand that Babylon is noted after her fall to be a literal "*home for demons.*" Babylon and Edom (which will be discussed next), will become protected areas, reserved for the confinement of the demonic hosts during the millennial kingdom while Satan alone will be in the Abyss.

Edom is prophesied the same sorts of judgments in Isaiah 34:8-14.

> [8] *For the LORD has a day of vengeance, a year of retribution, to uphold Zion's cause.*
> [9] *Edom's streams will be turned into pitch, her dust into burning sulfur; her land will become blazing pitch!*
> [10] *It will not be quenched night and day; its smoke will rise forever. From generation to generation it will lie desolate; no one will ever pass through it again.*
> [11] *The desert owl and screech owl will possess it; the great owl and the raven will nest there. God will stretch out over Edom the measuring line of chaos and the plumb line of desolation.*
> [12] *Her nobles will have nothing there to be called a kingdom, all her princes will vanish away.*
> [13] *Thorns will overrun her citadels, nettles and brambles her strongholds. She will become a haunt for jackals, a home for owls.*
> [14] *Desert creatures will meet with hyenas, and wild goats will bleat to each other; there the night creatures will*

also repose and find for themselves places of rest.

Verse 8 sets the timeline with a description of the Lord's day of vengeance, followed by an almost identical judgment in Edom as was given to Babylon.

Verse 9 states her streams turn to pitch, her dust into burning sulfur, her land blazing pitch. Verse 10 notes her fire will not be quenched, smoke will rise forever, and that she, too, will be desolate forever. No human will ever pass through her lands again. Edom, like Babylon, is noted to be a land which is not only desolate, but is incapable of sustaining life. It is burning, smoking and emanating pools of blazing pitch.

Additionally, the same strange animals are seen in Edom as were noted to live in Babylon. Verse 13 notes "*jackals*," which once again come from Hebrew, *tannin,* or "dragons" (KJV again uses the term "dragons"). Verse 14 notes the same "*wild goats*" from the Hebrew, *sair,* or literally, "goat demons." And, once again, all animal descriptions are non-descript and described with strange creaturely terms not normally affiliated with the animal kingdom.

Edom and Babylon have been sentenced to house demons throughout the millennial kingdom. In both cases, their judgment of desolation, burning, barrenness and demonic creatures has a duration of "*forever*." In the context of this study, "forever" on this earth lasts only shortly longer than the one-thousand year Millennial Reign, after which this earth will be destroyed and a new earth will be created to endure for eternity.

The First Resurrection

Noted earlier was an inference to the first resurrection, when Daniel would rise to receive his allotted inheritance. Revelation 20 speaks of this event, which will occur very early in the millennial kingdom.

Revelation 20:4-6

Chapter 9: The messianic kingdom

> *⁴ I saw thrones on which were seated those who had been given authority to judge. And I saw the souls of those who had been beheaded because of their testimony for Jesus and because of the word of God. They had not worshiped the beast or his image and had not received his mark on their foreheads or their hands. They came to life and reigned with Christ a thousand years. ⁵ (The rest of the dead did not come to life until the thousand years were ended.) This is the first resurrection. ⁶ Blessed and holy are those who have part in the first resurrection. The second death has no power over them, but they will be priests of God and of Christ and will reign with him for a thousand years.*

At this point in time, the martyrs of the great tribulation are to be raised from the dead physically, and will be allowed to reign with Christ for one thousand years; the time frame of the Kingdom. As noted in chapter 2, resurrections and judgments correspond to one another in scripture. Verse 4 notes the preparation for the judgment of those who are to be raised at this point, "*I saw thrones on which were seated those who had been given authority to judge.*" Just as the church will be judged at the time of the rapture, the tribulation saints will be judged for their acts of righteousness upon their resurrection. Judgments for believers are always judgments concerning reward, unlike the judgments upon non-believers, which are judgments of punishment. Upon completion of this resurrection and judgment, the statement is made "*this is the first resurrection.*"

The notation of "*the first resurrection*" does not refer to the first in a series of resurrections, but rather the first of two *types* of resurrections. One type of resurrection is the resurrection of the righteous. Another resurrection, which will occur at the very end of history, will be a resurrection of the unrighteous. The first resurrection is not completely represented by these martyrs alone, however, as other New Testament texts report that the first resurrection actually begins much earlier, with Christ himself. Thus, the "*first resurrection*" refers to the first of a *type* of resurrection, which is completed in the text with the raising of the tribulation martyrs. They are the final group to be raised in the first resurrection. One should not conclude that the tribulation martyrs are the sole recipients of this resurrection, but that their being raised *completes* the first resurrection.

Others who are part of the first resurrection have formerly been resurrected by this time. The fullness of the first resurrection can be compiled through several scriptural texts which teach that the first resurrection is indeed a process spanning millennia.

The "*first resurrection*," being the first *type* of resurrection, is in fact a series of resurrection events, beginning with Christ himself.

> ***1 Corinthians 15:20-23***
> *[20] But Christ has indeed been raised from the dead, the firstfruits of those who have fallen asleep. [21] For since death came through a man, the resurrection of the dead comes also through a man. [22] For as in Adam all die, so in Christ all will be made alive. [23] But each in his own turn: Christ, the firstfruits; then, when he comes, those who belong to him.*

Christ is the *firstfruits* of the first resurrection. He is the first among all who participate in the first resurrection, or the resurrection of the saved. Through his resurrection, all other believers have life and the promise of their own future resurrection. Just as the firstfruits of a fruit-bearing tree are the first of many, so Jesus, being the firstfruits of the resurrection of the righteous (the first resurrection) is the first of several groups of the righteous which will be raised physically.

It should be noted that the first resurrection produces a new and permanent status to its recipients. It is not the same as the resurrection of Lazarus, for example, or others in scripture who were raised to life only to die again at a later time. This resurrection in Christ is the resurrection of permanence, through which those raised receive a glorified body, which cannot die, become sick or sin as noted in Chapter 2. Of this "first

Chapter 9: The messianic kingdom

resurrection" group of the permanent and final resurrection, Christ was the *firstfruits*.

The next group to follow are those who are resurrected in the rapture event.

> ***1 Thessalonians 4:16-17***
> *[16] For the Lord himself will come down from heaven, with a loud command, with the voice of the archangel and with the trumpet call of God, and the dead in Christ will rise first. [17] After that, we who are still alive and are left will be caught up together with them in the clouds to meet the Lord in the air. And so we will be with the Lord forever.*

As noted in Chapter 2, the rapture event begins with "*the dead in Christ.*" Those who are dead in Christ today, as a result of whatever cause of death occurred to them, will be raised at the moment of the rapture. Following them, according to this text, are the glorification of the bodies of those "*who are still alive and are left.*" While the term "resurrection" may not seem the likely terminology to refer to the glorification of those who never died, the idea of the resurrection is fully met in those who are raptured. They will receive their resurrection body; the glorified body which cannot die. While they never officially will have experienced physical death, they will still participate in the first resurrection by merit of their body of death being replaced by a new and glorious body of life.

Also noted in Chapter 2, "*in Christ*" is a uniquely New Testament idea representing those who have the indwelling Holy Spirit; the church. For that reason, the rapture should be understood not to include the Old Testament saints. However, it will next be observed that they too will be part of the first resurrection and will receive an inheritance in the millennial kingdom.

Isaiah spoke concerning the resurrection of the Old Testament saints to which he prophesied.

> ***Isaiah 26:19***
> *But your dead will live; their bodies will rise.*
> *You who dwell in the dust, wake up and shout for joy.*
> *Your dew is like the dew of the morning; the earth will*
> *give birth to her dead.*

This text does not specify the timing of the resurrection of the Old Testament saints, but does speak to the fact that they will be resurrected. The timing of this resurrection, however, is referenced earlier in the same chapter, as Isaiah 26:1 states, *"In that day this song will be sung in the land of Judah...."*

"In that day" is a theme of several preceding chapters, detailing the events of the day of the Lord and the glory following it. The *"song"* which *"will be sung"* in Judah includes the lyric of verse 19, *"but your dead will live; their bodies will rise."* Thus, this text indicates a millennial kingdom resurrection of the Old Testament Saints, because it is a resurrection which follows the period of *"the day of the Lord."* However, this text does not detail the timing of the resurrection of the Old Testament saints beyond its being in conjunction with the millennial kingdom.

Daniel 12, as observed earlier, does, however.

> ***Daniel 12:13***
> *"As for you, go your way till the end. You will rest, and then at the end of the days you will rise to receive your allotted inheritance."*

It was noted earlier that Daniel was promised to *"rise to receive your allotted inheritance"* at the *"end of the days,"* or after the 1,335 days, which is 75 days into the millennial kingdom. This text gives us the timeline for the resurrection of Old Testament saints, for Daniel was one of them. That date is the 75th day of the millennial kingdom. Thus, *"the first resurrection,"* noted in Revelation 20 to conclude with the resurrection of the tribulation martyrs, must also be on or after the 75th

Chapter 9: The messianic kingdom

day of the Kingdom. The tribulation saints are the final group to be resurrected to salvation. All others have been raised by that time: Christ, the dead in Christ at the rapture, the raptured living, and the Old Testament saints will all have been resurrected by the time the tribulation martyrs are raised.

Concerning the second resurrection, Revelation 20 continues,

> **Revelation 20:5**
> *"(The rest of the dead did not come to life until the thousand years were ended.)"*

This stipulates that not all are resurrected at this time, but only those belonging to the first resurrection; the righteous. *"The rest of the dead"* refer to those of the second resurrection, the lost without Christ. There will have been no resurrection at this time of the lost. But, one will come. All who ever lived will be resurrected at their appointed times.

Daniel 12:2, in the context of the completion of the great tribulation states, *"Multitudes who sleep in the dust of the earth will awake: some to everlasting life, others to shame and everlasting contempt."*

Indeed, all will rise at their allotted time. The second resurrection group will be detailed in chapter eleven.

With the completion of the first resurrection, all of the righteous of history will have been raised to participate in the millennial kingdom. While Christ is indeed the coming King of Israel, and shall reign as the King of Israel, all of those who have placed their allegiance in him will be invited into the kingdom to serve. The Old Testament saints will rise to receive their *"allotted inheritance"* in the Kingdom.[72] The raptured church will *"be with the Lord forever."*[73] And, the tribulation saints *"will*

---

[72] Daniel 12:13
[73] 1 Thessalonians 4:17

reign with him for a thousand years."[74]

At this point, a note concerning the timing of the one thousand years of the Kingdom should be made. There have been a couple of one thousand year intervals noted relating to the messianic kingdom. Satan is to be bound for one thousand years in Revelation 20. Also in Revelation 20, the first resurrection, completed by the tribulation martyrs, will all rise to reign with Christ for one thousand years. The actual timing of the reign of Christ has been historically understood from these one thousand year intervals to also be specifically a "one thousand year" reign. However, there still remains a seventy five day period immediately after the tribulation period ends to be accounted for, as noted earlier, concerning Daniel 12.

Some understand that the millennial reign of Christ officially begins at the end of the seventy five days, beginning with the completion of the first resurrection. Yet, it seems apparent that Christ's return as King began when he established his authority over the earth and destroyed the enemies of Antichrist. While this would make Christ's millennial kingdom slightly over one thousand years, scripture never specifies the amount of time for the entirety of the millennial kingdom. Scripture only specifies that *Satan will be bound* for one thousand years and that the *first resurrection will reign with Christ* for one thousand years. Christ's reign, itself, will have begun 75 days earlier, for a total millennial kingdom duration of one thousand years and seventy five days. The one thousand year intervals in scripture do not limit Christ's kingdom from beginning slightly prior to the one thousand years which the first resurrection will reign *with* Christ.

The one thousand year specification does, however, seem to relegate Satan's bondage in the Abyss to begin on the same day as the first resurrection. This would mean that Satan's bondage did not begin immediately after the Battle of Armageddon, but seventy five days later. Revelation 20:7 notes, *"when the one thousand years are over, Satan will*

---

[74] Revelation 20:6

Chapter 9: The messianic kingdom

be released from his prison." It seems incomprehensible that the one thousand years of the first resurrection's reign with Christ and Satan's one thousand year imprisonment would be anything but simultaneous. Thus, Christ's reign, itself, will likely be seventy five days longer than the one thousand years for which the millennial kingdom draws its title. And, if that is the case, then Satan himself may not be formally bound in the Abyss until the seventy fifth day.

Still others have maintained that the one thousand year specification is general in nature. However, in light of the precision of the dating related to eschatology, down to the very day in so many instances, that seems improbable. Rather, the one thousand years should probably be understood to be strictly literal regarding the imprisonment of Satan and the time of the reigning "with Christ" of the tribulation saints. It is only the actual computation of the time of Christ's reign which is not limited to a stringent one thousand year period.

Marriage Feast of The Lamb

The Marriage Feast, in Jewish tradition, is a seven day fest commemorating a new marriage. The imagery of a wedding feast in Revelation 19 demonstrates metaphors used in both the Old and New Testaments.

In the Old Testament, Israel was metaphorically referred to as the "wife of Jehovah." The book of Hosea, for example, equates Hosea's unfaithful wife with Israel's unfaithfulness to God. Likewise, Jeremiah 3:14 says,

> *"Return, faithless people," declares the LORD, "for I am your husband. I will choose you--one from a town and two from a clan--and bring you to Zion.*

Similarly, in the new Testament, the church is referred to as "the bride of Christ." In 2 Corinthians 11:2, Paul says,

> *"I am jealous for you with a godly jealousy. I promised you to one husband, to Christ, so that I might present you as a pure virgin to him."*

Jesus told parables comparing the Kingdom of God to weddings[75].

This coming feast, then, draws it metaphorical understanding from a culmination of many biblical images demonstrating the consummation of a pure relationship between man and God through Christ in the millennial kingdom.

> ***Revelation 19:7-9***
> *[7] Let us rejoice and be glad and give him glory! For the wedding of the Lamb has come, and his bride has made herself ready.*
> *[8] Fine linen, bright and clean, was given her to wear."*
> *(Fine linen stands for the righteous acts of the saints.)*
> *[9] Then the angel said to me, "Write: 'Blessed are those who are invited to the wedding supper of the Lamb!'"*
> *And he added, "These are the true words of God."*

Concerning the preparation for the wedding, verse 7 notes, " *his bride has made herself ready.*" At this point in history a unique purity exists among God's chosen bride; those who have received his invitation to Lordship. Israel, the wife of Jehovah, is regenerated and pure. The raptured saints, or the bride, are pure, with new sinless bodies and minds. The tribulation saints are greatly refined, having endured tremendous persecution and demonstrated great endurance during the tribulation. The beginning of the millennial kingdom is a unique circumstance in human history not observed since the first family of Adam and Eve: all who exist on the earth at the beginning of the Kingdom are righteous and belong wholly to the Lord. The whole of his collective wife and bride are present with their King to begin his reign on earth.

---

[75] Matthew 22:1-14, Matthew 25:1-13

Chapter 9: The messianic kingdom

Verse 8 notes, "*Fine linen, bright and clean, was given her to wear.*" Seemingly contrary to the phrase "*the bride has made herself ready*", these two phrases beg the questions: Has the bride made herself ready or was she *given* fine linen to wear? The answer seems to be "both."

The next phrase reveals, "*(Fine linen stands for the righteous acts of the saints.)*" In this context, while fine linen was given to her to wear, the linen given to her was her righteous acts of service to her betrothed. Her clothing is both "given" and to some degree an act of her own response in faithfulness by her righteous acts. The bride's readiness to wed seems to be a compilation of the two. She has been purchased by Christ, having been given the opportunity to serve him and has responded to his Lordship by righteous acts on her part in obedience to His call.

"*Blessed are those who are invited to the wedding supper of the Lamb!*" To be on earth at this time is to be both Christ's possession and party to the wedding itself. To be present is the blessing of assured eternal life, both in the coming millennial kingdom and the eternal state of Heaven which waits thereafter. To be present at this wedding will be to see first-hand the fruition of the hope which the redeemed have longed for; the beginning of the kingdom of Christ on earth.

Life In The Messianic Kingdom

The First Resurrection: Reigning With Christ

> **Revelation 20:6**
> ⁶ *Blessed and holy are those who have part in the first resurrection. The second death has no power over them, but they will be priests of God and of Christ and will reign with him for a thousand years.*

Among the blessings of being invited to the wedding feast, the first resurrection are given an additional honor. They are given positions of authority in the newly established millennial kingdom. They will "*reign*

with Christ," having a special place of authority in the new kingdom.

Remaining on the earth are still the numbers of those who endured the tribulation. They are the Gentiles who passed through the judgment of the Gentiles invited to *"'Come, you who are blessed by my Father; take your inheritance, the kingdom prepared for you since the creation of the world.'"*[76] They are also those Israelites who survived the Battle of Armageddon, to whom God will say, *"'They are my people,' and they will say, 'The LORD is our God.'"*[77] The reconciliatory purpose of the great tribulation will bear fruit which will bring forth a righteous line of humanity which enter the Kingdom.

These will repopulate the earth under Christ's rule and be the subjects of the Kingdom, beginning a new life as citizens of Christ's government. This government itself will be compiled at Christ's pleasure as he assigns various positions of authority necessary to run the earth in his new program. These positions will be granted to the first resurrection.

Of those positions, verse 6 specifically notes, *"they will be priests of God and of Christ."* In the Old Testament, priests conducted all aspects of worship. They taught, governed and provided all aspects of sacrificial worship. In the New Testament, each believer has a priesthood through Christ, the mediator. Christ himself is the high priest by which all have access to God the father. In the millennial kingdom, a new form of priestly office will exist, requiring servants of that order. These positions of authority will be assigned to those of the first resurrection.

While the text does not specify all of the potential positions of priests in the millennial kingdom, the position of priestly service is uniquely named as a primary vocation by which the first resurrection may serve Christ. Some have difficulty accepting this designation, deeming it uncharacteristic of New Testament worship. However, scripture teaches that worship in the millennial kingdom will indeed be uncharacteristic of

---

[76] Matthew 25:34
[77] Zechariah 13:9

Chapter 9: The messianic kingdom

both Old and New Testament worship. The millennial kingdom will bring about an entirely new process of worship which will be conducive to the worship of Christ during his physical reign on the earth.

In the Old Testament, God was worshipped somewhat from afar, through his determined processes involving a Temple where his glory dwelt.[78] In the New Testament, the indwelling Christ was worshipped individually, though still to some degree from afar, as he was not *physically* present with his worshippers. Though Christ's spirit indwells believers, his physical presence has not been observed on the earth since the first century. In the millennial kingdom a new form of worship is prescribed which entails certain elements recognizable from both former worship systems.

A fundamental change from New Testament worship will be wrought in that millennial worship will involve once again a physical Temple, with God literally present in Christ Jesus. Yet, one should not presume millennial worship to be a return to Old Testament Temple worship. It is not Old Testament Temple worship, but millennial Temple worship.

> ***Ezekiel 43:7***
> *⁷ He said: "Son of man, this is the place of my throne and the place for the soles of my feet. This is where I will live among the Israelites forever. The house of Israel will never again defile my holy name--neither they nor their kings--by their prostitution and the lifeless idols of their kings at their high places.*

Ezekiel 40-43 describe a Temple which has never existed on the earth. It is understood to be the coming Millennial Temple, as no other Temple is prophesied in scripture. With the advent of the Kingdom will come the institution of a new Temple worship system, different from the former Old Testament system. This worship system is the one in which God proclaimed he would "*live among the Israelites forever*" and at a time

---

[78] 2 Chronicles 5:13-14

when "*the house of Israel will never again defile my holy name.*" The details of these chapters is beyond the scope of this study, but several observations can be noted here concerning the nature of millennial worship.

The first observation is that this new Temple worship is not the same as the Old Testament Temple worship, nor is the description of the temple in Ezekiel 40-43 the same as the description of any temple which has ever existed.

This biblical fact being noted, secondly it should be established that there *will be* a sacrificial system of some sort implemented in millennial temple worship.[79]

While there *will be* animal sacrifices, Christ himself has paid for all sin for all time. Thus, this system should not be construed as a reinstitution of the Old Testament sacrificial system nor a replacement of the blood of Christ. Hebrews 10:10 clearly states, "*we have been made holy through the sacrifice of the body of Jesus Christ once for all.*"

In the Old Testament, sacrifices had various purposes. Some sacrifices were given as atonement for sin, but others were given as homage, thanksgiving and celebratory worship. Atonement is granted forevermore through the shed blood of Christ, and will not be a purpose of the sacrifices of the new system of Temple worship. Yet, just as there were varying purposes for sacrifices in the Old Testament, so there surely will be in the millennial worship system. The new Temple worship of the millennial kingdom undoubtedly will have its own purposes which are not fully defined within Ezekiel's text. The reader is encouraged to work through Ezekiel 40-43 to gain some insight into the nature of millennial worship.

Regardless of Christ's processes in this new worship system, the end result is that there will be a new form of Temple worship in the

---

[79] Ezekiel 43:18-24

Chapter 9: The messianic kingdom

millennial kingdom, and the first resurrection will be drawn upon to serve as priests in this worship system, performing the various tasks related to the new priestly office. Yet, unlike the Temple worship of the Old Testament, the living Christ will be present in this Temple as both God and King. If Christ had chosen to dwell in a common household during his Kingdom, surely even that house would become a center for worship; for where Christ dwells, his followers will desire to gather.

Christ Will Rule Supremely

Beyond aspects of worship in the Kingdom is the reality of the government being on Christ's shoulders. He will be the ever-present God, but will also be the King who rules the earth. The overwhelming characteristic of this Kingdom is very simply the realization that Christ will rule the earth with absolute power. Gone is democratic process forever, as a righteous and just King will have risen to power without resistance from his new kingdom.

Revisiting Revelation 12, speaking of the woman (Israel) who gives birth to the male son (Jesus), it is stated in Revelation 12:5, *"She gave birth to a son, a male child, who will rule all the nations with an iron scepter."*

Revelation 19:15 states, *"Out of his mouth comes a sharp sword with which to strike down the nations. 'He will rule them with an iron scepter.'"*

Both of these texts mirror the messianic prophecy of Psalm 2:9, *"You will rule them with an iron scepter...."*

The overwhelming characteristic of the millennial kingdom is simple: Christ will rule supremely as an absolute King of Kings. There will be no messy senatorial debating nor will there be any semblance of democracy. The earth will yield completely to the rule of Christ.

> ***Jeremiah 23:5***
> [5] *"The days are coming," declares the LORD, "when I*

will raise up to David a righteous Branch, a King who will reign wisely and do what is just and right in the land.

Christ will be a King, who "*will reign wisely and do what is just and right.*" What need will there be for any other governmental system of checks and balances when the King is the righteous God of eternity? He will seek no counsel, need no advisory board nor require focus groups to gather community opinion. He is the very light of the life of men. In the true sense of the glory so many former kings of the earth sought, who *thought* they were gods, this King will indeed be. His word, which created all that exists and which destroyed the powers of Antichrist in an instant will be spoken into immutable law. What a day that will be.

Characteristics of Christ's Rule

Under Christ's rule, the earth's info structure will be profoundly redesigned.

> ***Isaiah 2:1-4***
> *[1] This is what Isaiah son of Amoz saw concerning Judah and Jerusalem:*
> *[2] In the last days the mountain of the LORD's temple will be established as chief among the mountains; it will be raised above the hills, and all nations will stream to it.*
> *[3] Many peoples will come and say, "Come, let us go up to the mountain of the LORD, to the house of the God of Jacob. He will teach us his ways, so that we may walk in his paths." The law will go out from Zion, the word of the LORD from Jerusalem.*
> *[4] He will judge between the nations and will settle disputes for many peoples. They will beat their swords into plowshares and their spears into pruning hooks. Nation will not take up sword against nation, nor will they train for war anymore.*

Chapter 9: The messianic kingdom

Jerusalem will be established as the new capital city of the world. *"The mountain of the LORD's temple will be established as chief among the mountains; it will be raised above the hills, and all nations will stream to it."* "*All nations will stream to it*" refers to the central importance of Israel in the world. Christ will rule from Jerusalem in person. Likewise, Christ will be worshiped in Jerusalem in person. Perhaps both are understood from verse 3, *"Many peoples will come and say, "Come, let us go up to the mountain of the LORD, to the house of the God of Jacob. He will teach us his ways, so that we may walk in his paths."* Opportunities unique to history will exist with Christ himself as King and Savior from a common office. People will have opportunity *learn directly from Christ*! People will make pilgrimages to Jerusalem, saying, *"let us go up to the mountain of the LORD, to the house of the God of Jacob."*

Verse 3 states *"The law will go out from Zion, the word of the LORD from Jerusalem."* This *"law"* refers not to the Mosaic Law of the Old Testament, but literally the "law of the land," the legislation of Jesus' kingdom. As absolute King, Christ will speak the law into existence from Jerusalem which the entire world will follow.

Furthermore, the art of warfare will be ended. *"⁴He will judge between the nations and will settle disputes for many peoples. They will beat their swords into plowshares and their spears into pruning hooks. Nation will not take up sword against nation, nor will they train for war anymore."* With a singular King over the entire earth, there is no necessity for warfare. The King will speak to disputes and settle them without interference from other powers.

It is important to observe that there *will* still be disputes. One must not confuse the millennial kingdom with the purity which will exist in Heaven. There is still a sin nature in fallen man, who will be the citizens of this kingdom. This is not Heaven on earth but the millennial kingdom on earth. Yet, Christ will judge between the nations rather than nations warring among themselves to settle such disputes. His law will be equally just to both sides of any possible dispute and his power will keep even the sinful natures of man, which may lead to conflict, absolutely under the control of his hand.

Verse 4 notes, "*They will beat their swords into plowshares and their spears into pruning hooks.*" Ironically, this is the complete opposite of Joel's prophecy of the world prior to Christ's rule. Joel 3:10 is a call to the armies of Antichrist to come against Israel so that Christ can destroy them. God calls them to, "*Beat your plowshares into swords and your pruning hooks into spears. Let the weakling say, 'I am strong!'*" In this kingdom, however, there is no need for the instruments of war. Christ will rule equally over all. At this point, only one war remains for all history: the final war against Satan after the millennial kingdom.

The restoration of the natural world

In Christ's kingdom, not only are disputes among men under his full control, but nature itself rejoices in obedience to its King as the animal kingdom itself aligns with Christ's will.

> ### Isaiah 11:6-9
> [6] *The wolf will live with the lamb, the leopard will lie down with the goat, the calf and the lion and the yearling together; and a little child will lead them.*
> [7] *The cow will feed with the bear, their young will lie down together, and the lion will eat straw like the ox.*
> [8] *The infant will play near the hole of the cobra, and the young child put his hand into the viper's nest.*
> [9] *They will neither harm nor destroy on all my holy mountain, for the earth will be full of the knowledge of the LORD as the waters cover the sea.*

Animosity is gone from the animal kingdom as natural enemies lose interest in the destruction of one another. Even the food chain is redesigned, as "*the lion will eat straw like the ox.*" Returning to what appears to be an Edenic state, the animal kingdom is restored along with humanity to a sense of order. As part of this new rule of law, neither will animals harm humans, for, "[6]*the calf and the lion and the yearling*

Chapter 9: The messianic kingdom

together; and a little child will lead them." Similarly, *"⁸ The infant will play near the hole of the cobra, and the young child put his hand into the viper's nest. ⁹ They will neither harm nor destroy on all my holy mountain, for the earth will be full of the knowledge of the LORD as the waters cover the sea."*

The noting of the earth being *"full of the knowledge of the Lord"* indicates a restoration of the entire earth to the command of its creator and King. While it is not explicitly stated in this text, the understanding of the earth being full of the knowledge of the Lord also lends one to understand the very obedience of weather systems to the voice of the King. Joel 2 demonstrates this very sentiment.

> *Joel 2:23*
> *²³ Be glad, O people of Zion, rejoice in the LORD your God, for he has given you the autumn rains in righteousness. He sends you abundant showers, both autumn and spring rains, as before.*

Speaking clearly within the context of the restoration of Israel after the "day of the Lord," Joel states the specific *sending* of rain showers to water the earth as needed.

The Lifespan of Man is Reinstated

> *Isaiah 65:20*
> *²⁰ "Never again will there be in it an infant who lives but a few days, or an old man who does not live out his years; he who dies at a hundred will be thought a mere youth; he who fails to reach a hundred will be considered accursed.*

In Jesus' kingdom, infant death will be unheard of. It will literally not be allowed by the King. *"Never again"* is a statement of absolute and fundamental essence. Likewise, *"old men will live out their years."* In modern terms, this is a confusing statement. To live out one's years may seem just if one were to die at 80 or 90 years of age. Yet, in this kingdom 100 years old will be "*thought a mere youth.*"

It is important to remember that while this sounds very heavenly, what is being described by Isaiah is not Heaven, but the millennial kingdom. In Heaven, there is no death. In the millennial kingdom, people can still die, and will still die under certain circumstances. Those circumstances are also noted in this text, though it is challenging to exegete.

The second half of this text notes in the NIV, "*he who dies at a hundred will be thought a mere youth; he who fails to reach a hundred will be considered accursed.*" The literal Hebrew renders, "*the young man shall die a hundred but the sinner a hundred shall be accursed.*" The KJV states it this way, *"for the child shall die an hundred years old; but the sinner being an hundred years old shall be accursed."* Likewise the ASV states, *"for the child shall die a hundred years old, and the sinner being a hundred years old shall be accursed."* This is a more literal translation from the Hebrew.

As noted, this is a difficult passage to exegete. However, the literal rendering of the text indicates a specific circumstance whereby one would die at one hundred years of age and be considered a youth. That circumstance is that he is a "*sinner.*"

While it has been established that the inhabitants of earth will still have a sin nature, the biblical concept of one being "*a sinner*" is the idea of one who has denied the Lord as the authority of his life. A "sinner," in biblical thought, is one who is not a believer in Christ, to establish it in New Testament terms. While it seems unthinkable that anyone living on the earth with Christ himself present as King would refuse to accept Christ as their Lord and savior, it will be clear by the end of this chapter that there will, in fact, come into existence a line of rebellious people on earth once again. While the millennial kingdom begins with none present but believers, those believers will repopulate the earth. Just as people today must chose their King for themselves, so those in the

Chapter 9: The messianic kingdom

millennial kingdom must receive Christ as their personal Lord and Savior. And, just as it exists today, some will refuse, though given every opportunity and proper teaching. As time progresses, an increased number of unbelievers will arise.

The idea of "*the sinner being a hundred shall be accursed*" speaks of the deaths of those who refuse to receive Christ as their personal Lord and savior. He *will undeniably* be their earthly King, but each person on earth will still have to receive him as their personal Lord and Savior from their sin. Those who refuse will be "*the sinner*" who "*shall be accursed.*"

The text seems to indicate that this death of a "*young*" one hundred year old man would only occur to those who have rejected Christ as their Lord and God. While one hundred is understood to be young, the text continues "*the sinner being an hundred years old shall be accursed.*" If taken literally, Isaiah indicates a sort of "cut off" time for one to make his proclamation to the divinity of Christ as his personal Lord and savior. Thus, the life-span of one hundred years will be the norm for the lost.

Likewise, the conclusion of this text seems to indicate that there will be no death for the saved at all; only the lost, at around 100 years of age. This makes the full text more sensible. "*[20]There shall be no more thence an infant of days, nor an old man that hath not filled his days; for the child shall die a hundred years old, and the sinner being a hundred years old shall be accursed.[80]*"

If this is not the interpretation of this text, then a new question arises: what happens to the saved of the millennial kingdom when they die? Would they go to an empty Heaven? The fullness of Heaven, the Old Testament saints, the church, the tribulation martyrs and saved Israel, all who were part of the first resurrection are on the earth in the Kingdom. They serve as priests and officials! Would a righteous man die and then become a priest?

---

[80] *American Standard Version*. 1995 (Is 65:20).

Logic, and the text seem to indicate that the saved will not die in the millennial kingdom. They are here for the duration of eternity, because when the millennial kingdom ends, the eternal order begins, as will be discussed in chapter 12.

Lastly, this text also demands what has already been observed. People will still be born with a sin nature during the millennial kingdom and will require salvation in Christ to endure into eternity in Heaven proper.

The "Good Life" Ensues

> *Isaiah 65:21-24*
> *[21] They will build houses and dwell in them; they will plant vineyards and eat their fruit. [22] No longer will they build houses and others live in them, or plant and others eat. For as the days of a tree, so will be the days of my people; my chosen ones will long enjoy the works of their hands. [23] They will not toil in vain or bear children doomed to misfortune; for they will be a people blessed by the LORD, they and their descendants with them. [24] Before they call I will answer; while they are still speaking I will hear.*

There is hardly a better description of common life in the millennial kingdom than "the good life." The things man commonly desires to acquire during his life are exemplified as customary and granted in Christ's kingdom.

One's work will be productive.

> *[21] They will build houses and dwell in them; they will plant vineyards and eat their fruit.*

Never again will one work themselves to the bone, only to be a failure. The fruition of one's labor will be realized.

Chapter 9: The messianic kingdom

> ²² *No longer will they build houses and others live in them, or plant and others eat.*

One's lifespan increase will guarantee their work's success.

> *For as the days of a tree, so will be the days of my people; my chosen ones will long enjoy the works of their hands.*

Note, once again, the promise of the extended life is granted for believers only, as it is "*my people*" and "*my chosen ones*" who will reap this promise of a long enjoyed life.

In the course of Kingdom life is the promise that one's family will be blessed, as well.

> ²³ *They will not toil in vain or bear children doomed to misfortune; for they will be a people blessed by the LORD, they and their descendants with them.*

Work will be productive and children will have fortune rather than misfortune. Now, along with the promise of a child's life being guaranteed not to be cut short is added the promise of a child's avoidance of misfortune. How many nights the author lays in his bed and pleads with the Lord to keep his children safe! How glorious life will be when the King is God incarnate, and he *assures* his people of safety, prosperity in their labor and the safety of their children. These are promises that no king has ever been able to afford his people. But the King of Kings will not only be able to make such promises, he will be able to deliver them. The very King of the earth will personally hold the power of life, death, success and productivity in life.

Moreover, God's presence will permeate the life of the believer in a more pure way that has been experienced in the church age.

> ²⁴ *Before they call I will answer; while they are still*

speaking I will hear.

Rather than praying, waiting and yearning, the text indicates Christ's immediate response to one's needs. This idea is contrary to the New Testament church age principles of patient endurance in suffering. In this new dispensation is a life very different from what one knows today. Just as the dispensation of grace, or the life New Testament believers live, differs greatly from the lives Old Testament believers experienced, so the dispensation of the Kingdom will bring another monumental shift in one's relationship with God. He will be intimately connected with his people, so much so that he will provide for their needs before even asked.

In preparation for the next chapter, it should once again be noted that the population of the earth will flourish and rebound during the one thousand years of the messianic kingdom. With enduring life spans of believers, families could conceivably be exceptionally large. Even among unbelievers, a 100 year life span is greatly increased from that of today, giving rise to the possibility of huge enduring families stemming even from those who will choose to reject Christ as Lord and Savior.

While this kingdom begins with believers only, even with Christ physically present on earth, ruling with absolute integrity and providing a life beyond the wildest dreams of anyone alive today, still the heart of man is sinful. An increasing number of people will reject their Savior, creating a large group of unbelievers on earth. As unimaginable as it seems, man, in large numbers, will once again gravitate toward his sinful nature. Many will refuse to relinquish control of their lives to their loving King.

This understanding should not come as a surprise. It is no more inconceivable than the fall of Adam and Eve. Who would guess than a perfect, sinless man and woman, given a bountiful food supply and full life would choose to refuse to obey a command as simple as "do not eat the fruit" from a single tree? Perhaps it should seem more incredible, as Adam and Eve were tempted directly by Satan; a reality impossible in

Chapter 9: The messianic kingdom

the millennial kingdom since Satan is bound. Yet, unlike Adam and Eve, man in the millennial kingdom has his own demons, so to figuratively speak, in that he must contend with a sin nature. That nature is strong. It will claim a multitude before the kingdom of Christ on earth comes to its final days. Many will be prepared to join Satan when he is released to deceive the earth once again.

Chapter 10: The Final Battle

While a general description of life in the Kingdom is given in scripture, there are no real narratives to follow concerning specific events during that season. However, as earth repopulates and unbelievers increase in number, the Kingdom dispensation will come to its close with once again a mixed earth. There will be believers and unbelievers living together once again on the earth. In preparation for the final division between the righteous, who will enter Heaven proper for all eternity, and the unrighteous, who will enter the lake of fire, the earth must once again be separated, just as the sheep were separated from the goats prior to the Kingdom. This final division of mankind will come as the result of a concluding war on the earth.

The Loosing of Satan From The Abyss

> *Revelation 20:7-10*
> *[7] When the thousand years are over, Satan will be released from his prison [8] and will go out to deceive the nations in the four corners of the earth--Gog and Magog--to gather them for battle. In number they are like the sand on the seashore. [9] They marched across the breadth of the earth and surrounded the camp of God's people, the city he loves. But fire came down from heaven and devoured them. [10] And the devil, who deceived them, was thrown into the lake of burning sulfur, where the beast and the false prophet had been thrown. They will be tormented day and night for ever and ever.*

After the millennial kingdom, Satan is released from his 1,000 year "*prison*" sentence from the Abyss. Being freed, Satan will do what he has always done. He will resume his career deceiving the nations, gathering them for his final assault against the Lord and his people.

Chapter 10: The Final Battle

It is noteworthy that the demonic kingdom is not specifically referenced in this text. It is not specified from scripture if they are released from their captivity in Babylon and Edom at this time or not, but logic and biblical historical inference would conclude that they would serve Satan in his final deception as they have in his former deceptions. The passages speaking of Edom and Babylon in the millennial kingdom, as the place of demonic dwelling, do not specify that the demons will be bound at these locations for any certain period of time. The do speak of these cities remaining abandoned for all eternity, and being places of smoke and fire for all eternity, but the possibility of the release of demons in conjunction with Satan's release are not referenced.

Logically, however, they may be released to join the final battle and the judgment which accompanies it. This presumption is gathered from what is noted of Satan himself; that he will "*go out to deceive the nations.*" The idea of Satan deceiving the nations alone is less tenable, of course, than the idea that his demonic hosts would assist him in this pursuit as they have always done. Historically, Satan's deceptive work among the nations depended on his demonic horde's support, such as in Daniel 10.

> **Daniel 10:20-21**
> [20] So he said, "Do you know why I have come to you? Soon I will return to fight against the prince of Persia, and when I go, the prince of Greece will come; [21] but first I will tell you what is written in the Book of Truth. (No one supports me against them except Michael, your prince.

Daniel 10 involves another of Daniel's visions. In this vision, the man speaking, which may be the angel Gabriel who had spoken with Daniel on other occasions, informs Daniel that he must leave to engage "*the prince of Persia*" and the "*prince of Greece*" in battle. He also notes that no one supports him in his battle with them except the archangel over Israel, Michael, "*your prince.*"

Satan's historic campaign of deception has been conducted in the same manner that he once learned as an angel of the Lord; in rank and file. Angels are demonstrated in scripture to be creatures of varying ranks and positions of organized mobility. That the archangel Michael is called a "chief prince" in Daniel 10:13 is indicative of such rank and file in the angelic realms. Likewise angelic "hosts" are referred to in scripture, such as in Psalm 148:2. Such terms indicate that angels commonly work together in an organized structure to accomplish their goals. To this end, one may assume the demonic legions of Satan will be released to assist him in the gathering of the wicked which have accumulated on the earth, as angelic missions have been historically prone to function in this manner.

While troubling to some, Satan's purpose is clearly outlined in the text to "*deceive the nations*" once again, much as he did during the great tribulation through the counterfeit ministry of Antichrist. Clearly, God's providence is steering this initiative. In the first place, God had John to write about it in advance in his vision. One must always understand that God is a God of infinite control. He could easily have put Satan into the lake of fire when he placed the Antichrist and the false prophet there. He would never have heard from Satan again. Yet, it is clear that it is God's intention for Satan to once again engage the world in deception in order to produce a final division on earth between the righteous and the wicked. Secondly, God, foreknowing what Satan's plan will be, will choose to release Satan to conduct that very plan. This should lead one to understand that it is in fact God's will that Satan be released to conduct his business of enticing the unbelievers on earth to a great revolt, that he may again divide humanity in preparation for the eternal order of Heaven.

Furthermore of interest in this text is the re-use of the terms "*Gog and Magog*." The use of Gog and Magog in Revelation 20 is a different use than that of Ezekiel 38, however. In Ezekiel 38, Gog "*of the land of Magog*" is referenced as the leader of the coalition assault against Israel commonly known as the Gog-Magog invasion. Here, however, Gog is referenced as a geographical inference rather than the identity of a world leader. It appears that the use of Gog and Magog in Revelation refers to the heathen people of the earth in general, rather than a specific ruler of a

Chapter 10: The Final Battle

nation.

The purpose of Satan's deception is clearly articulated in the text. He is not merely to deceive and confuse the unrighteous of the millennial kingdom, but he is *"to gather them for battle."* Once again, just as in the tribulation, God is preparing a battle as the means to cleanse the earth of his enemies. This battle, however, will be Satan's very last stand. He will have no further opportunities to attempt to usurp God's authority over the earth. The focus of his last stand is once again Israel, the city of God's people, *"the city he loves."*

Psalm 2 was earlier demonstrated to detail Satan's purposes for attacking Israel during the Battle of Armageddon. It is Satan's thought that by eradicating Israel, God will lose his vested interest in the earth. It is entirely possible that Psalm 2 speaks of Satan's interest in Israel at this final battle as well. Yet, Satan has other profound reasons for focusing his final battle on Israel. Israel is the very seat of Christ's rule. It is in Israel that Christ, the King of the earth will be reigning. It is in Israel that Christ, the God of the people of earth will dwell. Israel is the most logical place for Satan to attack, as it is the heart and soul of his enemy, the King, and is the physical location of the one he must overthrow to have his own evil desires carried out.

In his deception, Satan gathers an enormous army. Verse 8 says, *"In number they are like the sand on the seashore."* How sad that so many on earth will have succumbed to their sin nature and will have rejected their gracious God-King's spiritual authority in their lives. In their lost state, their subjection to Satan will be unavoidable. He will gather them all for this final battle, and will lead them all to their final and eternal destruction.

It is also an interesting thought concerning this battle that it will be a first of sorts. All battles in the history of the earth have been fought by fighting men; armies who are trained in battle and who have gained proficiency with their weapons of designation. In the millennial kingdom, however, there will be no weapons, soldiers or training for military conflict. The weapons will have all been beaten into plows!

Satan's gathering will by necessity involve not military organizations, but rather a compilation of the citizens of earth who have rejected the spiritual authority of their King. There is little hope for them to have any degree of fighting expertise or excellence, not that it would do them any good if they had. How does one fight an enemy who can "speak" one's demise? Their lack of preparation will be irrelevant. There is no training available to ready one to fight against the invincible Christ. And their utter inability to fight against him will quickly relegate them to sudden and uncompromising destruction.

Revelation 20:9 says simply, *"But fire came down from heaven and devoured them."* Unlike the Battle of Armageddon, there is no calculated pace in this battle. Judgment is instantaneous and swift. They are all destroyed by fire upon the simple will of the Lord. Once again the earth stands completely purged of all who have rebelled against Christ's Kingship. All who are evil are simultaneously destroyed.

Concluding the battle, Revelation 20:10 states, that Satan *"was thrown into the lake of burning sulfur."* He now joins the Beast and the false prophet, and Satan's career is ended forever. Unlike the Abyss, the Lake of Fire is a permanent place of confinement. All who enter, never escape but are judged, as verse 10 states, *"tormented day and night for ever and ever."*

Once again, the fate of the demonic hordes are not specifically mentioned. Yet, logic demands that they will join the fate of their leader, Satan at this time. Jesus states in Matthew 25:41 that the eternal fire of Hell, or the lake of fire, was *"created for the devil and his angels."* It is certain from scripture that the demonic angels will indeed end up in the lake of fire, but it is not specifically noted as to when that occurs. It is, however, presumed to be at this time, for reasons which will be discussed next.

Chapter 10: The Final Battle

Final Prophecies Fulfilled on earth

Once again the earth is full only of the righteousness of God and his people. But, for the first time in history, the earth is now also permanently free of the threat of demonic intervention. At this point, distinctively, the enemies of Christ are now removed in totality, never to return; being eternally sentenced to the lake of fire. This condition prepares the way for Christ to return the authority of the earth to God the Father.

> *1 Corinthians 15:24-28*
> [24] *Then the end will come, when he hands over the kingdom to God the Father after he has destroyed all dominion, authority and power.* [25] *For he must reign until he has put all his enemies under his feet.* [26] *The last enemy to be destroyed is death.* [27] *For he "has put everything under his feet." Now when it says that "everything" has been put under him, it is clear that this does not include God himself, who put everything under Christ.* [28] *When he has done this, then the Son himself will be made subject to him who put everything under him, so that God may be all in all.*

Verse 27 notes what is now historically experienced as the normative state, "*God himself, ... put everything under Christ.*" Indeed even now during the preparation and writing of this work, all is under Christ's authority. He simply waits for the appointed time to begin the events described in this work. Philippians 2:9 states that Christ has been "*exalted to the highest place.*" Jesus himself stated in Matthew 28:18 that, "*all authority in heaven and on earth has been given to me.*" Likewise, Ephesians notes that God's strength,

> *Ephesians 1:20-23*
> [20] *which he exerted in Christ when he raised him from the dead and seated him at his right hand in the heavenly realms,* [21] *far above all rule and authority,*

> *power and dominion, and every title that can be given, not only in the present age but also in the one to come.* [22] *And God placed all things under his feet and appointed him to be head over everything for the church,* [23] *which is his body, the fullness of him who fills everything in every way.*

Christ was exalted by God to the position of authority over all things. He "*placed all things under his feet*" not "*only in the present age but also in the one to come.*" The present age speaks of the age of the writing of Ephesians, or the age prior to the millennial kingdom; the church age. The age to come, in Jewish thought, always referred to the age of the kingdom, which is now concluded.

Just as God placed all things under Christ's feet, Paul states in 1 Corinthians 15:24-25 that Christ will hand the kingdom back to the Father only after the destruction of Christ's enemies is complete. Specifically, this will be after he has destroyed all dominion, authority and power, "[25]*For he must reign until he has put all his enemies under his feet.*" Thus, God placed all things under Christ's feet until such a time as Christ has placed all of his *enemies* under his feet.

At this point in the timeline, Christ's enemies are "*under his feet.*" The unrighteous who stood against him were consumed by fire. Only the saved remain on earth. Satan was cast into the Lake of Fire. While the demons were not specifically noted to enter the lake of fire with Satan, clearly at the time of Christ's enemies *all* being placed under his feet, they are now so placed. According to the text, "*death*" is all that remains; "[26]*The last enemy to be destroyed is death.*"

Death exists on earth as God's sentence for sin. Prior to sin there was no death. God's warning to Adam in Genesis 2:17 concerning eating the forbidden fruit in disobedience was, "*the day you eat of it you will surely die.*" Indeed, death came into being as the very manifestation of God's wrath against sin. Now, in preparation for the eternal order, sin and its sentence, death, are to be removed in the final judgment of the great white throne.

Chapter 10: The Final Battle

Chapter 11: The Great White Throne Judgment

Several judgments have been observed in the timeline leading to this final moment of earth's history. The church was judged at the judgment seat of Christ following the moment of the rapture. The old testament saints were judged upon their resurrection on the seventy fifth day of the Kingdom. The tribulation saints were judged that same day most likely, as they were resurrected. All non-Jews who lived to the end of the tribulation were judged at the judgment of the Gentiles. The righteous entered the Kingdom, the unrighteous were destroyed.

A key group that has not yet received their judgment are the unrighteous dead from all of history, other than those judged at the judgment of the Gentiles. Beyond that group, however, all dead in their sin remain in Hades. Hades should not be equated with the lake of fire, as some incorrectly assert. Rather, Hades is the location where all dead were held until the time of Christ's resurrection. At that time the righteous were taken into Heaven, and the unrighteous remained. From the time of Christ's resurrection in roughly 30 AD, Hades has contained only the souls of those who are lost, without Christ. It is at the great white throne judgment that this group will be resurrected and will enter into judgment.

> ***Revelation 20:11-15***
> *[11] Then I saw a great white throne and him who was seated on it. earth and sky fled from his presence, and there was no place for them. [12] And I saw the dead, great and small, standing before the throne, and books were opened. Another book was opened, which is the book of*

Chapter 11: The Great White Throne Judgment

> *life. The dead were judged according to what they had done as recorded in the books. *^{13}* The sea gave up the dead that were in it, and death and Hades gave up the dead that were in them, and each person was judged according to what he had done. *^{14}* Then death and Hades were thrown into the lake of fire. The lake of fire is the second death. *^{15}* If anyone's name was not found written in the book of life, he was thrown into the lake of fire.*

The setting for this judgment is described as Christ seated upon a great white throne. It is clear that the one seated is Christ himself from verse 6, where this one on the throne states, "*I am the Alpha and Omega, the Beginning and the End.*" While one could presume God the father being on the throne, it was established in the previous chapter that Christ would reign until all of his enemies are placed under his feet, the last of which is death. It is at this judgment that death will be indeed placed under Christ's feet, as death will be destroyed.

In the presence of Christ's white throne of judgment, something very interesting occurs. Verse 11 notes, "*earth and sky fled from his presence, and there was no place for them.*" What appears to be observed in this moment is the fundamental change from the old order of things to the new. In the old order of things, sin had corrupted not only mankind, but the very earth itself.[81] In the new order of things, it will shortly be observed, new skies and a new earth are to be created which are free from such corruption. The old earth and skies were tainted by sin. And, as 1 Corinthians 15:50 notes, "*I declare to you, brothers, that flesh and blood cannot inherit the kingdom of God, nor does the perishable inherit the imperishable.*" The corrupted and perishable earth is incapable of inheriting the eternal order just as the perishable body is.

Paul teaches that the earth is corrupt and awaits this final restoration.

> **Romans 8:19-21**
> *^{19} The creation waits in eager expectation for the sons of*

---

[81] Romans 8:19-23

> God to be revealed. ²⁰ For the creation was subjected to frustration, not by its own choice, but by the will of the one who subjected it, in hope ²¹ that the creation itself will be liberated from its bondage to decay and brought into the glorious freedom of the children of God.

Likewise, Peter teaches that,

> **2 Peter 3:7 (NIV)**
> ⁷ ... the present heavens and earth are reserved for fire, being kept for the day of judgment and destruction of ungodly men.

This will be that day of judgment. It is specifically the judgment against man's sin which will be pronounced on a personal basis, and the sinfulness of a corrupted earth, which will flee into nonexistence in the face of the righteous judge. The fleeing of the earth will be in preparation for a new earth which will be free from sin and decay which will be presented in Revelation 21.

At this moment, all that has been tainted by sin is to be finally and utterly destroyed; removed from God's presence that the final enduring hope of Heaven may be entered by the righteous which remain.

The Second Resurrection

Noted in chapter nine was the first resurrection, which was a resurrection of believers only. At this time will be observed the second resurrection, which is the resurrection of all non-believers whose souls remain in Hades. From the beginning of time, the bodies of all non-believers have turned to dust in the bowels of the earth, while their souls endured in Hades. Yet, the resurrection of the dead is a reality for all whom ever lived, whether righteous or unrighteous. The righteous are resurrected to a glorified body, the unrighteous are resurrected to their former bodies of death, which are made of physical materials, yet will be supernaturally preserved for eternity in the lake of fire. Jesus describes this state of the

Chapter 11: The Great White Throne Judgment

unbeliever in Hell in the book of Mark.

> *Mark 9:47-48*
> *[47] And if your eye causes you to sin, pluck it out. It is better for you to enter the kingdom of God with one eye than to have two eyes and be thrown into hell, [48] where "'their worm does not die, and the fire is not quenched.' Everyone will be salted with fire.*

Both ideas are present in Jesus' warning. First, that unbelievers will resurrect to their former bodies, since he warns them to not attempt to enter Hell with two eyes. Clearly the same eyes will follow one into eternal punishment. Second, he affirms the idea of the former body of death being preserved in the lake of fire as he notes that "*their worm does not die.*" The idea of the worm not dying is an idea of eternal destruction, yet without the elimination of the worm's food source, the body of death. Let the reader fully understand, Hell is a grisly and frightening place of eternal punishment. In this lake of fire, one will dwell with the very same physical body one has now; capable of experiencing the pain of fire and the continued grief of physical anguish, yet without being consumed or destroyed. It is a place to be avoided at all costs!

Verse 13 speaks of the process of the resurrection of the unrighteous dead, once again, as is God's character, conducted in an orderly fashion.

> *[13] The sea gave up the dead that were in it, and death and Hades gave up the dead that were in them, and each person was judged according to what he had done*

The sea giving up its dead clearly depicts the resurrection of the lost bodies of all the unrighteous who died at sea. Just as fascinating as the conception of a bodily resurrection is for those raptured, so it is fascinating in light of the unrighteous dead. The God who formed the first man out of the dust of the earth will once again reconstitute man's flesh from the collective dust to whence it decomposed. Bodies will recompile from whatever level of disintegration and dispersion those bodies have endured throughout history.

Death and Hades, commonly listed together in scripture, are noted as a pair which give up their dead next. While the sea uniquely refers to those whose bodies are under the ocean, "*death*" refers to a general condition of those which remain. Death and Hades are referenced together throughout the book of Revelation. Revelation 1:18 notes Jesus having the keys of death and Hades. Revelation 6:8 speaks of the rider on the pale horse, whose name was Death, and Hades followed him. Here, death and Hades are once again paired, speaking of the resurrection of the dead.

In this pairing of death and Hades, the physical and spiritual attributes of man are represented. Death is the natural state of the sinful body. Hades is the spiritual state of man's existence beyond the body. All resurrections in scripture involve the rejoining of the body with the spirit. 1 Thessalonians 4:16 notes the joining of the bodies and spirits of the dead in Christ who will be the first to be raptured. He notes that "*the dead in Christ will rise first.*" This rising speaks of their bodies, as their spirits will have been in Heaven. As Christ returns, their spirits will return with him and be rejoined with the body. Similarly, death and Hades will couple together as they "*give up the dead that are in them.*" The dead bodies will rise as the spirits join them from Hades for this judgment and eternal assignment to a position in the lake of fire.

Two processes are granted to death and Hades, or the reconstituted body and spirit of the unbelievers of history. Verse 13 notes they are judged, and verse 14 notes that they are cast into the lake of fire. While the *general* state of all unrighteous dead is the same in that death and Hades are cast into the lake of fire, the *specific* state is determined by the great white throne judgment. The standard of this judgment is stated to be what a person had done to warrant his specific degree of punishment, as verse 13 notes, "*and each person was judged according to what he had done.*"

"*What he had done*" is the certain indictment of man's sinfulness. The

Chapter 11: The Great White Throne Judgment

actions of all men are sinful. Without Christ's forgiveness to those who will choose him as Savior, all mankind's actions would be judged as unrighteous to varying degrees. Romans 3:11-12 says *"[11] there is no one who understands, no one who seeks God. [12] All have turned away, they have together become worthless; there is no one who does good, not even one."* Thus, being judged "*according to what he had done*" was a sure sentence of condemnation for these remaining in Hades, who are without Christ's forgiveness for their sin. But, more than the certainty of sin leading one to eternal destruction, this phrase also notes that a *degree* of punishment is to be rendered upon each soul entering the lake of fire. *"According to what he had done,"* a man will receive his eternal punishment. One's eternal sentence in Hell will match the severity of his sin.

Being judged according "*to what he had done*" should not lead one to an understanding of a works-based salvation. Rather, the results of this judgment should be understood to be a pronouncement of the degree of punishment which one will endure for eternity. The general punishment of the lake of fire has already been determined for this group by merit of their failure to receive Christ as their Lord while they lived. Verse 15 says: *"If anyone's name was not found written in the book of life, he was thrown into the lake of fire."* Yet, Hell is clearly presented as a place which is not to be an equal sentence for all.

"*The book of life*" is a book containing the names of all of those who belong to the Lamb, or to Christ. Revelation 13:8 states, *"All inhabitants of the earth will worship the beast--all whose names have not been written in the book of life belonging to the Lamb that was slain from the creation of the world."* The "*book of life*" is, in effect, a roster of all who have found salvation in Christ by receiving him as their Lord and receiving his forgiveness for their sin. It is those whose names are not found in the book of life who's sinfulness will not be covered by Christ's payment for their sin. It is this group alone who have not yet been resurrected by merit of their lack of a relationship to Christ. This group is judged by the fact that their works, like the works of all men, is unsatisfactory in God's sight to achieve a place in Heaven, in the presence of God's glory. And, without the forgiveness of Christ, brought by a confession of his deity and submission to his lordship, no one could enter eternal life.

Thus, one's eternal destiny is already determined at this point. The nature of the great white throne judgments is not to determine who will enter Hell, but is rather to determine the nature of one's punishment *while in* Hell.

The Substance of The Judgment

While it is not stipulated fully in this text, the substance of this judgment can be determined from other scriptures.

> ***Matthew 11:20-24***
> *[20] Then Jesus began to denounce the cities in which most of his miracles had been performed, because they did not repent. [21] "Woe to you, Korazin! Woe to you, Bethsaida! If the miracles that were performed in you had been performed in Tyre and Sidon, they would have repented long ago in sackcloth and ashes. [22] But I tell you, it will be more bearable for Tyre and Sidon on the day of judgment than for you. [23] And you, Capernaum, will you be lifted up to the skies? No, you will go down to the depths. If the miracles that were performed in you had been performed in Sodom, it would have remained to this day. [24] But I tell you that it will be more bearable for Sodom on the day of judgment than for you."*

In Matthew, Jesus clearly depicts varying degrees of judgment to be prescribed in Hell. He states that it will "*be more bearable on the day of judgment*" for some cities than for others. To be more bearable for some than for others clearly demonstrates varying degrees of judgment will exist in Hell. Likewise Paul notes a tiered punishment in Hell.

> ***Hebrews 10:29-31***

Chapter 11: The Great White Throne Judgment

> *²⁹ How much more severely do you think a man deserves to be punished who has trampled the Son of God under foot, who has treated as an unholy thing the blood of the covenant that sanctified him, and who has insulted the Spirit of grace? ³⁰ For we know him who said, "It is mine to avenge; I will repay," and again, "The Lord will judge his people." ³¹ It is a dreadful thing to fall into the hands of the living God.*

Without going into too much detail, Paul asserts that having "*trampled the Son of God under foot*" and having "*treated as an unholy thing the blood [of Christ]*" is grounds for a worse punishment than is deserved for those who have not done such a thing. Additionally, Paul demonstrates that it is God who is in charge of the judgments of Hell, rather than Satan, as some mistakenly believe. Hell, as every other part of the creation, belongs to God and serves his purposes. Jesus noted that God created Hell for the devil and his angels, but all who have served them will join their punishment there. Yet, not all will be punished equally, as there clearly are levels in Hell.

> ### *Luke 12:46-48*
> *⁴⁶ The master of that servant will come on a day when he does not expect him and at an hour he is not aware of. He will cut him to pieces and assign him a place with the unbelievers. ⁴⁷ "That servant who knows his master's will and does not get ready or does not do what his master wants will be beaten with many blows. ⁴⁸ But the one who does not know and does things deserving punishment will be beaten with few blows. From everyone who has been given much, much will be demanded; and from the one who has been entrusted with much, much more will be asked.*

In this parable, Jesus speaks of the master returning and assigning the servant who fails to do as he should "*a place with the unbelievers*." The place of unbelievers, of course, is the lake of fire; the very substance of this point in the timeline. Likewise, Jesus states that more blows will be distributed to those who know the master's will and do not do it than will be given to those who do not know the master's will.

Deductions from these texts clearly indicate that some parts of Hell are worse than others, and that at least one aspect of the judgment is one's knowledge of right and wrong. While more can be determined from scripture on this subject, sufficient understanding is demonstrated in these texts as to the nature of the great white throne judgment. The great white throne judgment is not the determination of who will enter Hell and who will not. That has been determined by one's relationship to Christ. All whose names are not found in the book of life *will* enter Hell. The substance of this judgment is instead the determination of exactly what degree of punishment one will receive in Hell.

As Hebrews states it,

> **Hebrews 10:30-31 (NIV)**
> ³⁰ *For we know him who said, "It is mine to avenge; I will repay," and again, "The Lord will judge his people."* ³¹ *It is a dreadful thing to fall into the hands of the living God.*

Indeed, "*to fall into the hands of the living God*" is a state of absolute helplessness. He judges with knowledge and finality. He is just; giving more severe punishments to those who are deserving of them.

May the reader be more concerned with having his name written in the book of life than with attempting to negotiate a higher existence in Hell, however. For no level of Hell will be bearable but for the shear inability to escape it. Chapter thirteen will concern itself with one's preparedness to face these final days. The chief focus of that preparedness is to have one's name written in the book of life. Anything less is to have utterly failed for all eternity. Hell will literally be the eternal destruction of body and soul. It many times is entered into by the fool who ignores the warnings of scripture, as with all of God's judgments of wrath.

Chapter 11: The Great White Throne Judgment . . . .

Chapter 12: Eternity

Concerning the timeline of this work, all things have been set into place for the eternal order. It is at this point that the story reaches its true climax and the final restoration of all things is at hand. Satan, and all who rebelled with him are in an eternal state of destruction. All sin, and its penalty, death, are also in the lake of fire. Even the corrupted skies and earth are now gone. With all enemies under his feet, Jesus has handed authority back to the Father. Thus, outside of the lake of fire, sin has been permanently removed and the fullness of God's glory will permeate the eternal order.

Revelation 21 details the process whereby the eternal order is ushered in.

> ***Revelation 21:1-4***
> *[1] Then I saw a new heaven and a new earth, for the first heaven and the first earth had passed away, and there was no longer any sea. [2] I saw the Holy City, the new Jerusalem, coming down out of heaven from God, prepared as a bride beautifully dressed for her husband. [3] And I heard a loud voice from the throne saying, "Now the dwelling of God is with men, and he will live with them. They will be his people, and God himself will be with them and be their God. [4] He will wipe every tear from their eyes. There will be no more death or mourning or crying or pain, for the old order of things has passed away."*

A chief area of confusion surrounding this text involves a misunderstanding of the term "*heavens*." The term translated "heaven" or "heavens" comes from the Greek term *ouranos* in the New Testament. *Ouranos* is commonly translated into several English words, such as "heaven," "air," "sky" or "heavenly" depending on its usage. Just as a word may have several different usages in English, so they may have varying meanings in Greek. The English word "love," for example can refer to the affection given to a mate, or one's regard for one's job. Certainly the same meaning is not employed in both usages!

Chapter 12: Eternity

Ouranos has three very similar usages in biblical Greek, all pertaining to the expanse beyond the physical grounds of earth. *Ouranos* refers to either of the three "heavens" depending on its usage. At times biblical writers will specify which heaven they speak of, and at times they will allow the context of their writing to determine how one interprets their meaning.

The first heaven refers to the skies of the earth where the birds fly and clouds accumulate. In Matthew 8:20, *"Jesus replied, 'Foxes have holes and birds of the air* (Gk. *ouranos* - or "heavens") *have nests, but the Son of Man has no place to lay his head.'"* The NIV translates *ouranos* in this text as "air," or the heaven which the birds fly in. Though the author, Matthew, did not specify which heaven he was speaking of, it was clear from the context that it was the heaven the birds fly in. To that end, the NIV translators rendered the term "air" for *ouranos*.

The second heaven could properly be understood by a modern reader as outer space; that expanse beyond the first heaven. Jesus speaks of this heaven in Matthew 24:29.

> *"Immediately after the distress of those days '"the sun will be darkened, and the moon will not give its light; the stars will fall from the sky (Gk. ouranos - or "heavens"), and the heavenly (Gk. ouranos - or "heavens") bodies will be shaken.'"*

In this text, *ouranos* is used twice, both times referring to the second heaven, or outer space. Once again, the context determines for the reader which heaven is intended. It is the second heaven, the heaven of the moon and stars, or "outer space" in modern thought.

The third heaven is what the author refers to as "Heaven proper," the home of God, where his throne dwells. Paul speaks of this heaven in 2 Corinthians 12:2-4.

> *"I know a man in Christ who fourteen years ago was caught up to the third heaven (Gk. ouranos - or*

> *"heaven"). Whether it was in the body or out of the body I do not know--God knows. ³ And I know that this man-- whether in the body or apart from the body I do not know, but God knows-- ⁴ was caught up to paradise. He heard inexpressible things, things that man is not permitted to tell.*

In this text, Paul specifies precisely which heaven he refers to in two different ways. First, he notes that it is specifically the *"third heaven,"* so as to inform the reader that this man, which happens to be himself, was actually taken to Heaven proper, the home of God. Secondly, to make certain his context is known, he states another name for the third heaven as he notes that he was *"caught up to paradise."* Thus, he leaves no room for misunderstanding.

In Revelation 21, however, some have found room for misunderstanding, believing that the text teaches that Heaven proper is to be replaced. This is not what John is teaching. Heaven proper, God's home, is perfect in condition and will never be made new. It is without sin and incorruptible. It is new as it sits, being perfectly preserved in its original condition. The new heaven and new earth in Revelation 21 refer instead to a new creation of the earth and the "skies" which surround it.

It was noted in chapter 11 that the old earth and heavens passed away in the presence of the great white throne. The old creation was corrupted by sin and passed away in preparation for the eternal order. At this time a new earth and heaven, or "sky," are created. Unlike the former earth and heavens, this new earth has only one additional *"heaven"* beyond its land mass. Thus, a distinction between the first and second heavens is not noted for the new earth, but only a singular heaven. There will be one sky, rather than an atmospheric heaven which gives way to the darkness of outer space.

This new earth and sky will be conducive for eternal life in God's presence. Thus, it will be an incorruptible earth and sky, utterly incapable of the presence of sin. And, unlike the former earth, on the new earth *"there was no longer any sea."* This fact is a personal point of

Chapter 12: Eternity

anguish to the author, as he loves fishing very much and has often longed to spend eternity on an off-shore fishing vessel! However, it is most certain that one will not miss the sea in the glory that will be the new earth. While there will be bodies of water on this new earth, there will not be a sea, or a common ending place for flowing water.

The essence of the new earth is that it will be the eternal location for Heaven proper. Verse 2 notes, *"I saw the Holy City, the new Jerusalem, coming down out of heaven from God."*

Once again, the term *"heaven"* causes some to miss what is being stated. Heaven, refers to the sky of the new earth. However, *"the Holy City, the new Jerusalem"* refers to Heaven proper, God's home. Thus, Heaven proper comes down out of the sky to rest upon the new earth. The idea of a *"new Jerusalem"* is observed in scripture as a term referring to Heaven proper. Hebrews 12 references Heaven proper as a "heavenly" Jerusalem.

> **Hebrews 12:22**
> *²² But you have come to Mount Zion, to the heavenly Jerusalem, the city of the living God. You have come to thousands upon thousands of angels in joyful assembly,*

Likewise, Galatians speaks of a heavenly Jerusalem.

> **Galatians 4:26**
> *²⁶ But the Jerusalem that is above is free, and she is our mother.*

This *"Holy City, the new Jerusalem"* is one and the same as Heaven proper, as it exists today. This new Jerusalem is the dwelling of all believers, righteous angels, and God for eternity, in God's presence. The idea of Jerusalem being the "new" Jerusalem does not denote Heaven proper being recreated, but rather its replacing the former Jerusalem which existed on the former earth. In the millennial kingdom, Christ's throne was in the earthly Jerusalem. In eternity, Heaven proper will be the "new" Jerusalem, the city where Christ will reign with the Father.

The end result, then, is a new creation whereby Heaven itself will reside on a new earth. As Jesus notes in verse 5, all is to be recreated new.

> ***Revelation 21:5***
> *⁵ He who was seated on the throne said, "I am making everything new!" Then he said, "Write this down, for these words are trustworthy and true."*

In light of Revelation 21, the phrase "Heaven on earth" is indeed a biblical concept.

Some have taken this phrase, "*I am making everything new*" to mean that Jesus is in fact restoring the former earth at this time rather than creating a new earth. Some veins of eschatology teach that the work of Christ on the earth will gradually overcome Satan's influence and create a world conducive to Christ's return. In that sense, they believe that "*I am making all things new*" refers to a rebuilding or a renovation rather than the destruction of the old earth and creation of a new earth.

There are two problems with this view. The first problem is that Revelation 20 clearly teaches the destruction of the former heavens and earth. Revelation 20:11 states of the current earth and skies that "*they fled from his presence, and there was no place for them.*" Being corrupt, the old earth and skies were incapable of existing in the presence of God's manifest glory. They, in fact, were destroyed in his presence.

The second problem with this view stems from a misunderstanding of the Greek term "*poieo*," which is translated "making." *Poieo* is a term with numerous nuances. While "*making*" all things new sounds akin to a mere renovation of the former earth, the term denotes not the transformation but the raw construction of another earth; a "new" earth. *Poieo* is used in the book of Hebrews to literally mean "creating" from scratch, rather than upgrading something already in existence.

Chapter 12: Eternity

Hebrews 1:2 (NIV)
² but in these last days he has spoken to us by his Son, whom he appointed heir of all things, and through whom he made (poieo) the universe.

In this usage of *poieo* the meaning of "*made*" refers to the initial formation of the universe, for it speaks of Christ as the creator of the original cosmos which was created out of nothing.[82] Thus, *poieo*, or "*making*" all things new indicates not the overhaul of the former earth, but the *new creation* of a *new* earth and sky.

Thus, Christ will not systematically "improve" the current earth by means of Christianizing of society. Indeed, this current earth will pass away before the Lord's presence in flames! Peter unconditionally states that at the moment of the great white judgment the current earth will be destroyed, just as Revelation 21 demands.

2 Peter 3:7 (NIV)
⁷ By the same word the present heavens and earth are reserved for fire, being kept for the day of judgment and destruction of ungodly men.

Continuing the examination of Revelation 21, a loud voice speaks in verse 3-4, saying, "*Now the dwelling of God is with men, and he will live with them. They will be his people, and God himself will be with them and be their God. ⁴ He will wipe every tear from their eyes. There will be no more death or mourning or crying or pain, for the old order of things has passed away.*"

Indeed, all things will be new! The dwelling of God will be joined with the reconstruction of earth, the dwelling of man. Just as God walked with Adam and Eve in the purity of this creation before the fall, so he will once again literally dwell with men on the new earth, which will

---

[82] Hebrews 11:3

house Heaven proper.[83]

"The dwelling of God...with men" is an expansion of the principle used in conjunction with the Temple in the Old Testament.

> ***Exodus 25:8***
> [8] *"Then have them make a sanctuary for me, and I will dwell among them.*

In the sanctuary, God's glory resided in the temple. In the New Jerusalem God's glory will reside with man in his normal abode of Heaven, which will be upon the new earth, unhindered by sin. However in the eternal order God's dwelling in glory will not be concealed behind the veil of the Holy of Holies, but will be at large among his creation. As unique as the millennial kingdom will be to have Christ ruling and being worshipped in the flesh, the new earth will have the fullness of the trinity present, including God the father dwelling with man in his full glory. Such coexistence is only possible because of the absolute absence of sin which will permeate eternity.

With the absence of sin also comes a life not formerly possible for man, even within the exceptional conditions of the millennial kingdom. In the millennial kingdom, man still had a sin nature and the earth was still corrupted, although greatly renewed by the presence of Christ. In the eternal city, however, all that has been known as the results of the judgment of sin will have passed away. Sorrow will not exist, as *"He will wipe every tear from their eyes."* Verse 4 determines that *"there will be no more death, mourning, crying or pain"* for *"the old order of things has passed away."* In short, Heaven will be everything man could possibly desire in the purest state of existence.

> ***Revelation 21:6-8***
> [6] *He said to me: "It is done. I am the Alpha and the Omega, the Beginning and the End. To him who is*

---

[83] Genesis 3:8

Chapter 12: Eternity

> *thirsty I will give to drink without cost from the spring of the water of life. [7] He who overcomes will inherit all this, and I will be his God and he will be my son. [8] But the cowardly, the unbelieving, the vile, the murderers, the sexually immoral, those who practice magic arts, the idolaters and all liars--their place will be in the fiery lake of burning sulfur. This is the second death."*

Beginning in verse 6, the reader is encouraged concerning the trials noted throughout the book of Revelation. The objective is to overcome. *"He who overcomes will inherit all this, and I will be his God and he will be my son."* Along with encouragement comes a warning concerning those who will not be allowed into the city.

> *[8] But the cowardly, the unbelieving, the vile, the murderers, the sexually immoral, those who practice magic arts, the idolaters and all liars--their place will be in the fiery lake of burning sulfur. This is the second death."*

May the reader heed the warning and be part of the Holy City of Heaven proper.

A Description of Heaven

> **Revelation 21:9-14**
> *[9] One of the seven angels who had the seven bowls full of the seven last plagues came and said to me, "Come, I will show you the bride, the wife of the Lamb." [10] And he carried me away in the Spirit to a mountain great and high, and showed me the Holy City, Jerusalem, coming down out of heaven from God. [11] It shone with the glory of God, and its brilliance was like that of a very precious jewel, like a jasper, clear as crystal. [12] It had a great, high wall with twelve gates, and with twelve angels at the gates. On the gates were written the names of the*

twelve tribes of Israel. [13] There were three gates on the east, three on the north, three on the south and three on the west. [14] The wall of the city had twelve foundations, and on them were the names of the twelve apostles of the Lamb.
[15] The angel who talked with me had a measuring rod of gold to measure the city, its gates and its walls. [16] The city was laid out like a square, as long as it was wide. He measured the city with the rod and found it to be 12,000 stadia in length, and as wide and high as it is long. [17] He measured its wall and it was 144 cubits thick, by man's measurement, which the angel was using. [18] The wall was made of jasper, and the city of pure gold, as pure as glass. [19] The foundations of the city walls were decorated with every kind of precious stone. The first foundation was jasper, the second sapphire, the third chalcedony, the fourth emerald, [20] the fifth sardonyx, the sixth carnelian, the seventh chrysolite, the eighth beryl, the ninth topaz, the tenth chrysoprase, the eleventh jacinth, and the twelfth amethyst. [21] The twelve gates were twelve pearls, each gate made of a single pearl. The great street of the city was of pure gold, like transparent glass.
[22] I did not see a temple in the city, because the Lord God Almighty and the Lamb are its temple. [23] The city does not need the sun or the moon to shine on it, for the glory of God gives it light, and the Lamb is its lamp.
[24] The nations will walk by its light, and the kings of the earth will bring their splendor into it. [25] On no day will its gates ever be shut, for there will be no night there. [26] The glory and honor of the nations will be brought into it. [27] Nothing impure will ever enter it, nor will anyone who does what is shameful or deceitful, but only those whose names are written in the Lamb's book of life.

An overriding characteristic of the eternal kingdom of Heaven is the results of the very presence of God's glory. Verse 11 notes, *"It shone*

Chapter 12: Eternity

with the glory of God." That Heaven shines, because of the presence of God's glory is indicative of a presence of God not commonly experienced in history. This measure of God's glory was formerly seen in some circumstances, however, such as Moses' encounter with God on Sinai.

> **Exodus 34:29-30**
> [29] *When Moses came down from Mount Sinai with the two tablets of the Testimony in his hands, he was not aware that his face was radiant because he had spoken with the LORD.* [30] *When Aaron and all the Israelites saw Moses, his face was radiant, and they were afraid to come near him.*

Moses' encounter with God was exceptionally up close and personal. The end result was that his face remained radiant, even after his journey back down the mountain and away from God's presence. Clearly, the radiance of his face would not be likened to a radiance that may be described from a school girl who just had an exciting date, as this was a radiance that was visible to others as a literal glow. The Israelites were afraid to even come near Moses because of this luminosity, which indicates this radiance must have been visually perceptible from a distance.

The glow on Moses face from his encounter with God will be the common reality in Heaven. Heaven will be full of God's glory, which will give it a permanent shine. From that shine, verse 23 notes, the entirety of Heaven will draw it's light. There will be no need for a sun, *"for the glory of God gives it light."*

A General description of heaven is given next in the text. In verses 12-14, its walls are noted to be very high, with twelve foundations upholding the wall itself. Each of the foundations will bear the name of one of the apostles, and will be decorated with precious stones. The wall is made of jasper, which is a highly ornamental type of silica. The wall measures 144 cubits thick, which is roughly 200 feet.

Verse 16 notes, *"the city was laid out like a square, as long as it was wide."* Furthermore, *"he measured the city with the rod and found it to be 12,000 stadia in length, and as wide and high as it is long."* Thus the city, being as wide and high as it is long, may be representative of a cubical design, or may perhaps have some very tall elements while not quite resembling a cube. At any rate, it is an impressive city, being 12,000 stadia, which is about 1,400 miles in each direction.

The gates of the city receive a considerable amount of description in the text. Verse 12 notes that Heaven will have twelve gates, three on each wall, with an angel posted at each gate. It is a curious detail that an angel is to be posted at each gate, being that no one will ever be allowed into the city who is not redeemed. Perhaps the angels posted at each gate are a demonstration of God's glory and control over his domain. The substance of each gate is that of a single pearl. Pearls are traditionally interpreted as symbols of suffering, as an oyster is understood to suffer greatly in the production of a pearl. The gates, or the entrance to Heaven, then, are frequently understood to represent the suffering of Christ who himself is the gate, providing access to the city for all who enter it.[84]

Other characteristics of the city include the infamous *"street of gold."* The gold is noted to be so pure that it is translucent *"like glass."* Coupled with the walls made of jasper and a foundation covered in jewels, this city, indeed will be a masterpiece of the literal reflections of the glory of God, as the light of his glory is able to reflect off of an array of shimmering surfaces.

Verse 22 articulates, *"I did not see a temple in the city, because the Lord God Almighty and the Lamb are its temple."* Temple worship lacks a general appreciation in the church age. In the current dispensation of the church age, believers in Christ have his very spirit living within their hearts. Yet, in the Old Testament, the Temple was the "house" for God's presence and glory on the earth. It was a dwelling place whereby man

---

[84] John 10:7

Chapter 12: Eternity

could draw near to God in a physical manner. Likewise, a Temple will play a key role in millennial worship. In millennial kingdom, not only is God's *name*, or his glory in the Temple, but Christ himself will be bodily available for the nations to approach him in worship. In Heaven, however, the presence of God and Christ will be so pervasive that a Temple is an unnecessary medium. The Lord God and Christ *are* the Temple, permeating every square inch of the city. Thus, in Heaven, the purest of all possible worship experiences will exist. There will be no Temple necessary to experience God's present glory as it will saturate one's existence at all places one should go in equal measure.

Verse 24 states, "*the nations will walk by its light, and the kings of the earth will bring their splendor into it.*" It is unclear if these nations refer to some division into heavenly nations, or if they reference the people of former earthly kingdoms. The kings of earth are said to bring their splendor into it, yet once again, it is unclear if the kings refer to the kings from historical earth who knew Christ, or if it refers to people of a certain authority on the new earth, who perhaps would be allowed to enter and exit the city for life on the new earth, where the city resides.

The text seems to imply that the latter is a possibility, however. Verse 26 states, "*the glory and honor of the nations will be brought into it,*" and verse 27 continues, "*Nothing impure will ever enter it, nor will anyone who does what is shameful or deceitful, but only those whose names are written in the Lamb's book of life.*" Thus, it seems plausible that while the Holy City will exist on the new earth, people will have the ability to enter and leave the city to traverse the new earth for various activities. While this idea is certainly not conclusively determined from the text, it does seem a possibility.

In all fairness, day to day life in Heaven does not appear to be the focus of this text, but rather, the overwhelming reality of the glory of God's presence. As sensational as the millennial kingdom will be, Heaven will be that much more.

In the millennial kingdom, although Christ is present, so is man's base desires for evil, conflict, and by the end of the millennial reign there will be a great number who have rejected Christ and turned completely to their own ways once again. Contrarily, Heaven will be a place devoid of sin. No one will have a sin nature. Never again will there be rebellion. Never will there be a need for Christ's judgments to be handed out. All will live in full harmony in the presence of the very manifest glory of God for eternity.

More can be gleaned from scripture about Heaven, but concerning the timeline of eschatology, the end has come in a sense, and will never come in another sense. While Heaven is the final destination for those who have had their names written in the book of life, "the end" is hardly a fitting conclusion to the account. One may rather desire to conclude with, "the beginning," for Heaven is the eternal and enduring state. After the entirety of the clock which human history existed has passed once again, no less time will remain for those who enjoy Heaven. In light of eternity, all human history is a mere short breath. The real chronicle, it seems, is not one's adventures prior to the eternal state, but rather, the circumstance of eternity itself, for it is that state which will be the immeasurable duration of one's existence.

Each soul of history, thus, will find himself living an incalculable percentage of his life, the eternal existence, either in a beautiful city full of God's glory or in a lake of fire, full of God's wrath.

Chapter 12: Eternity
. . . .

Chapter 13: Our Response

The ultimate question asked of student and teacher alike upon completion of a body of study in scripture should always be, "what shall my response be?" Scripture, unlike historic human literature, has as its purpose to point man to God, that he may do God's good pleasure and receive the blessings noted in this work rather than the curses of God's wrath. Peter warns,

> **2 Peter 1:19**
> [19] *And we have the word of the prophets made more certain, and you will do well to pay attention to it, as to a light shining in a dark place, until the day dawns and the morning star rises in your hearts.*

To say it another way, scripture is not akin to fine human literature with is read, pondered and filed away as a beautiful thought which may or may not bring any real substance to one's life. Irrevocably, what one does with scripture is decisive in one's life. God's revelation of himself will be heeded or it will be rejected. To ponder scripture and not heed its teachings, by definition, is to have rejected them. God, in his graciousness has given mankind the Bible to point him toward God's good and pleasing will. All man must do is respond affirmatively to the leading of scripture. Having seen God's future plans for the earth, and eternity afterward, one must only ask the question, "what shall I now do?"

Overwhelmingly, the biblical warning which permeates eschatological teachings could be stated in two simple terms; "be ready."

If one is not ready for the rapture event, that one will be doomed to live out all other events described in the biblical body of prophecy concerning the great tribulation. If one is not ready, by merit of having received Christ's lordship before his or her departure from this earth by

Chapter 13: Our Response

death, that one can only expect to wait in Hades for the great white throne judgment to determine the extent of his or her eternal punishment in the lake of fire. The only way to choose one eternal destiny over the other, is to be ready.

Jesus, in Matthew 24 speaks of readiness for the yet future events described in this work. That warning is the strongest of all warnings which could be given in light of this study.

Matthew 24 is a somewhat complicated chapter, which answers three questions which are asked at the beginning of the chapter. This dialogue, The Olivet Discourse, is recorded in Matthew 24-25, Mark 13, and Luke 21. The dissection of the Olivet Discourse is beyond the intention of its reference in this chapter, but this portion of it serves as a clear sounding of Jesus' warning to "be ready."

Jesus warns the disciples in verses 1-2 of the destruction of the city at a future time. The disciples then ask the questions which the remainder of the discourse will answer.

> **Matthew 24:3**
> *"As Jesus was sitting on the Mount of Olives, the disciples came to him privately. "Tell us," they said, "when will this happen, and what will be the sign of your coming and of the end of the age?"*

The disciples asked three different questions. Each question is separated by the Greek term, *kai*, which is rendered "and" in English. This term separates distinct, but connected thoughts, such as our word "and."

The first question is, *"when will this happen?"* This question is the question of the immediate context; when will *"this"* happen. Jesus had just predicted the destruction of the temple. They are asking, "when will the temple be destroyed."

The second question is *"what will be the sign of your coming?"* This question is a change from the immediate context. The question asks for a sign of Christ's coming. It could be debated which "*coming*" the disciples are asking about; the rapture, or the second coming to establish his kingdom upon the earth. Yet, Jesus' answer demonstrates that it is the coming for rapture that they are asking of.

The third question is, "(what will be the sign) *of the end of the age?*" As noted earlier, Jewish though was broken into two ages: this age, and the age to come. "This age" was thought of as the current age, and still is in Jewish thought, while "*the age to come*" was the age which Messiah would set up his kingdom on earth, or the age of the millennial kingdom.

Jesus' answer to the question "*what will be the sign of your coming*" is what is noted in verses 36-44. This can be deduced by his answer.

> ### *Matthew 24:36-41*
> *³⁶ "No one knows about that day or hour, not even the angels in heaven, nor the Son, but only the Father. ³⁷ As it was in the days of Noah, so it will be at the coming of the Son of Man. ³⁸ For in the days before the flood, people were eating and drinking, marrying and giving in marriage, up to the day Noah entered the ark; ³⁹ and they knew nothing about what would happen until the flood came and took them all away. That is how it will be at the coming of the Son of Man. ⁴⁰ Two men will be in the field; one will be taken and the other left. ⁴¹ Two women will be grinding with a hand mill; one will be taken and the other left.*

Jesus clearly is answering one of the latter two question, either concerning his coming to rapture the church, or his coming to establish his millennial kingdom. Jesus' statement, "*no one knows about that day or hour,*" however, is not true of the second coming of Christ, but is true of the rapture. Daniel and Revelation both narrow the return of Christ to establish his kingdom down to the exact day in light of the great tribulation. There will be 1,260 days (the first half of the tribulation) followed by 1,260 days (the second half of the tribulation) which would

Chapter 13: Our Response

precisely inform one of the day of his return to reign as King once the tribulation begins. To that end, those who may read Jesus' response during the coming tribulation *could* in fact calculate the day of his return to reign. It is his return to rapture the church which no one can know the day or the time. Thus, Jesus is speaking in this part of the text concerning his return to rapture the church.

The comparison of people "*eating and drinking, marrying and giving in marriage,*" likewise, does not fit the attitude prior to the second coming, but will fit the attitude prior to the rapture. At the time of the second coming the Battle of Armageddon will have been raging for some period of time. Babylon would have been destroyed and the armies of Antichrist will have surrounded Israel. The earth will be under the in exhaustive travail of war, starvation, famine and death. Thus the description of the carefree nature of humanity is certainly not answering the question "when will the second coming be," but rather "when will your coming for the rapture be." The rapture will come at a time when people are utterly carefree, while the second coming will come at a point of great anxiety.

Continuing the discourse, "be ready" is the clear warning of Jesus with regards to our understanding of the coming of the rapture. Unlike in the days of Noah, when, "*they knew nothing about what would happen until the flood came,*" man has been given foreknowledge concerning the coming of Christ to rapture his church and are issued a warning.

> ### Matthew 24:42-44
> [42] "*Therefore keep watch, because you do not know on what day your Lord will come.* [43] *But understand this: If the owner of the house had known at what time of night the thief was coming, he would have kept watch and would not have let his house be broken into.* [44] *So you also must be ready, because the Son of Man will come at an hour when you do not expect him.*

That warning is to "*keep watch*" in verse 42 and to "*be ready*" in verse 44. Keeping watch is likened to a home-owner having full knowledge of the arrival of a thief. Had a homeowner been granted foreknowledge of a pending break-in, *"he would have kept watch and would not have let his house be broken into."* Man is being given by Jesus a forewarning that this thief *will come*. Jesus *will return* to take those who know him out of the way prior to the great tribulation. One who knows a thief is definitely coming will make appropriate preparations to be ready for that event. Mankind, having been warned of the coming of Jesus' return to rapture the church are likewise instructed to be ready at all times, *"because you do not know on what day your Lord will come."*

How to be ready

Jesus does not leave man with only a warning. He next stipulates what exactly man must do in order to be ready.

> ***Matthew 24:45-51***
> *45 "Who then is the faithful and wise servant, whom the master has put in charge of the servants in his household to give them their food at the proper time? 46 It will be good for that servant whose master finds him doing so when he returns. 47 I tell you the truth, he will put him in charge of all his possessions. 48 But suppose that servant is wicked and says to himself, 'My master is staying away a long time,' 49 and he then begins to beat his fellow servants and to eat and drink with drunkards.*
> *50 The master of that servant will come on a day when he does not expect him and at an hour he is not aware of.*
> *51 He will cut him to pieces and assign him a place with the hypocrites, where there will be weeping and gnashing of teeth.*

Readiness is simple in this text. It is to be doing the master's will when he returns. The servant in Jesus' metaphor is charged with the *"care of the servants in his household to give them their food at the proper time."* Readiness is defined by it being *"good for that servant whose master finds him doing so when he returns."* Thus, Jesus states that being ready

Chapter 13: Our Response

is to be doing what the master had required at the time he returns. In short, when Jesus comes to rapture his church, it is the obligation of man to be doing what Jesus has asked him to do.

So what has Jesus asked man to do? To shorten it to a simple phrase, he has asked man to accept his Kingship and to serve him.

> **John 8:12**
> *12 ... "I am the light of the world. Whoever follows me will never walk in darkness, but will have the light of life."*

Readiness is also tested in the text. Jesus supposed that the servant became weary of the master's delay "*and he then begins to beat his fellow servants and to eat and drink with drunkards.*" The servant will be tested when the master "*will come on a day when he does not expect him and at an hour he is not aware of.*" The test yields either faithfulness or hypocrisy.

The servant who fails to observe the masters instructions, the master will "*cut him to pieces and assign him a place with the hypocrites, where there will be weeping and gnashing of teeth.*" Once again, works salvation is not being taught, but rather a test is being administered to determine the faithfulness of the servant. This servant, having failed to do what his master instructed him to do, is assigned a place with the hypocrites. A hypocrite is one claims certain principles for himself but does not live according to them. He is one who says one thing and does another. This servant claimed to be a good servant, but his lifestyle indicated that he indeed was not. Readiness, then, is to live in a state which is favorable by the master. It is not to *claim* to serve the master, but to actually be found serving the master when he returns. The distinction between those who claim Christ is their King and those for whom Christ actually *is* their King is determined by one's *actions* rather than one's words. Salvation is not defined in scripture as one who *understands* the teachings concerning Christ, but as one who exhibits by faith a life submitted to the Lordship of his King.

Any who presume themselves to be a servant of Christ in this age, then, should hear and understand Jesus' warnings that the true test of one's allegiance to him as King is not one's claims, but one's actions. One is not considered a follower of Christ because of a religious affiliation with a church or because of words spoken in homage to Christ. Rather, one is considered a follower of Christ if one does what Christ asked him to do; to serve him as King.

God's Offer: Now, and To Come

At this time the author chooses to intentionally convert to the first person writing style. I'd like to speak freely, as the author of this work, as a minister of the gospel of Christ and as one who very personably desires to share God's outstanding offer of salvation to you, the reader.

An interesting note which was omitted at the beginning of Chapter 3 is that God's two purposes of the great tribulation, *judgment* and *redemption,* represent two options which have been in existence for man from the very beginning of time. In the tribulation, God will simply begin to execute judgments on mankind early, that perhaps these judgments will serve as an indicator for what he has in store should one continue to reject Christ as his King. While this is a bit of an oversimplification, the point is tenable; you and I have the same choices today that will be offered during the great tribulation: we will be redeemed or we will be judged.

In the great tribulation it appears that God will increase the intensity of the knowledge of that choice by giving mankind a taste of his wrath while still offering redemption. He will forewarn them of what lies ahead should they refuse to receive his redemption. Yet, while the choices are the same now as they will be then, they exist without the same measure of perceived urgency. Most people think "I have time" to make the most essential decision of life; to choose to receive and serve Christ as King.

As compassionately as I can, let me encourage you to understand that

Chapter 13: Our Response

. . . .

God has been a gracious God to us, yet we have utterly trampled his goodness underfoot.

Imagine owning a plot of acreage and giving half of it to a dear friend. Additionally, you build him a nice custom home on it adjacent to your own homestead so that you can live together in harmony as the great friends that you are. This dear friend has nothing, yet you are able to grant this gift to him out of your wealth, because you love him and greatly desire to give to him this gift.

This land is given to him freely, save for one stipulation: there are to be no animals kept on the property. After all, this is your land, which you are giving generously, and you do not desire to live next to pigs, chickens and the general by-product of a barnyard.

Now imagine that you and your neighbor live together in great accord for a time, but a day comes when the neighbor begins to resent your restrictions over him. He becomes so comfortable in his provisions that he takes ownership over it in a way that defies your agreement. He first brings in some pigs who create a foul stench for the entire area. He adds chickens and allows them to roam freely. He gets a dozen goats and allows them to roam because he does not care for mowing grass. In his power stupor he then adds every type of animal imaginable to litter the property in wanton disrespect to your graciousness.

Your friend has always been dear to you. You love him as your own family. Yet, he has taken great care to egregiously demonstrate that you will no longer have authority over his homestead. He openly defies your restrictions on the property.

At this point you consider your options. The simplest and most efficient option is to go to court and easily redeem that which was once yours for the flagrant breach of contract. Your friend would be cast off the property forever and you could then clean it up to your own standards. Yet, because of your love for your friend, you instead give him an option to not be evicted: you will forgive all past trespasses if he will only submit himself to the agreement and clean up the property.

The above parable is not without fault, but is a good beginning to understand what God has done for you and I. He has granted to us what we could not possibly have acquired without him. He alone granted the very bones, sinew and blood which makes up our physical lives. He provided the earth, in all of its glory to compliment our existence. He granted us the intellect to master and be creative with that environment. No living soul can claim to have what he or she has by merits of his or her own actions. It is a gift from God.

Yet, God's gift came with stipulation. To Adam and Eve, he offered the full abundance of the Garden of Eden for their own consumption. They were only not to eat the fruit of the trees in the middle of the garden. The rest, as it is said, is history. From the time of Adam and Eve's decision to deliberately rebel against God's "deed restrictions" our lives have continued down the path toward greater depravity and stronger demonstrations of our perceived independence from God's ownership over us. People today commonly assert their "freedom" from God's control by doing whatever seems best in their own eyes. Even those who live "clean" lifestyles, according to scripture, are sinful from birth and are worthy of removal from God's presence. Each of us has lied, cheated and been obstinate against authority at some time in our lives. We have no idea what it is to live a pure and sinless life, for sin is within us. No one taught us how to disobey our parents or how to harbor envy against others. No one taught us as two year olds how to lie when presented with the option in order to avoid discipline. It is simply in us to do so. We are overcome by sin, even if we feel that we compare higher than others.

Yet, God, loving us as his dear children, instead of evicting us eternally into judgment and away from his presence has offered us a choice: be reconciled to him and his lordship, or receive the judgment which is due for our actions.

The choices of the great tribulation, judgment or redemption, are the choices man has had from the beginning. It is the choice you have this very day.

Chapter 13: Our Response

Perhaps the intensity of this decision between judgment and redemption will be magnified in the tribulation years because of its known time factor, not to mention the pouring out of horrible retributions, albeit judgments significantly less than those of eternity. In that seven year period people will be granted a mild vision of the chastisement to come, and will only have those years with which to make their choice. Yet, much is the same today. While judgments are not being poured out upon the earth as in the tribulation, we all are slowly giving into death, that final hour of choice. And, that final hour is not guaranteed to linger; for not all live to a ripe old age. As tragic as it is to see a young person die, how much more tragic to see a young person die without having chosen their King, thinking that much time still remained to make life's ultimate choice.

As God has a clear purpose outlined for the great tribulation, so my presentation of eschatology has had clear purposes. As God's servant, I have been called to a specific teaching ministry to explain biblical teachings as clearly as I can. It is for that purpose I engaged this study and have produced this work. But, as a believer in Christ, I also have a broader calling to inspire you to choose God's exceptionally gracious offer of redemption from your sin, which is common in us all. Some who read this will not even have seven years to do so, and should not ignore this opportunity. For when one's time is gone, the choice has been made by default, and an eviction from God's presence- for all of eternity- will result; plunging the procrastinator into the same eternal lake of fire which Satan, Antichrist, the False Prophet and all the lost of creation will share.

How to Receive God's Offer

Romans 6:23 sums up our affirmative choice better than perhaps any single verse in the Bible:

> *²³ For the wages of sin is death, but the gift of God is eternal life in Christ Jesus our Lord.*

"*Wages*" are defined as what one earns from one's labor. Wages are contrary to a gift, which is also mentioned in the text. You would not hire onto a job, complete the work, then receive payment as if it were a gift. It was in fact earned. You worked for it. You deserve payment. This text informs you and I that we *have earned death* because of our sin. We are subject to an eternal lake of fire, because we earned it by our sinful actions. God, being a just God, does not allow sin to go unpunished. If he did, he could not be called just.

"***Sin***" is most simply stated as *disobedience to God*. It is the breach of his will. Being the life-giver, he alone has the option to put restrictions on what he has given. No one has the right to claim their life as their own because it was in fact given to them without any action of their own. Yet, sin, stated another way is exactly that; it is man choosing to own his life and serve his own ways, contrary to God's desires. Adam's sin in the garden wasn't about him needing more food. It was about him believing the deception of Satan and choosing his own path, which he thought was better, rather than God's.

Many in our culture struggle with the concept of sin. Some say that sin is a product of guilt which organized religion has attempted to impress upon the rest. Yet, even those would admit having failed on some level at achieving even their own self-imposed standards. And, even those demand justice to be brought when another imposes upon their own rights, which in itself is the beginnings of an understanding of what sin is.

The Bible teaches that all are born into sin from the time of Adam and Eve. That truth is evident in that parents do not teach their sons and daughters how to lie, for example. They figure that out quite on their own from the wealth of inherent sin in their nature. In fact, all manners of righteousness necessitate being taught to children, for they will not figure "good" out on their own. They are *taught* to share, or they will spend their lives being greedy. They are *taught* patience (at least some are) else they spend their lives in tantrums. They are *taught* to nicely administer disagreement or they will naturally incline themselves to fight with the other children. The simple truth is, sin exists in us from birth, and is something to be *overcome* rather than to be embraced.

Chapter 13: Our Response

"***Death***," in Romans 6:23, refers to the penalty which God has established as a worthy response to sin. Death is a two-fold principle in scripture: physical deterioration and spiritual punishment. All will be subject to the former in this life, but are offered redemption from the latter. And, even physical death will be reversed with the glorification of the resurrected bodies of those who receive salvation, as noted in Chapter 2. All life will be resurrected at some point in history. The first resurrection, which is entirely for believers, will result in a new glorified body which cannot die and will never decay. In that case, even the body is re-born into Christ for those who receive him. Those who participate in that resurrection will have even the physical manifestations of death revoked when they receive their new bodies. The second resurrection, which is entirely for unbelievers, will result in a continually and permanently marred body of death. Those without redemption will receive the fullness of death for all eternity; physical and spiritual.

Some believe this sentence to be unfair or to not match the crime. Yet the penalties of laws are granted by their makers, not those who are found guilty. The same God who created the standard has created the due punishment for its trespass according to his own measure. Clearly, in God's uniquely perfect understanding, the distance between righteousness and sinfulness is as great as the chasm which exists between the splendor of Heaven and the despair of the lake of fire, which is the epitome of spiritual "death" referred to in this text. In short, the wages of sin, then, is to die physically *and* spiritually forever in the lake of fire.

So far, Romans 6:23 has painted an utterly hopeless picture. If the wages of sin is death, then anyone who sins will be sentenced to the lake of fire discussed in this study. And, sadly, the Bible also teaches that all sin. I sin, and you sin. Romans 3:23 says "*for all have sinned and fall short of the glory of God.*" Thus, all of mankind is rightly due an eternity of agony in the lake of fire without mercy. Mankind has been the ungrateful neighbor who has squandered the gift of his landlord. Graciously, the text continues and offers hope for us. For God is gracious and kind to us, not wanting us to perish for our sin.

The pivotal term "***but***" in Romans 6:23 is a welcome hope for remedy. There is another option. For those who are deserving of judicial action have been offered a means of making amends with their offended benefactor. Perhaps the most renowned scripture of all time is John 3:16,

> *"For God so loved the world that he gave his one and only Son, that whoever believes in him shall not perish but have eternal life."*

While physical and spiritual death is the just and default state of man's future, God has always offered grace in the face of certain judgment to those who would receive it. Just as he will offer salvation during the judgments of the great tribulation to those who will repent, so he offers salvation to us now.

Thus, the wages of sin is death, *but* the gift of God is eternal life through Christ Jesus our Lord.

A "***gift***" is completely contrary to a wage. While wages are earned, a gift cannot be. No one opens a Christmas or birthday present while asking which action was performed in the previous year to have rendered such a payment. A gift is not the response to one's actions, but is the response to the grace and love of the giver. Children may have in fact earned a bundle of switches, as my father used to jokingly warn me that I may receive at the next Christmas, yet when the time comes grace is extended even to the willfully disobedient child and gifts will surely await them under the tree. God offers such a gift to you, his beloved creation. It is a gift which is available to all but is not guaranteed as will be noted shortly.

This gift is "***of God***" in the text, reminding us that God and God alone has right to offer compassion on those he has judged as sinful. It is he who was offended and it is he alone who can offer grace to the offender. He alone is the judge who can determine an appropriate penalty for our crimes.

Chapter 13: Our Response

"*Eternal life*", likewise, is the antithesis of "*death*." Death results in the permanent state of bodily and spiritual suffering in the abode of Hell. Eternal life reverses both: a new body is given at the resurrection of the saints and the spirit/body combination will live eternally in a harmonious state with God in the New Jerusalem, or Heaven. As noted earlier, however, eternal life is not automatic nor universal. It is granted in the text specifically "*through Jesus Christ our Lord*."

"*Through*" indicates the course by which this eternal life is arrived at. There is but one path: **Jesus Christ our Lord**. It is well documented in this study that Israel has experienced a national separation from God because of their rejection of this one "path" of Christ. There are strong numbers of individual Israelites who have accepted their savior, but as a whole, the nation has not and will not do so until the end of the great tribulation. As a people, the Jews have done what many individuals have chosen to do. They have charted their own course toward God. Yet, in scripture they are clearly condemned for doing so, as Christ is the granted path which alone will be accepted by God. Romans 9:31-32 says,

> "...Israel, who pursued a law of righteousness, has not attained it. [32] Why not? Because they pursued it not by faith but as if it were by works."

The path is by faith in Christ alone. Israel attempted to achieve salvation by works, as many Gentiles attempt to do today as well. Many think that "being a good person" will grant them favor with God and somehow convince him to excuse their sin, which they also have done. However, only faith in Christ is the accepted path to redemption, as Jesus notes in John 10:7-9,

> "I tell you the truth, I am the gate for the sheep. [8] All who ever came before me were thieves and robbers, but the sheep did not listen to them. [9] I am the gate; whoever enters through me will be saved."

He also notes in John 14:6,

> *"I am the way and the truth and the life. No one comes to the Father except through me."*

It is only through Christ that one can receive God's gift of grace. Even Israel, God's chosen people, the very family of Christ's human heritage are rejected and judged if they refuse to serve Christ as their King.

The reasons for this, simply stated, can be observed from God's own law. God, who established the law and the penalty for breaking it, has stipulated that death *will be administered* as payment for sin in every instance. Hebrews 9:22 says,

> *"In fact, the law requires that nearly everything be cleansed with blood, and without the shedding of blood there is no forgiveness."*

Death *must* follow the trespass of sin. God, in his mercy, allowed a substitution to be made, however. In the Old Testament, animal sacrifices were stipulated which would cover man's sin. Leviticus 17:11 states,

> *"For the life of a creature is in the blood, and I have given it to you to make atonement for yourselves on the altar; it is the blood that makes atonement for one's life."*

Those who chose to receive God's grace in that day were allowed to offer an animal sacrifice for their sin, and be spared the penalty of eternal death for themselves. As such, the animal was a substitution for the death demanded upon the sinner. Yet, as people continued to sin, sacrifices were continually required to cover their sin. When God sent Jesus to earth, he did so to provide a singular blood sacrifice by which the whole of mankind could find a substitutionary replacement in death for their own sin.

The wages of sin is death, and those wages will be paid. They will be paid by you, or by a worthy substitution. New Testament theology

Chapter 13: Our Response

clearly teaches that Christ is the fulfillment of the Old Testament law. He is the final blood sacrifice by which men may be saved, and is the *only* substitutionary atonement acceptable to God. No longer are animal sacrifices required nor acceptable now that the perfect sacrifice has been offered. Unlike the blood of animals, Christ's blood endures as a continual offering for sin; past, present and future. Hebrews 10:10b-11 states,

> *"...we have been made holy through the sacrifice of the body of Jesus Christ once for all. Day after day every priest stands and performs his religious duties; again and again he offers the same sacrifices, which can never take away sins. [12] But when this priest had offered for all time one sacrifice for sins, he sat down at the right hand of God."*

Christ, unlike the former priests who administered the animal blood sacrifices, offered *"for all time one sacrifice,"* and rendered complete the payment of death required by God's law. To that end, this gift of God, which is eternal life, is only available *"through Jesus Christ our Lord."*

The last term one must grasp firmly from Romans 6:23 is "**Lord**." This term is the same concept as the term "King" demonstrated throughout this work. It is perhaps this title which causes so many to give pause in receiving God's gracious gift. A lord or king is one who rules over another's life completely. The King is the ultimate and uncompromising authority of life. This sentiment is of great concern to the willfully sinful spirit of man. As noted earlier, sin can be simply understood as man's persistence to rule himself, outside of the constraints of God's oversight. This text clearly teaches, however, that a restoration of God's rule in one's life is required for the acceptance of God's offer of salvation through Christ. To receive salvation, you must understand that it comes through the submission to Christ as Lord. Romans 10:9 states,

> *"if you confess with your mouth, "Jesus is Lord," and believe in your heart that God raised him from the dead, you will be saved."*

Christ is the King. It is he who will destroy the work of evil on earth. It is he who will reign supremely during the millennial kingdom. It is he who is the worthy recipient of the glory in this study. And, it is the acceptance of his Lordship which is a fundamental key to one's salvation. You *cannot* experience the forgiveness of Christ outside of the willful laying of your life at his feet to serve him as your Lord and King.

Contrary to widely misunderstood notions, simply believing that Christ was God's son and that he died in your stead is not sufficient for the acceptance of God's gift. One must place Christ as his Lord, allowing Christ to rule his life. James 2:19 states,

> *"You believe that there is one God. Good! Even the demons believe that--and shudder."*

Simply believing the historical facts of Christ's death, burial and resurrection makes one no different than Satan himself. In fact, the demons have more than belief of Christ's deity, crucifixion and resurrection; they have knowledge. They were present on earth when Christ was crucified. They were able to observe his resurrection from the dead to demonstrate his authority over death. They much more than believe in the logistical realities of Christ's substitutionary death and sequential resurrection; *they know it.* Yet they are condemned and will be cast into the lake of fire, all-the-while knowing who Christ is. Like the demonic kingdom, man cannot be saved by his mere belief. Man is saved by his *response* to his belief. Do not misinterpret John 3:16 stating *"whosoever believes in him shall ...have everlasting life"* to indicate that an intellectual belief can uphold one outside of acting upon that belief.

The Bible calls this principle of acting on one's belief "faith." Faith is believing something to the point of acting upon it. Belief without action is what the book of James calls "dead" faith. To exercise faith, for example, in a chair, one must first believe the chair will hold his weight, then one must choose to *exercise* that belief and sit upon the chair. Without sitting on the chair one has not demonstrated faith, but only a stated academic belief. Biblical belief is much more than cerebral. It is

Chapter 13: Our Response

experiential. One who sincerely believes the chair will hold him will not hesitate to sit. Likewise, if warned while driving down a highway that a bridge was out ahead, one's true belief will inspire an appropriate action. It if is *truly believed* that the bridge is out, one must still make the decision to stop the car before getting to that point in the road. If you, sincerely believe that Christ is King, then it is imperative that you act upon that belief and live your life accordingly: call on him today, proclaim him as your Lord and serve him.

To biblically believe in Christ demands that one respond to him. That response is to make him the Lord of one's life. Upon establishing submission to Christ's rule, one receives the removal of sin which Christ's substitutionary death has made available. The commitment of a believing person to the Lordship of Christ is the commitment unto salvation. It is through "*Christ Jesus our Lord*" that one is redeemed.

In conclusion, to "*be ready*" for the return of the King is to make him King of your life *now* rather than waiting for his coming to rapture up his believers. Once the rapture occurs, all who have put off their commitment to the lordship of Christ, and who live long enough are assured to endure the fullness of the fury of the great tribulation. God has promised protection from some of his judgments to believers, but not all of them. And, he also has promised that those who become believers between the times of the rapture and his return will be subject to great personal persecution. A multitude of them which no one can count will be beheaded for their faith. How wise is the one which does not procrastinate. It is Jesus' desire for you to place him in your heart today rather than tomorrow. Hebrews 9:28 reminds us,

> "*so Christ was sacrificed once to take away the sins of many people; and he will appear a second time, not to bear sin, but to bring salvation to those who are waiting for him.*"

If you desire to conclude this study by making the commitment of faith to Christ, may I suggest the sincere communication of this prayer to the Lord:

Lord, Jesus, I do believe you are who the Bible says. You are God's Son, and our only path to salvation from sin. I believe you died to be a substitute for man's sin. I admit that I am a sinner and need your forgiveness. Please forgive me for my sin and help me to live as you desire. I proclaim you as the Lord of my life and will serve you to the best of my abilities.

Upon your commitment to the Lordship of Christ, I strongly suggest that you find a good church to join and learn with. A good church is one which teachers the Bible, and the Bible alone as the source of the revelation of God to man. Beyond that, a good church is one which interprets the Bible literally, rather than symbolically. Men will fall and will fail. Their leadership is always to be tested biblically. But, God's Word will remain intact, and is absolutely trustworthy to lead you in pursuit of the Lordship of Christ. A good biblical teacher will always begin with the Bible itself as the source of truth, and will teach what the Bible teaches, rather than attempting to teach another agenda while using the Bible as support material. Find a pastor who will preach the text of the Bible purely and you will surely find a good church to learn and grow in.

Until the King returns, may his grace lead you to readiness and great anticipation of his redemption.

Chapter 13: Our Response
. . . .

Scripture Index

Genesis
2:17, pp. 84, 283
3:1, p. 191
3:8, p. 301
3:15, pp. vi, 58, 59, 65
5:24, p. 120
6, pp. 60, 61, 63, 64, 65
6:1–4, p. 60
6:4, p. 67
6:5–8, p. 65
6:11–12, p. 66
12:2-3, p. vi
15:18–21, p. 241
37, p. 172
37:9–11, p. 171
46:21, p. 25

Exodus
25:8, p. 301
33:20, p. 84
34:29–30, p. 304

Leviticus
17:11, p. 323

Numbers
10, p. 82
10:8–10, p. 82
13, p. 61

Deuteronomy
18:21–22, p. 14

2 Kings
2:11, p. 120

2 Chronicles
5:13–14, p. 264

Job
1:6, p. 63
1:6–7, p. 63
38:6–7, p. 63

Psalms
2, pp. 101, 172, 192, 193, 194, 280
2:1–6, p. 192
2:5–6, p. 194
2:6–9, p. 172
2:9, p. 266
83:14–16, p. 95
110, p. 128
118, p. 206
118:22–26, p. 206
148:2, p. 279

Isaiah
1:18, p. 126
2, pp. 242, 243

2:1–4, p. 267
2:2–4, p. 242
9, p. 193
9:2, p. 193
9:6–7, p. vi, vii, 193, 235
11, p. 243
11:6–9, p. 269
13, pp. 186, 249, 251, 252
13:9, pp. 102, 249
13:19–22, p. 249
13:21–22, p. 251
14:12, p. 134
14:14, p. 191
17:13, p. 125
26:1, p. 257
26:19, p. 257
28, p. 167
28:15, p. 107
28:15–18, p. 167
34:8–14, p. 252
52–53, p. 9
53:4-5, p. vi
53:11, p. vi
63:1–4 1, p. 215
63:3, p. 218
65:20, p. 270
65:21–24, p. 273

Jeremiah
2:20, p. 124
3:14, p. 260
23:5, p. 267
31, pp. 17, 18
31:31–33, p. 17
33:14–21, p. 238
51:43, p. 250

Lamentations
1:13, p. 95

Ezekiel
16:15–41, p. 124
20, pp. 16, 18, 209
20:32–38, p. 16
20:34–38, p. 209
23:5–44, p. 124
28:14, p. 248
28:16, p. 175
38, pp. 23, 30, 31, 279
38:1–6, p. 24
38:7–9, p. 26
38:8, pp. 34, 36
38:10–13, p. 27
38:13, p. 29
38:14–16, p. 30
38:17–18, p. 32
38:19–23, p. 32
39:9–12, p. 35
40–43, pp. 264, 265
43:7, p. 264
43:18–24, p. 265

Daniel
2, pp. 37, 42, 43, 44, 47, 48
2:26–45, p. 37
2:37–38, p. 42
2:40, p. 46
2:44, pp. 45, 47
7, pp. 37, 42, 43, 44, 48, 71, 109, 142
7:1–28, p. 39
7:7, p. 47

7:20–22, p. 50
7:21, 24–25, p. 109
7:22, p. 110
7:23, pp. 45, 46, 49
7:23–25, p. 48
7:24–25, p. 50
9, pp. 21, 107, 155, 167
9:24–27, p. 54
9:25–27, p. 153
9:26, p. 109
9:27, p. 162
9:27, pp. 20, 21, 107, 108, 162, 166
10, p. 278
10:13, p. 279
10:20–21, p. 278
11, pp. 141, 142, 148
11:40–45, pp. 141, 167
11:41, p. 177
11:45, p. 143
12, pp. 245, 257, 259
12:2, p. 258
12:9–10, p. 2
12:11–13, p. 245
12:13, pp. 258, 259

Hosea
1:2, p. 124
5, p. 202
5:9, p. 202
5:14–15, p. 202
5:15, p. 206

Joel
2, pp. 211, 227, 270
2:23, p. 270
2:28–32, p. 210
3, pp. 227, 228
3:1–2, pp. 226, 227
3:2, p. 228
3:3, p. 228
3:10, p. 269

Micah
2, p. 215
2:12–13, p. 215

Nahum
1:2, p. 220

Zephaniah
2:3, p. 104

Zechariah
12:1–3, p. 194
12:4–9, p. 196
12:9–14, p. 203
12–13, p. 210
12–14, p. 194
13, pp. 199, 201
13:1–6, p. 199
13:7–9, p. 201
13:8, p. 199
13:9, pp. 213, 263
14:2, p. 198
14:3, pp. 211, 222
14:3–4, pp. 223, 225
14:4, p. 229
14:4–5, p. 76
14:12–13, p. 221

Malachi

4:5, p. 121

Matthew
3:11, p. 95
4, p. 173
4:3,006, p. 191
5:14, p. 241
5:19, p. 96
8:20, p. 296
10:41–42, p. 96
11:14, p. 121
11:20–24, p. 291
12, p. 204
12:23, p. 204
12:24, pp. 204, 205
12:31–32, p. 205
17:11–13, p. 121
21, p. 207
21:33–45, p. 207
22:1–14, pp. 208, 261
22:30, p. 64
23, pp. 9, 205
23:37–39, p. 205
24, pp. 8, 25, 31, 119, 152, 155, 156, 157, 168, 176, 177, 192, 213, 214, 310
24: 3–16, p. 155
24:3, pp. 170, 229, 310
24:3–8, p. 8
24:4–25, p. 157
24:9, p. 174
24:9–14, p. 12
24:14, p. 119
24:15, p. 21
24:15–28, p. 168
24:23, p. 68
24:23–24, p. 111
24:23–25, p. 68
24:23–26, p. 145
24:26–27, p. 213
24:28, p. 214
24:29, p. 296
24:36–41, p. 311
24:42–44, p. 312
24:45–51, p. 313
24–25, pp. 206, 310
25, pp. 229, 232
25:1–13, p. 261
25:31, p. 218
25:31–40, p. 230
25:34, p. 263
25:41, p. 281
25:41–45, p. 231
26, p. 46
26:39, p. 126
26:57, p. 46
27:11, p. 46
28:18, p. 282

Mark
9:47–48, p. 288
10:35–40, p. 96
13, pp. 169, 310
13:26, p. vii

Luke
1, p. 240
1:30–33, p. 240
6:35, p. 96
8:30–31, p. 138
12:46–48, p. 292
13:2–3, p. 104

14, p. 96
14:12–14, p. 97
17, p. 169
21, pp. 86, 310
21:12, p. 89
21:34–36, pp. 86, 106
21:35–36, p. 97
24:39–41, p. 86

John
3:16, pp. 321, 325
5:28–29, p. 93
8:12, p. 314
8:44, p. 161
10:7, p. 305
10:7–9, p. 322
14, pp. 73, 74, 75
14:1–4, p. 74
14:6, p. 322
15:21, p. 89
16:33, p. 89
19:2, p. 126
20:19, p. 85

Acts
3:19, p. 104
4:10–12, p. 201
9:36–41, p. 120

Romans
1, p. 89
1:18–20, p. 89
2:5, p. 89
3:11–12, p. 290
3:23, p. 320
5:9, p. 88

6:23, pp. 84, 318, 320, 321, 324
8:1–4, p. 88
8:19–21, p. 286
8:19–23, p. 286
9:17, p. 31
9:31–32, p. 322
10:9, p. 324
11:25–27 25, p. 208

1 Corinthians
1:24, p. 85
3:11–15, p. 94
4:5, p. 95
12:3, p. 203
15, pp. 80, 83
15:5, p. 84
15:20–23, p. 255
15:24–25, p. 283
15:24–28, p. 282
15:35–49, p. 83
15:50, p. 286
15:50–58, p. 80

2 Corinthians
5:10, p. 94
11:2, p. 261
12:2–4, p. 296

Galatians
4:26, p. 298

Ephesians
1:20–23, p. 282
5:18, p. 127
6:17, p. 219

Philippians
2:9, p. 282
2:10-11, p. v

1 Thessalonians
1:7, p. 52
1:9–10, p. 87
4:13–18, p. 77
4:16, p. 289
4:16–17, pp. 97, 256
4:17, pp. 218, 259
5, p. 89
5:1–3, p. 70
5:1–10, pp. 88, 102
5:10, p. 91

2 Thessalonians
1, p. 52
2, p. 53
2:1–4, p. 50
2:3, p. 57
2:3–4, pp. 21, 159
2:4, pp. 109, 163
2:8, pp. 110, 219
2:9, p. 58
2:9–10, p. 162

2 Timothy
4:7–8, p. 96

Titus
3:5, p. 203

Hebrews
1:2, p. 300
4:12, p. 219
7, p. 128
7:17, p. 129
9:22, p. 323
9:27, p. 120
9:28, p. 326
10:1–18, p. 154
10:10, pp. 265, 324
10:15–16, p. 203
10:29–31, p. 292
10:30–31, p. 293
11:3, p. 300
12, p. 298
12:22, p. 298

James
2:19, p. 325

2 Peter
1:19, p. 309
2:3, p. 15
2:4, pp. 67, 140
3:7, pp. 287, 300
3:9, p. 104

Jude
1:6–7, p. 66
6, pp. 67, 140
7, p. 67

Revelation
1:10, p. 99
1:11, pp. 99, 181
1:18, p. 289
2:11, p. 91
3:3, p. vii
3:5, p. 91

3:10, p. 90
5, p. 108
6, p. 108
6:1–2, p. 109
6:2, pp. 109, 217
6:3–4, p. 111
6:5–6, p. 112
6:7–8, p. 113
6:8, p. 289
6:9–11, p. 114
6:12–17, p. 115
7, p. 127
7:1–4, p. 117
7:9, p. 118
7:13–14, pp. 105, 118
8:1–5, p. 131
8:6–7, p. 132
8:8–9, p. 133
8:10–11, p. 134
8:12, p. 135
8:13, p. 136
9, p. 228
9:1–12, p. 136
9:13–21, p. 139
9:20–21, p. 105
11, pp. 120, 122
11:2, p. 122
11:3–6, p. 119
12, pp. 170, 171, 173, 174, 175, 177, 191, 192, 266
12:1–6, p. 170
12:5, p. 266
12:7–9, p. 174
12:12, pp. 127, 192
12:13–17, pp. 175, 191
13, pp. 143, 148, 159, 160, 162

13:3–8, p. 151
13:8, p. 290
13:11–15, p. 160
13:14, p. 162
13:14–15, p. 162
13:16–18, p. 163
14:6–7, p. 103
16, pp. 195, 210, 226
16:1–2, p. 180
16:3, p. 181
16:4–7, p. 183
16:8–9, p. 184
16:10–11, p. 185
16:12–16, p. 189
16:17–21, p. 224
17, pp. 50, 128, 186, 225
17:1–6, p. 123
17:13, pp. 128, 143
17:15–18, p. 186
17:18, p. 128
18:2, p. 252
18:3, pp. 129, 130
18:9–10, p. 187
18:10, p. 131
18:11–13, p. 130
18:23, p. 130
19, pp. 110, 260
19:1–3, p. 250
19:7–9, p. 261
19:11–12, p. 110
19:11–16, p. 217
19:15, pp. 219, 266
19:17–18, p. 220
19:19–21, p. 222
19:20, p. 223
20, pp. 3, 232, 235, 240, 247,

254, 258, 259, 279, 299
20:1–3, p. 247
20:4–6, p. 254
20:5, p. 258
20:6, p. 259
20:6, p. 262
20:7, p. 260
20:7–10, p. 277
20:9, p. 281
20:10, p. 281
20:11, p. 299
20:11–15, p. 285
21, pp. 287, 295, 297, 299, 300
21:1–4, p. 295
21:5, p. 299
21:6–8, p. 301
21:9–14, p. 302

Made in the USA
Charleston, SC
09 January 2010